CCCC STUDIES IN WRITING & RHETORIC
Edited by Steve Parks, University of Virginia

The aim of the CCCC Studies in Writing & Rhetoric (SWR) Series is to influence how we think about language in action and especially how writing gets taught at the college level. The methods of studies vary from the critical to historical to linguistic to ethnographic, and their authors draw on work in various fields that inform composition—including rhetoric, communication, education, discourse analysis, psychology, cultural studies, and literature. Their focuses are similarly diverse—ranging from individual writers and teachers, to work on classrooms and communities and curricula, to analyses of the social, political, and material contexts of writing and its teaching.

SWR was one of the first scholarly book series to focus on the teaching of writing. It was established in 1980 by the Conference on College Composition and Communication (CCCC) in order to promote research in the emerging field of writing studies. As our field has grown, the research sponsored by SWR has continued to articulate the commitment of CCCC to supporting the work of writing teachers as reflective practitioners and intellectuals.

We are eager to identify influential work in writing and rhetoric as it emerges. We thus ask authors to send us project proposals that clearly situate their work in the field and show how they aim to redirect our ongoing conversations about writing and its teaching. Proposals should include an overview of the project, a brief annotated table of contents, and a sample chapter. They should not exceed 10,000 words.

To submit a proposal, please register as an author at www.editorial manager.com/nctebp. Once registered, follow the steps to submit a proposal (be sure to choose SWR Book Proposal from the drop-down list of article submission types).

D1739072

TEACHERS TALKING WRITING

PERSPECTIVES ON PLACES, PEDAGOGIES, AND PROGRAMS

TO: KYLE
YOUR TIME & ENERGY TO ANSWERING MY QUESTIONS & YOUR WILLINGNESS TO LISTEN IS GREATLY APPRECIATED. THANK YOU FOREVER.

Shane A. Wood
University of Southern Mississippi

Conference on College
Composition and
Communication

National Council of
Teachers of English
www.ncte.org

The WAC
Clearinghouse
wac.colostate.edu

Staff Editor: Kurt Austin
Manuscript Editor: Don Donahue
Series Editor: Steve Parks
Interior Design: Mary Rohrer
Layout: Mike Palmquist
Cover Design: Pat Mayer
Cover Image: John Perry

Print ISBN: 978-0-8141-5276-8; epub ISBN: 978-0-8141-5278-2; PDF ISBN: 978-0-8141-5277-5

It is the policy of NCTE in its journals and other publications to provide a forum for the open discussion of ideas concerning the content and the teaching of English and the language arts. Publicity accorded to any particular point of view does not imply endorsement by the Executive Committee, the Board of Directors, or the membership at large, except in announcements of policy, where such endorsement is clearly specified.

NCTE provides equal employment opportunity (EEO) to all staff members and applicants for employment without regard to race, color, religion, sex, national origin, age, physical, mental or perceived handicap/disability, sexual orientation including gender identity or expression, ancestry, genetic information, marital status, military status, unfavorable discharge from military service, pregnancy, citizenship status, personal appearance, matriculation or political affiliation, or any other protected status under applicable federal, state, and local laws.

Every effort has been made to provide current URLs and email addresses, but because of the rapidly changing nature of the web, some sites and addresses may no longer be accessible.

This book is copublished with the WAC Clearinghouse. It is available in open-access digital formats at wac.colostate.edu.

Library of Congress Cataloging-in-Publication Data

A catalog record of this book has been requested.

CONTENTS

Acknowledgments   vii

Introduction: Conversations on Composition   1

PART I. PLACES   23
Pathways and Reflections on Teaching   25
Two-Year Colleges   39
Historically Black Colleges and Universities   61
Hispanic-Serving Institutions   85

PART II. PEDAGOGIES   107
Classroom Writing Assessment   109
Multimodality   129
Social Justice   145
Disability Studies   161
Community Literacies   179

PART III. PROGRAMS   199
Writing Program Administration   201
Basic Writing   221
Second-Language Writing   241
Writing Across the Curriculum   263
Writing Centers   281
References   305
Author   321
Contributors   323

v

Acknowledgments

I want to acknowledge, first, the fifty-two teachers who sat down and talked to me about their teaching and research for this project. This book exists because of their willingness to share their stories and knowledge about teaching writing. Thanks to Linda Adler-Kassner, Chris M. Anson, Chuck Bazerman, Melvin Beavers, Susan Naomi Bernstein, Dev Bose, Carolyn Calhoon-Dillahunt, Les Hutchinson Campos, Suresh Canagarajah, Christina V. Cedillo, Frankie Condon, Steven J. Corbett, Ginny Crisco, Harry Denny, Jay Dolmage, John Duffy, Candace Epps-Robertson, Bryna Siegel Finer, Laura Gonzales, David F. Green Jr., Jennifer Grouling, Cody Hoover, Asao B. Inoue, Karen Keaton Jackson, Darin Jensen, Lisa King, Eunjeong Lee, Neal Lerner, Alexandria Lockett, Paula Mathieu, Paul Kei Matsuda, Temptaous Mckoy, Cruz Medina, Sharon Mitchler, Beverly J. Moss, Jessica Nastal, Beatrice Mendez Newman, Rebecca S. Nowacek, Steve Parks, Staci Perryman-Clark, Mike Rose, Todd Ruecker, Iris D. Ruiz, Alisa Russell, Cecilia Shelton, Jody Shipka, Nancy Sommers, Chris Thaiss, Howard Tinberg, Stephanie Vie, Elizabeth Wardle, and Tara Wood.

I would like to extend special thanks to Steve Parks, who had faith in this project and took a risk on a book integrated with a podcast. Steve has been such a valuable friend, editor, and mentor throughout this process. He was also one of the first to express confidence in *Pedagogue* and the potential it had for meaning making and community building in the field of rhetoric and composition. His goodwill and generosity have made possible a lot of the work I do. I'm grateful for the Conference on College Composition and Communication (CCCC), National Council of Teachers of English (NCTE), and the WAC Clearinghouse for helping publish this book, too.

Thanks to Paula Mathieu and John Duffy for helping me imagine what this book could be—their support and good cheer motivated me to take up this project. I'm thankful for my good friend and mentor, Asao B. Inoue, who continues to encourage me as a teacher and learner. He took me under his wing as a grad student. I'm also grateful for Mike Palmquist, Nobert Elliot, Mya Poe, and Chris M. Anson. They each read earlier pages and configurations of this book and offered good guidance and great feedback. I'm thankful for Wes Berry, my undergrad mentor. His enthusiasm for teaching inspired me to learn, and he was the first teacher who talked to me about rhetoric and composition.

I also want to thank Mike Rose for responding to my email asking him to be the first guest on *Pedagogue*. Your good-heartedness and enthusiasm has meant a lot to me, Mike. I'll always remember our conversations on teaching, writing, and life. There are some wonderful people who have supported *Pedagogue* since the beginning: Stephanie Vie, Christie Toth, Jessica Nastal, Sharon Mitchler, Les Hutchinson Campos, Christina V. Cedillo, Staci Perryman-Clark, and Candace Epps-Robertson, to name a few. Thanks to everyone who has taken time to listen to *Pedagogue* and to all the people who have shared the podcast with their colleagues and friends. Your support means a lot to me. Thank you for finding the podcast valuable and for using it in your writing classes and programs. Many thanks to all the *Pedagogue* contributors. I'm humbled by your kindness. I've learned so much from our conversations.

I'm extremely grateful for my students and colleagues at Fresno State, the University of Kansas, Haskell Indian Nations University, and the University of Southern Mississippi. I've been fortunate to learn alongside so many good people in so many different places. My students and colleagues inspire me. I'm thankful for all the classroom, hallway, and office conversations.

My mom and dad helped facilitate a love for learning at an early age. Thanks for cultivating curiosity and fostering imagination. My brother has been a source of encouragement since we were little kids. Thanks for always being there for me, Dusty. My family has always been so supportive, and I'm forever thankful for their love.

I'm only able to teach and write because of my wife, Melody Wood. Mel sacrifices her time and energy to let me do this work. She's the best mom to our daughters, Rose and Eleanor. She's loving, patient, and kind, and I feel blessed to do life alongside her.

Pedagogue, and now this book, are products of her support. Mel encouraged me to start the podcast, and she's given me all the space and time to interview, edit, and write. I'm the beneficiary of her love—and so are Rose and Elle, who light up every room with joy.

Introduction
Conversations on Composition

Teachers Talking Writing (TTW) is a *collection of conversations* about the theory and teaching of writing in postsecondary contexts. It might also be considered a composition anthology focused on practices and pedagogies in the 21st century. What makes such anthologies appealing are the overviews and insights they provide teachers who want to better understand approaches to teaching. And yet we are all aware of the issues such anthologies produce. For instance, many anthologies include single-authored chapters around a theory or practice. For example, 84 of the 95 essays (88.4%) in *Strategies for Teaching First-Year Composition* are single-authored. In *Cross-Talk in Comp Theory* (2011), 36 out of 42 (85.7%) are single-authored. Eleven of the 13 chapters (84.6%) in *First-Year Composition: From Theory to Practice* are written by a single author. Many anthologies also include established scholars in the field, or teachers who are tenured. This orientation offers a limited range of perspectives, especially when it comes to teaching writing in the 21st century. For example, every contributor (100%) in *First-Year Composition: From Theory to Practice* is either a professor or associate professor, so tenured faculty. Twenty-six of 30 (86.6%) contributors in *A Guide to Composition Pedagogies* are professors or associate professors. Thirty of 33 (90.9%) are professors or associate professors in *Naming What We Know*. Twenty-one of 22 (95.4%) are professors or associate professors in *Exploring Composition Studies: Sites, Issues, Perspectives*. And as is well known, almost all anthologies exist as printed words on (increasingly thin) paper.

TTW is structured and designed as a *conversation on composition*. As such, this book diverges from traditional constructions of rhetoric and composition anthologies. Instead of relying on alphabetic text, this book integrates multimodality and invites readers to listen to the embodied voices of its contributors. Rather than formal academic biographies, this collection has personal narratives of contributors (see back of book). Instead of offering perspectives primarily from R1 universities, this book represents a range of institutional contexts and programs that are often underrepresented, such as two-year colleges, Historically Black Colleges and Universities, and Hispanic-Serving Institutions. Moreover, rather than put pressure on one voice to capture a pedagogical issue of the entire field, each chapter in this book includes at least four voices and perspectives. Finally, in place of a concise conclusion at the end of each chapter, this book offers questions to encourage deeper reflection and conversation. *TTW*, then, reconsiders how knowledge can be reconstructed and redistributed in composition and rhetoric. Clearly the field has benefited from composition anthologies. *TTW* suggests that technologies have afforded new forms of conversation to occur.

TTW is interconnected with *Pedagogue*, a podcast I created in April 2019. *Pedagogue* is designed to amplify teacher-scholar perspectives on composition across contexts and positions. I started the podcast with the hopes of building a space for teachers to talk about teaching, to foster a collaborative and supportive community curious about composition pedagogies and practices, and to celebrate the labor teachers do inside and outside the classroom. Each episode is a conversation with a teacher (or multiple teachers) about their experiences teaching writing, their work, inspirations, assignments, assessments, successes, and challenges.

Pedagogue reminded me that conversation is a meaning-making, community-building activity. Gary A. Olson and Irene Gale's (1991) *(Inter)views: Cross-Disciplinary Perspectives on Rhetoric and Literacy* situates conversation as "an especially fruitful source of social understanding, a preferred way of learning, of thinking with others, of testing received thought. Conversations help to promote the feeling that, yes, there *is* a heartbeat on the pages of our intellectual lives" (Bleich, p. 1). Having a conversation with another teacher brings to life scholarship and makes more tangible our work in the writing classroom. Listening to different perspectives and experiences on teaching writing contributes to my understanding of the field and what it means to teach. I'm energized and encouraged every time I talk with a *Pedagogue* contributor because they challenge me to (re)consider my own practices and beliefs about teaching writing.

These conversations with teachers on *Pedagogue* eventually led me to reimagine what it might look like to engage with composition theories and pedagogies and practices through a multimodal-centered anthology on teaching writing:

- What would it look like to complement traditional alphabetic text with digital mediums (e.g., audio, visuals) to distribute and circulate writing instruction knowledge and to build a more diverse, inclusive community of teacher-scholars?
- What would it look like to reimagine the single-authored chapter on a specific approach to teaching, and to amplify a range of voices across institutional contexts? So instead of one perspective (e.g., often established teacher-scholars) in one context (e.g., R1s), how about four or five voices in different locations?
- What would it look like to craft stories and experiences around teaching writing and to do so in a more accessible way mediated through technology?

Ultimately, I asked myself, "What might it mean to remix or re-invent the traditional anthology as a conversation across print and audio platforms? How might that replicate the very conversations that have always supported my own teaching?"

TEXT AND SOUND (TOGETHER)

My interest in sound, orality, and aurality go back to when I was a kid. I went to speech therapy once a week for two years due to a speech impediment. I was naturally frustrated with words and at the same time amazed by other peoples' abilities to use them to tell stories. I loved hearing people *talk*. I liked the attitude and tonality, and the ebb and flow of radio programs like National Public Radio's (NPR) *All Things Considered* and *Car Talk*. I enjoyed staying up to watch *The Tonight Show with Jay Leno*, *The Late Show with David Letterman,* and *The Late Late Show with Craig Ferguson*. There's cadence and rhythm involved in conversation, and those radio and television programs offered a unique kind of interactive performance for me as a listener. There's something special about the improvisation that happens when two people talk. The interaction branches off in different directions even if questions are scripted and interviewees are informed beforehand because that's how conversations happen.

As a grad student, I learned a lot about teaching composition through conversations in hallways and offices talking with peers or sitting around chatting about classroom practices before and after grad seminars. I would argue some of my most beneficial learning experiences happened outside conventional academic structures. It wasn't in rhet/comp seminars grappling with dense theoretical texts. It wasn't taking comps. It wasn't writing a dissertation or defending it. Sure, those things helped build my knowledge about teaching writing, but they weren't where I felt most comfortable as a student. I learned a lot about praxis from talking with other teachers. I was—and still am—drawn to Q&As after conference presentations, pedagogy and professional development workshops, and informal conversations with colleagues and students. I still have a difficult time duplicating that same kind of interactivity and engagement with alphabetic texts. Those more casual spaces have always felt more personal and inviting to me as a learner. Text and sound offer different affordances, and I believe we gain a lot when we combine the two. New opportunities for learning are made possible when we see how these meaning-making activities interact.

This book situates conversation as knowledge-building practice and relies on the interconnectivity between text and sound to capture composition in the 21st century. Rather than an anthology of singular voices speaking, *TTW* provides curated conversations about places, pedagogies, and programs by teacher-scholars in rhetoric and composition who have contributed to *Pedagogue*. The original interviews on *Pedagogue* offer further insight on contributors' teaching and research. I see *Pedagogue* as a monologue and *TTW* as the full script for a play. *Pedagogue* focuses on individual actors; each episode is a center stage spotlight on teacher-scholars talking about their teaching and institutional context. *TTW*, on the other hand, is interwoven scenes that comprise a full production and collaborative performance that consists of a much larger plot. For this reason, *TTW* invites readers and listeners to navigate back and forth between alphabetic text and audio of *Pedagogue*.

I understand how tradition might seem to dictate that *TTW* is scholarship, whereas *Pedagogue* is an interesting creative side project. I would argue that both *TTW* and *Pedagogue* should be considered equally important to knowledge making and community building. Interviews are rich and reflective. Consider the fact that interviews as a method for research provide a unique experience for readers and listeners because they capture thinking in real time—whether in print or through audio. Consider the nuanced information, ideas, feelings, and relationships formed through interviews. I'm reminded of Wade Mahon's (2005) thoughts on the importance of interviews to our field:

> [Interviews] have a value as preserving institutional or disciplinary memory, documenting the development of a field over time: particularly in composition studies, since it's a relatively young field . . . you get to trace scholars' developing thought processes, and basically see them as human beings to a certain degree. I think it's very valuable in understanding different scholars and the work they do, why they do it, the struggles they themselves have had behind the scenes, and how their thinking develops, how that fits in with the changes in the discipline as a whole. (https://kairos.technorhetoric.net/10.1/ interviews/rhetoric-and-composition.htm)

The richness of interviews can also be seen in academic journals that invite and publish these scholarly contributions (e.g., *Composition Forum*, *The WAC Journal*, *Kairos*, *The Journal of Multimodal Rhetorics*). Yet valuing interviews alone does not fully resolve the hierarchies and biases that exist between print and digital scholarship in English departmental guidelines and documents (Lee & Selfe, 2008), where digital scholarship is often seen "outside the purview of knowledge making" (Purdy & Walker, 2010, p. 178). As compositionists and rhetoricians, though, we understand how important multimodality has been to extending definitions of literacy and the teaching of writing in the past twenty years (Alexander & Rhodes, 2014; Selfe, 2007; Shipka, 2011; Palmeri, 2012).

As Richard J. Selfe and Cynthia L. Selfe (2008) say, "We learn about, act in, and understand the world using multiple channels of communication" (p. 84). As writing teachers, we know that reading and composing in multiple ways offers greater affordances to more students. We design curriculum and use multimodal activities to cultivate learning in hopes of inspiring students to engage and think critically. We ask students to play with/in different modes and mediums to build knowledge. We invite students to explore different rhetorical situations and genres and ways of communicating meaning. We encourage students to consider different audiences. Our writing classes are even interconnected with digital tools and technologies (e.g., learning management systems). Theory and research on multimodality has transformed teaching practices. While some teacher-scholars have talked about integrating sound studies and podcasting in writing classes (Dangler et al., 2007; Jones, 2010; Krause, 2006), podcasts have yet to be considered *as scholarship*. But what counts as scholarship, or better yet what has the academy ascribed as scholarship? Single-authored monographs? Peer-reviewed journal articles? What makes those texts scholarship? And who do they exclude?

Podcasting has made global the ability to construct and disseminate information. Most podcasts are intended for public consumption, designed for public audiences. Most are free and accessible. They have different formats and purposes: inform, educate, humor, entertain, broadcast news, engage in topical conversations, establish community, and so on. Like many academic and/or educational podcasts, *Pedagogue* is public scholarship that participates, builds, and circulates knowledge to larger audiences beyond academia. *Pedagogue* invites public audiences to listen to writing teachers talk about their classroom practices and contexts. *Pedagogue* deconstructs the walls of the classroom and makes accessible the theories and practices teachers use to teach writing. Podcasting, then, allows us to hear the thoughts of others and establishes new pathways for interaction and engagement. Podcasts intersect sound and dialogue as a tool for knowledge building. And they extend far beyond the reach of print-based scholarship situated behind paywalls and journal subscriptions with limited readership.

For these reasons, *TTW* and *Pedagogue* should be valued as scholarship that constructs and builds knowledge on teaching writing in the 21st century. By using text and sound together, we extend future possibilities and audiences in rhetoric and composition. This work offers a new form and format of academic/public scholarship. In 1996, Ellen Cushman asked compositionists and rhetoricians to consider "the civic purpose of our positions in the academy, of what we do with our knowledge, for whom, and by what means" (p. 12). Today, how are we making our knowledge public, for whom, and by what means? Cushman argues that "when we fail to consider the perspectives of people outside of the academy, we overlook valuable contributions to our theory building" (1996, p. 23). We build walls between the university and public when we publish theory in journals and don't consider how those theories and practices should move beyond those spaces. We distance ourselves from the students we teach when we don't engage with the technologies they use. We become exclusive when we don't pay attention to how communities are producing and distributing knowledge.

TTW and *Pedagogue* are academic and public scholarship that can be used to draw back the curtains of classroom pedagogies and practices. They can be used together to help make real the work we do as writing teachers in and outside writing classrooms.

AIMS AND INTERVENTIONS

It would be wrong, of course, to dismiss or undervalue the importance of traditional anthologies in the field. Teachers and scholars have for decades benefitted from rich anthologies on teaching writing: *Strategies for Teaching First-Year Composition* (edited by Roen et al., 2002); *The Norton Book of Composition Studies* (edited by Miller, 2009); *Exploring Composition Studies: Sites, Issues, Perspectives* (edited by Ritter & Matsuda, 2016); *Cross-Talk in Comp Theory* (edited by Villanueva & Arola, 2011); *A Guide to Composition Pedagogies* (edited by Tate et al., 2014); *First-Year Composition: From Theory to Practices* (edited by Coxwell-Teague & Lunsford, 2014); and *Naming What We Know* (edited by Adler-Kassner & Wardle, 2015). All of these collections have informed my own teaching practices. I believe each provides something valuable to our field. *A Guide to Composition Pedagogies*, for example, contributes original essays that highlight important contemporary pedagogies (e.g., "second-language writing," "genre"). *First-Year Composition: From Theory to Practice* offers sample syllabi which helps us see how teachers approach first-year writing classes with different frameworks and assignments. *Cross-Talk in Comp Theory* is a compilation of some of our field's most foundational texts. *Naming What We Know* uses threshold concepts as a lens to examine core values and key ideas in writing studies.

Such anthologies have been used in grad practicums and orientations to develop writing teachers for years—including my own practicums. We gain a lot from this good scholarship. For instance, we get a snapshot of the history of rhetoric and composition; we get to see what's changed over time; we get theories and pedagogies; we get praxis; we get a look inside institutions and composition classes. *TTW* exists because of the rich history and information found in these anthologies. And within that history, *TTW* hopes to model a conversation that achieves three aims:

1. To document a wide range of pedagogies, practices, conditions, and programs on teaching writing from diverse perspectives at various institutions (e.g., two-year colleges, Historically Black Colleges and Universities, Hispanic-Serving Institutions, public universities, and private universities);
2. To record the current state of composition studies and the teaching of writing as well as offer future directions for teaching and research; and
3. To be an inclusive, accessible, multimodal-engaged experience for readers, listeners, teachers, scholars, and activists.

Since these aims construct and guide this book, I'll explain each in more depth.

To Document a Wide Range of Pedagogies, Practices, Conditions, and Programs on Teaching Writing from Diverse Perspectives at Various Institutions

Anthologies often serve as guides for approaches to teaching writing and resources for best practices in the field. *TTW* is designed to amplify teacher-scholar voices across institutions and positions and to represent a range of conversations about teaching writing in different contexts while also showing the dynamic nature of pedagogical practices across these sites. In doing so, *TTW* includes established voices and early career teacher-scholars in rhetoric and composition. It strategically redirects conversations about who teaches writing and where teaching writing happens through the voices it includes. Hearing experiences from non-tenure-track positions and tenure-track, from lecturers to assistant professors to associate professors, ultimately creates a more dynamic picture of teaching writing and the realities and conditions that surround teaching. Teaching writing is not one dimensional. Places, pedagogies, and programs are not homogenous. Writing classes and programs and institutional labor conditions, including teaching loads and service requirements and research expectations, are different.

Here it is important to highlight that while there are many sites for teaching, traditional scholarship has long been dominated by a singular voice: teachers-scholars who teach at predominantly White institutions (PWIs) and/or White teacher-scholars. I hope *TTW* (and *Pedagogue*) can challenge gaps in scholarship and further examine power and race: "Racial discourse influences rhetoric and composition pedagogies, so not to examine its influence in the classroom not only reifies its dominance, but ignores the context in which writing is produced. It also completely ignores the marginalization of people of color" (Pimentel et al., 2016). In 2019, Karen Keaton Jackson, Hope Jackson, and Dawn N. Hicks Tafari talked about the silencing of Historically Black Colleges and Universities and Black teacher-scholars in conversations on race and writing: "This silence is deafening, for those who teach thousands of African Americans each year, specifically for us as African American female faculty at HBCUs, essentially have no voice in the relevant pedagogies and theories that dominate our field" (p. 185). *TTW* emphasizes social justice and antiracism (Inoue, 2019) and linguistic justice (Baker-Bell, 2020), but does so by including those voices and perspectives who have been doing this work—often outside the focus of "traditional scholarship."

And rather than put pressure on a singular scholar of color to "address racism," *TTW* utilizes curated interviews as a valuable source for constructing and circulating knowledge about contexts and pedagogies and practices. Such a strategy enables different voices from different institutional locations to be heard simultaneously—putting pressure on all those involved to be responsible. Curated interviews provided a chance to strategically resist the traditional structure and organization that authorized only singular voices, with singular responsibilities, and opened opportunities for different perspectives to contribute to the conversation together. Thus, *TTW* offers fifty-two perspectives across institutional status and rank: emeriti, professor, associate professor, assistant professor, director, chair, project manager, senior instructor, continuing lecturer, and instructor. This book includes observations and experiences from teacher-scholars in the National Council of Teachers of English (NCTE) American Indian Caucus, Latinx Caucus, Asian/Asian American Caucus, and Black Caucus. The first third of this book decenters PWIs and R1 contexts and amplifies perspectives from two-year colleges (TYCs), Historically Black Colleges and Universities (HBCUs), and Hispanic-Serving Institutions (HSIs).

Nor should diverse perspectives be limited to issues of cultural identity. When we consider how traditional composition anthologies are used in grad practicums and composition theory classes that develop first-year writing teachers, then we can observe what voices are being projected and heard. For example, TYC teacher-scholars are rarely included in traditional anthologies. I believe this creates a ripple effect on the job market and/or the perception of where teaching writing occurs and what opportunities are available after grad school for future teachers. Based on the construction and organization of many conventional anthologies, we might conclude that R1 contexts are the *only* place for teaching and research (again, based on the voices included in those collections). This creates a narrow view of teaching, and it also impacts how programs and grad students see themselves and their futures. It postulates a myth that R1s are "more prestigious" and if a grad student doesn't get a position at an R1, then they are somehow "unsuccessful." This framing is incredibly problematic. Moreover, it doesn't represent actual data that shows about half of all US undergraduates are enrolled in two-year colleges and two-year colleges are responsible for a lot of developmental writing and first-year writing instruction (see TYCA Guidelines for Preparing Teachers of English in the Two-Year College). *TTW* attempts to provide a more complete landscape of where teaching writing happens and offers different strategies and practices for teaching by incorporating a range of teacher-scholar voices.

To Record the Current State of Composition Studies and the Teaching of Writing as Well as Offer Future Directions for Teaching and Research
The origin of composition studies is often traced to the writing-as-process movement in the late 1960s at the Dartmouth Seminar, where teacher-scholars from the United States and United Kingdom met to discuss what it meant to teach writing. Teachers exchanged ideas, had arguments, and shared experiences engaging with students and talking about writing. From those conversations, and through subsequent years of theory and practice, it is often argued, composition studies emerged as a new professional field in English. First-year writing classes and across the discipline writing instruction became critical elements to university operations and sustainability. Teaching writing has seen substantial growth since the 1960s. Now, the notion of writing-as-process seems basic; writing instructors need a teaching philosophy to apply for academic positions; writing programs are everywhere; writing across the curriculum (WAC), writing in the disciplines (WID), writing centers, and other university faculty development initiatives for writing are leaders in innovation; and almost every student is exposed to at least one writing-focused course within their first year.

There are currently over 30 journals associated with rhetoric and composition. Composition studies has made strong commitments to recording histories in the teaching of writing (see Lunsford; Crowley; Connors; Miller), and composition anthologies are one way to observe how teaching has developed over time. While these journals and anthologies have advanced theory, research, and practice, many contain narrow histories and perspectives. They privilege teachers who have the affordances to conduct research and write. The histories that get recorded, then, are from teachers at R1s with fewer course assignments and more research support. So composition histories have gaps both in where teaching writing happens and who gets heard. For instance, most don't record teaching at HBCUs: "There has yet to be a comprehensive, meaningful treatment of composition instruction at HBCUs" (Relerford, 2012, p. 117). Put differently, many journals and anthologies don't do justice to the work of teaching writing because they're limited in scope and lack representation across contexts and positions. Additionally, information on composition theory and praxis is often situated behind paywalls and journal subscriptions, which means knowledge about teaching is inaccessible because of how information is being distributed. *TTW* intercedes as an open access text and offers a more robust depiction of present and historical understandings of composition.

This book asks us to listen to what teacher-scholars are doing and saying, and this book provides a means for us to look ahead at new opportunities and future possibilities. It attempts to disrupt the history of rhetoric and composition studies (Ruiz, 2016) that is fraught with White teacher-scholars theorizing about teaching and then writing scholarship about students who are often excluded from their very classrooms. *TTW* attempts to address this issue by amplifying teacher-scholar perspectives from the most racially and socioeconomically diverse institutions in higher education (e.g., TYCs, HBCUs, and HSIs). There are a lot of rich books that provide nuanced understandings about teaching that are also centered on race and language, such as *Bordered Writers: Latinx Identities and Literacy Practices at Hispanic-Serving Institutions* (Baca et al., 2019), *Reclaiming Composition for Chicano/as and Other Ethnic Minorities: A Critical History and Pedagogy* (Ruiz, 2016), and *Survivance, Sovereignty, and Story* (King et al., 2015). *TTW* is another resource for hearing perspectives and building knowledge about teaching. This book reflects the experiences of writing teachers across the field's disciplinary interests and labor conditions.

Teaching writing is always interconnected with politics and cultural and social systems. The curated interviews in this collection are the beginnings of an attempt to document the current state of composition studies in the 21st century, with all its nuances and differences. Interviews help preserve histories. The kind of record keeping *TTW* and *Pedagogue* provide is capturing real-time ideas about teaching that more accurately represent the complexities of teaching writing in this specific moment in time. These conversations aren't revised, edited, and rewritten like traditional alphabetic texts. There's a sense of vulnerability and honesty in interviews. Interviews as a method for collecting knowledge offer a unique understanding of pedagogies and practices as emerging and evolving. *TTW* and *Pedagogue* demonstrate this as teachers talk through their approaches to teaching writing and share their research. *TTW* and

Pedagogue are archives of conversations about the always evolving nature of pedagogies and practices.

To Be an Inclusive, Accessible, Multimodal-engaged Experience for Readers, Listeners, Teachers, Scholars, and Activists

The multimodal and open access nature of this book invites new ways to interact with writing instruction knowledge and casts future direction for composition studies. *TTW* and *Pedagogue* are interconnected. As you read, you'll notice every chapter is connected to *Pedagogue*. The easiest way to see that is through the hyperlink and timestamp next to every interview question in each chapter. The hyperlink will take readers to the *Pedagogue* episode. I chose to link to a blog post for usability purposes. Some readers/listeners might want to listen directly on the site, for example. Some might choose to listen through other platforms (e.g., Apple, Spotify), which are all linked in each post. Some readers/listeners might navigate to the transcripts on the site to read the full alphabetic text of the conversation. There are different opportunities for engagement this way as opposed to just embedding the mp3 into the book. Podcasts are more than audio files (Detweiler, 2021). Podcasts come in different formats and styles and are deeply networked genres that invite us to learn different kinds of literacies, to create, write, edit, produce, distribute, circulate, that require understandings of certain technologies (e.g., audio-editing software, audio interfaces, microphones), and that span across devices and spaces (e.g., phones, computers, streaming services, social media, websites). While most interview questions and answers in this book align with the audio, some have been modified for coherency and cohesion.

I also believe readers/listeners can use this book alongside other texts. For example, teachers might read (or assign) David F. Green Jr.'s (2016) "Expanding the Dialogue on Writing Assessment at HBCUs," or Christina V. Cedillo's (2018) "What Does it Mean to Move?: Race, Disability, and Critical Embodiment Pedagogy," or Laura Gonzales's (2018) *Sites of Translation: What Multilinguals Can Teach Us about Digital Writing and Rhetoric*, or Asao B. Inoue's (2019) *Labor-Based Grading Contracts*. Teachers and students, then, can listen to/read these teacher-scholar interviews in *TTW* or hear full episodes on *Pedagogue* to get a sense for the context and motivations behind these texts. Thus, by drawing on the affordances of the linguistic mode (e.g., text) and aural mode (e.g., audio), my aim is to sponsor a new form of conversational engagement with composition theories and pedagogies. *TTW* and *Pedagogue* can stand alone as scholarship and/or be linked with traditional alphabetic texts. Which is to say this book offers numerous interactive experiences designed for all kinds of teaching and learning environments.

Some might pick up this book and read it word for word. Others might choose to listen to the audio. And then some might choose to read alongside the text while listening to the audio. Each type of engagement offers its own affordances and can be understood differently due to its modality and the way information is being distributed and received. As a whole, *TTW* centers conversation as a tool for building knowledge and community, and prioritizes dialogue, inclusivity, and accessibility.

ORGANIZATION AND CHAPTERS

TTW is organized around three parts: Part I. Places; Part II. Pedagogies; Part III. Programs. Within these three sections, there are a total of 14 chapters and 52 contributors. Every chapter is built around a topic connected to composition studies and contains a brief, noncomprehensive introduction of historical and current relevance around the chapter theme. Each chapter offers resources and posits questions that can help facilitate conversations and future directions for teaching and research in rhetoric and composition based on the chapter topic. After the introduction, each chapter includes curated interviews from *Pedagogue* from at least four teacher-scholars sharing knowledge or strategies and practices based on the subject. Readers can click the hyperlinks embedded in the interviews to listen to the episode on *Pedagogue*. There's a timestamp that indicates the exact location of the question and answer in the episode. At the end of each chapter, I offer a "denouement." The denouement brings together the interviews and then offers a list of questions readers and listeners can consider based on the conversations. My hope is that these questions provide room for more conversation around each chapter's theme and present another opportunity to reflect and listen.

In developing the *Places, Pedagogies,* and *Programs* structure, I consulted traditional composition anthologies (many listed above) to see historic and current trends in composition theory and practice. Perhaps most notable in all the anthologies is attention to approaches (e.g., process, threshold concepts), practices (e.g., reflection, responding to student writing), and pedagogies (e.g., critical, feminist, multimodal). There tends to be a lack of attention to institutions/contexts for teaching. Since institutional sites and contexts inform approaches, practices, and pedagogies, I chose to emphasize the *places* where teaching writing happens first in this collection. Next, I focus on the *pedagogies* teachers use to teach writing. Teachers draw on different practices and approaches—and often several at the same time. I conclude with conversations around *programs* because teachers and scholars in rhetoric and composition work between and beyond writing classrooms to advance writing knowledge across colleges and universities in various administrative positions and roles.

Part I. Places

- Chapter 1. Pathways and Reflections on Teaching (interviews with Chris M. Anson, Chuck Bazerman, Beverly J. Moss, Mike Rose, and Nancy Sommers)
- Chapter 2. Two-Year Colleges (interviews with Carolyn Calhoon-Dillahunt, Sharon Mitchler, Jessica Nastal, and Howard Tinberg)
- Chapter 3. Historically Black Colleges and Universities (interviews with David F. Green Jr., Karen Keaton Jackson, Alexandria Lockett, and Temptaous Mckoy)
- Chapter 4. Hispanic-Serving Institutions (interviews with Steven Corbett, Ginny Crisco, Cody Hoover, and Beatrice Mendez Newman)

Places focuses on a range of institutional contexts, specifically two-year colleges, Historically Black Colleges and Universities, and Hispanic-Serving Institutions. Teaching is inextricably linked to communities and locations. Institutions shouldn't be generalized by their overarching designations because each context has its own unique affordances and challenges. In this section, teachers offer insight about their specific colleges and universities and talk about practices and strategies they use in their writing classrooms. They also critique myths and assumptions about their contexts and offer future directions for rhetoric and composition.

Chapter 1 explores how senior teacher-scholars found their way into teaching writing and how composition has developed over the years. They reflect on their personal pathways to teaching, key moments in composition studies, and how they continue to have passion for teaching writing. This chapter helps situate how teaching is energizing and also localized. It reveals how teaching is always connected to institutional sites and students. This chapter, then, encourages readers and listeners to self-reflect on their own contexts and pedagogical practices, as well as examine the diverse contexts around teaching writing, such as two-year colleges, Historically Black Colleges and Universities, and Hispanic-Serving Institutions.

Chapter 2 focuses on two-year colleges (TYCs). The contributors in this chapter talk about their classes, students, program goals and outcomes, research, and the importance of increasing TYC visibility in composition and rhetoric scholarship at large. Teachers reflect on the unique opportunities and demands of TYCs. They talk about teaching loads, transfer, and the joys of teaching a wide range of student demographics, from recent high school graduates to adult learners working multiple jobs and raising families. Some contributors talk about their pedagogical emphases, like the importance of teaching deep reading, while others share their research on writing placement and assessment, and teaching for transfer.

Chapter 3 highlights the rich rhetorical and pedagogical traditions of Historically Black Colleges and Universities (HBCUs). Teachers from Howard University, Bowie State University, Spelman College, and North Carolina Central University reflect on the culture and mission of HBCUs and chat about differences between institutions. Some illuminate how composition studies scholarship has silenced HBCU perspectives and experiences, and others cast future directions for HBCUs and rhetoric and composition as a field. These contributors also talk about classroom practices on race and language, including African American rhetorics, hip hop, amplification rhetorics, and curriculum on the intellectual traditions of Black women. Some teachers share their readings and writing assignments, for example, how they use literacy narratives and literacy artifacts to encourage students to engage with/in communities.

Chapter 4 focuses on Hispanic-Serving Institutions (HSIs), specifically teacher-scholar experiences at Texas A&M University, Kingsville; California State University, Fresno; Clovis Community College; and The University of Texas Rio Grande Valley. Teachers share common misconceptions about teaching at a minority majority institution, valuing community and cultural understanding in writing classes, and fostering linguistic diversity. They provide insight on approaches to teaching writing, such as culturally sustaining pedagogies, and how to best prepare for teaching in an HSI.

Part II. Pedagogies
Pedagogies centers on approaches and practices and strategies for teaching writing. In examining traditional composition anthologies and with my work on *Pedagogue*, I highlighted keywords and came up with chapter titles that best reflected what teacher-scholars talked about when they talked about teaching writing in the 21st century. These themes came across through hundreds of hours researching and writing questions, interviewing, and editing episodes. I noticed how most teacher-scholars talked about their teaching in what I noted as "evolving." Teachers and approaches to teaching writing adapt and evolve over time.

Pedagogies are informed by beliefs and assumptions about teaching writing that most teachers have learned either in grad school, via research and scholarship, and/or through experiences in the classroom. Yet every teacher-scholar has a unique pedagogical identity. Present constructions and orientations to teaching writing are informed by previous theories and practices but also by new research and data-based evidence on teaching writing. Through interviews, teacher-scholars often talked about how their current practices were informed by past and present research and theory. Likewise, most offered how their pedagogies and practices and their own research could shape the writing class and composition studies in the future. The chapters included aren't a full representation of composition pedagogies and practices; instead, they're a small sample of what teachers do in classes. Part II includes the following chapters:

- Chapter 5. Classroom Writing Assessment (interviews with Chris M. Anson, Jennifer Grouling, Asao B. Inoue, and Nancy Sommers)
- Chapter 6. Multimodality (interviews with Christina V. Cedillo, Laura Gonzales, Jody Shipka, and Stephanie Vie)
- Chapter 7. Social Justice (interviews with Frankie Condon, John Duffy, Asao B. Inoue, Cruz Medina, and Cecilia Shelton)
- Chapter 8. Disability Studies (interviews with Dev Bose, Christina V. Cedillo, Jay Dolmage, and Tara Wood)
- Chapter 9. Community Literacies (interviews with Les Hutchinson Campos, Candace Epps-Robertson, Lisa King, Paula Mathieu, Beverly J. Moss, and Steve Parks)

In Chapter 5, contributors talk about classroom writing assessment, such as teacher response to student writing and grading. Teachers talk about how assessment is at the center of their approach to teaching, discuss problems with traditional grading standards and offer alternatives, describe how their practices have changed over the years, and share how response can better reflect classroom values on language and literacy. This chapter is designed to offer strategies and reflections on the impact of classroom writing assessment.

Chapter 6 offers a multimodal orientation for teaching writing. Teachers describe how they incorporate multimodality and offer assignments and strategies. Contributors also reflect on digital practices and issues, such as privacy and surveillance, and how to responsibly use technology in the writing classroom. The chapter illuminates how pedagogies can be interlinked, too. For example, one teacher talks about how a disabilities studies approach to teaching informs how they frame multimodality in their class.

Chapter 7 explains how social justice can be centered through teaching writing and how teachers can create assignments and assessments that align with social justice aims. Contributors talk about antiracism, linguistic justice, investigating social, local, and cultural systems, and offer new futures for composition studies.

In Chapter 8, contributors describe accessible pedagogies and practices. Teachers talk about commonplace myths about disability and describe how ableism is attached to systems and policies (e.g., attendance, "late" work). Contributors reflect on universal design for learning and share strategies for constructing more inclusive, accessible writing classes.

Chapter 9 includes conversations on community-engaged pedagogies, cultural rhetorics, and Indigenous rhetorics. Contributors share best practices for building community partnerships, valuing intellectual and community spaces, cultural knowledges, traditions and practices, embracing rhetorical frameworks, relationality and reciprocity, and talk about the power of listening. They reflect on lived and embodied experiences of communities and talk about how teachers can work to deconstruct White, Eurocentric Western ideologies in writing classes.

Part III. Programs
After situating institutional sites (Part I) and describing different pedagogies (Part II), Part III incorporates perspectives on program administration. Writing classes are often situated in writing programs that help guide pedagogies and practices in ways that help complement program goals and outcomes. Writing programs usually conduct annual assessment to measure how classes are meeting certain aims and expectations. Of course writing instruction extends beyond English departments and programs, too. Writing happens across the university, and other programs are designed to help faculty and students with writing, whether that be generating workshops that integrate how to assess writing in other disciplines or helping students with their individual writing assignments. Programs like writing across the curriculum (WAC) and writing centers are sources for writing instruction knowledge and are often working within and between various campus stakeholders. This section includes conversations about different kinds of program administration as well as different practices within those programs.

- Chapter 10. Writing Program Administration (interviews with Jacob Babb, Melvin Beavers, Staci Perryman-Clark, Iris D. Ruiz, and Elizabeth Wardle)
- Chapter 11. Basic Writing (interviews with Susan Naomi Ber-

nstein, Carolyn Calhoon-Dillahunt, Darin Jensen, and Bryna Siegel Finer)

- Chapter 12. Second-Language Writing (interviews with Suresh Canagarajah, Eunjeong Lee, Paul Kei Matsuda, and Todd Ruecker)
- Chapter 13. Writing Across the Curriculum (interviews with Linda Adler-Kassner, Chuck Bazerman, Alisa Russell, and Chris Thaiss)
- Chapter 14. Writing Centers (interviews with Frankie Condon, Harry Denny, Karen Keaton Jackson, Neal Lerner, and Rebecca Nowacek)

Chapter 10 examines different writing program philosophies and frameworks. Contributors reflect on program values, challenges, training and developing first-year writing teachers, transitioning to writing program administration, and provide advice for future administrators. Some contributors talk about how their program practices interconnect with their pedagogical approaches to teaching, and how their evidence-based research informs what they do as program administrators.

In Chapter 11, contributors talk about basic writing programs and classes. This chapter offers practices and strategies for teaching basic writing and provides insight on outcomes and goals. Teachers share their experience and expertise in basic writing classrooms. Some take issue with the term "basic writing" and talk about advancements and developments in composition studies around the students served in those classes. Others mention successes and challenges to teaching basic writing and offer steps institutions can take to better support basic writing programs and classes.

Chapter 12 focuses on second-language writing. Contributors talk about critical approaches to language and literacy studies, key issues in the context of teaching second-language writing, misconceptions about second-language writers, and practices and strategies for building linguistically diverse writing classes. Some reflect on the histories of second-language writing programs in composition studies, while others cast future directions for teaching and research.

Chapter 13 provides insight on WAC programs and practices, including philosophies and models for developing programs. Some contributors share how WAC has progressed over the years and talk about trends in scholarship. Contributors also reflect on facilitating faculty workshops and generating conversations about writing across disciplines. They share strategies for faculty development and offer advice to help programs assess the effectiveness of workshops. Moreover, these teacher-scholars talk about challenges and successes they've experienced as administrators.

In Chapter 14, contributors discuss ongoing issues facing writing centers, antiracist and socially just writing center initiatives, program outcomes and goals, professional development, collaboration, and feedback to student writing. These teachers address constructing sustainable writing centers that align with their pedagogical values, and they describe how writing centers can be sites for activism and research. Additionally, they talk about fostering and facilitating community among writing tutors and students in writing centers.

INTERLUDE

This introduction doesn't end with a conclusion. This is an *interlude* to chapters that provide richer writing instruction knowledge and experiences. Better yet, this is an interlude to more nuanced *conversations*. The word *interlude* comes from the medieval Latin word *interludium*: *inter-* meaning "between" and *ludius* meaning "play." What follows this introduction are *acts*, or scenes that help comprise a fuller understanding of composition studies and teaching writing. This collection is a way to make meaning about places, pedagogies, and programs. This meaning making is always evolving because knowledge is always acting and being acted upon by people in social and cultural systems. Teaching is an embodied performance. Each chapter aims to deconstruct where and how teaching writing happens in this moment in time. The interviews illuminate individual teacher-scholar experiences and perspectives in institutions, writing classes, and programs. *TTW* and *Pedagogue* interplay. Because of this, readers and listeners can navigate between textual and digital mediums to survey composition studies in the 21st century.

PART I. PLACES

1

Pathways and Reflections on Teaching

> I cannot be a teacher without exposing who I am. Without re-
> vealing, either reluctantly or with simplicity, the way I relate to
> the world, how I think politically . . . as a consequence, one of
> my major preoccupations is the approximation between what I
> say and what I do, between what I seem to be and what I am
> actually becoming.
>
> —Paulo Freire, *Pedagogy of Freedom*

Through the hundreds of hours interviewing and editing involved
in the making of this book, I became aware of how often teachers talked about their past educators and mentors who ultimately
helped guide their paths to teaching. I heard teachers talk about
their pedagogies and practices as *becoming*, as not yet complete. I
listened to them share how they were inspired to teach because of
the communities around them. There is a degree of vulnerability in
the work we do as teachers. Teaching is personal. Every teacher has
a story, and that story is often connected to others: family, friends,
teachers-scholars, and of course, students. That sense of community is one of the most special things about teaching writing—we are
mentored by others and we mentor students by how we approach
teaching and learning. Teaching is inherently collaborative. I chose
to start this book with *pathways and reflections on teaching* because
all our stories are unique.

The word *pathway* is used to describe interconnectedness and se-
quential order in the natural sciences (e.g., physiology, biochemis-
try) and is used in the social sciences (e.g., archaeology, anthropology) to locate sites, societies, and human activity. Of course, it can
also be used as a metaphor. I see pathway connected to the classroom, which is a site or channel for learning that brings together

teachers, students, reading, writing, texts, languages, cultures, and identities. The classroom is one space, of many, that centers itself on exploration and discovery. The heart of this collection, *Teachers Talking Writing*, reveals the multilayered nuances of teaching writing, including the different pathways, sites, elements, and interactions that occur in teaching. This first chapter shows how teaching is a communal endeavor and a complex individual process. Teaching exposes us.

No one has to convince us that writing is meaningful and important. We already know how profound writing is to life. Peter Elbow (2004) describes writing as a powerful tool that helps students "converse with themselves, and tackle both cultural messages and peer pressures" (p. 12). Donald Murray (1972) says *writing is thinking* and tells teachers to "be quiet, to listen, to respond" (p. 5). The act of being in conversation with others and listening seems essential to our profession as writing teachers. It seems important in building a global community of teacher-scholars and central to building community with students in our classrooms. How are we listening, and who are we listening to? Conventional scholarship (e.g., peer-reviewed alphabetic texts) is one representation of listening and extending conversations about teaching writing. Digital scholarship (e.g., podcasts) is another way of producing and circulating writing instruction knowledge. Interviewing as a method of inquiry makes more visible *thinking and listening*. Through interviews, we hear the thought processes of people and see what informs and influences theory and praxis. This book relies on interviews to build knowledge about teaching writing.

This chapter, and really this collection, is about listening to stories and approaches to teaching writing. Stories unveil glimpses of identities, such as who we are, where we come from, and what we believe about teaching and language. It seems to me that teaching writing and learning about teaching is a metacognitive reflective practice. Unlike the other chapters in this book, this one doesn't begin with a theoretical overview of the conversation that exists in scholarship. The purpose of this chapter is to position interviewing and listening as a knowledge-constructing, meaning-making activity. Listening is a community-building practice, too. This chapter celebrates pathways to teaching and preserves voices in our field.

We learn a lot by reading teacher-scholars, especially those who have spent decades teaching writing. These archives are integral to the field's history and development. This chapter captures some perspectives that have made a significant impact on composition theory and practice. Unlike the other chapters in this section, this one isn't about a specific place (e.g., two-year college). The throughline in this chapter is how teachers are always being informed by and alongside past and present individuals and communities. The imprint we make on students in our own classes is a window into our past. As teachers, we can trace moments in our life that have shaped our praxis, and we can celebrate those who have come before us who have helped create pathways forward.

INTERVIEWS

The interviews[1] in this chapter serve as a small representation of narratives about first experiences teaching and recollections of theories and practices from five teacher-scholars, each having taught for at least thirty-five years in writing classes: Mike Rose, Nancy Sommers, Chris M. Anson, Chuck Bazerman, and Beverly J. Moss. Rose shares how "he didn't know what the hell [he] was doing" when he first walked in the classroom in 1968. He talks about how teaching challenges us to learn more about "human beings . . . about language and literacy." Sommers mentions her junior high language arts teacher, high school English teacher, a college literature professor, and her dissertation advisor as people who took "leaps of faith with [her]." She says these teachers inspired her to work with students who didn't have confidence in themselves as writers. Anson describes his graduate school experience in the late 1970s and early 1980s. He talks about two mentors who helped him develop as a writing teacher. Bazerman talks about how teaching first and third graders was a "revelation," and Moss ends our conversation by reflecting on the moment she realized she could study African American community literacies, which created a pathway for her to incorporate different methodologies and writing practices (e.g., ethnographies) in the classroom.

---

1   Transcriptions throughout this book have been slightly modified for coherency and cohesive purposes. Text/audio won't always align. I attempt to remain as faithful to the contributor's words and intentions as possible.

Shane to Mike Rose: I'd like for you to think back to 1968 when you first walked into the classroom as a teacher. What were you thinking and how were you feeling in that moment? What did you think teaching was going to be like? [Episode 1: 02:12–07:29]

You know, it was so long ago that I'm not sure my memory is going to be that specific, but I can tell you what the situation was and maybe as we talk about it some thoughts will come back to me. The first actual teaching I did was when I was twenty-four, and I had just joined the program called the Teacher Corps. It's no longer around, but it was one of the Johnson Era War on Poverty programs . . . Teacher Corps would place folks like me in communities of need and we would work with existing schools. There would be teams of four interns. Then, we would have what we called a "team leader." This was a person who was an experienced teacher in that district. It was sort of a guru, our guide, knew everything and knew everybody, and guided us four little ducklings around the community and the school.

So, there I was. I was twenty-four. I had started a PhD program in English and realized it wasn't for me. Then I had taken a year of courses in psychology because I thought, well, maybe that's the route I wanted to go, and that was at a time when academic psychology was still pretty heavily experimental in its orientation in a way that just didn't capture me. So . . . I joined this program and set out with my team to a community called El Monte which is east of East Los Angeles. At that time, it was a working-class White and Latino community and we were assigned to an elementary school . . . I had been meeting with my team for the whole summer. We organized around a local college or university, in our case, it was USC. For the whole summer, this team of four people with our team leader, Ben Campos, we spent that summer reading books, and talking with each other, and getting to know each other.

Ben took us through the community of El Monte. I mean we met everybody. We met the priest, we met the mechanic, we met parents, we met kids, we met teachers. And we just became deeply acquainted with the community, so by the time school started and I was ready to walk into the first day with this teacher who I would be working with, we already knew the community. That was a hugely important feature of this program—I wish teacher education programs today had more of that component.

I'm trying my best, Shane, to think back to what that was like, and I can tell you I had the really good fortune of being connected with a woman named Rosalie Naumann, who was just a magnificent 5th and 6th grade teacher. I think going into those first few weeks, I was probably pretty uncertain. I didn't know what the hell I was doing exactly. I felt comfortable in the community because we had been there. I felt comfortable with my teammates. I felt very comfortable with Ben and his advice, and I had gotten to know Rosalie the week or two before. But in terms of what I expected, I got to tell you, I didn't know much, and my recollection, hazy as it is, is that I was pretty green and pretty nervous and really willing to follow the lead of this teacher, Rosalie, who fortunately was just as skilled as could be.

Those were my first weeks of teaching . . . a bunch of 6th graders, primarily working-class White and Latino kids, so that was where I first cut my teeth on reading and writing, on teaching reading and writing with this group of kids. I was green. I was young. I didn't know what the hell I was doing and was kind of excited to see what would happen.

Shane to Mike Rose: How have you grown as a teacher? What has changed the most since teaching 6th graders in El Monte, California? [Episode 1: 07:40–13:17]

I've got to say I am so lucky that I love to teach probably more, actually, than I did then. I was eager to do it. I was scared. And trepidatious. I still have a little tinge of that anticipation, I guess, when I walk into a classroom.

But I'm just blessed that it means as much to me now or more as it did when I started out. So what has changed? Well, hopefully I have gotten better at it. You know, you just pick up so many tricks of the trade along the way: How to ask a question, how to give feedback, how to spot when someone is having a difficult time with something, how to see through and understand various kinds of reluctance or resistance. You know, there's just so much you pick up with time. Hopefully, I have learned a lot in that regard.

I'm still as excited, maybe even more so, about the kind of interaction teaching involves. There's something profoundly special it seems to me about having the good fortune to teach because you really are participating with other people in their development. I mean, what other kind of work allows you to do that? I guess certain kinds of pastoral counseling and therapy, maybe certain kinds of medicine or certain ways medicine is practiced. But you know, there's not many occupations that provide that opportunity to get close into people's lives and help them grow in a way they want to grow. So that just captivates me still and means so much to me.

. . . I've also come to appreciate how important listening is . . . I can't tell you what a fundamental pedagogical skill listening has become for me over the decades. I think the better you can hear what someone is asking when they ask a question, or the better you can hear what someone is trying to do with a piece of writing, and the better you are at remembering all that so that you're able to bring it up weeks later in connection with something somebody else says. That kind of really focused and targeted, serious listening is just so rare. Period. I mean think of it, how many people do you know that really listen to you when you sit down to talk with them? . . . I find myself desiring these close-knit and intimate interactions where you have to work really hard in a focused way to understand where somebody is at, where they are trying to go, what it is they are trying to do with a piece of writing, and how to help them get there.

Shane to Nancy Sommers: What led you to teach, and what was your first experience teaching like? [Episode 6: 02:07–06:09]

Oh, it's so much fun to think back on what led me to teaching. You know, we always have to be careful when we try to identify or tell the story of our origins, but if I were to try to look back all those years, I would look back all the way to junior high when we had Career Day and the boys and girls were separated, and the girls had the choices to learn about being a nurse, a homemaker, or a teacher. Those were the only choices, and you can only imagine the boys of course had much more exciting choices—doctor, lawyer, engineer. At that moment, I was very excited to think about teaching and what that might mean, so I formed very early in my mind this idea that I would be a teacher. I don't believe I really understood what that meant, but it was just part of my own identity as I went through high school and college.

I think partly, too, it's because I have had so many crazy, wonderful, idiosyncratic teachers who took leaps of faith with me. I wasn't an obviously promising student at various points in my career, but I had these wonderful teachers. I think of an eighth-grade language arts teacher, a high school English teacher, a college literature professor, and my dissertation advisor, who all took leaps of faith with me. There was something about that, that said to me, "I want to do that too. I want very much to find those students who don't believe that they have promise, academic or otherwise, and help them to see that." I think that became a mission.

In college we were all very, very political, and at a certain point, I realized that I was not actually going to solve all the problems, end the war or . . . create peace in the world, but that maybe I could help somebody write a good sentence, and maybe I could help somebody appreciate literature. That seemed like, again, a good direction.

My first teaching experience was teaching 8th grade, and I look back and smile when I think about that year. I was at Northwestern University and they had a program that took undergrad . . . or recent college graduates and said, "You can go into the classroom." I suppose there was a teaching shortage or otherwise we wouldn't have been able to do that. We had almost no training, and we were just plumped into classrooms in Chicago.

I had tremendous amount of enthusiasm and great passion, very much a person of my time. I just wanted the students to go outside, and read Walt Whitman, and conjugate the color green, and think about *Leaves of Grass*, and look under the microscope, and look at grass, and write about it, and write poems about it. I had just read *Pride and Prejudice*, and I wanted my 8th graders to read that, too. It was a crazy curriculum as I think about it, but students became very enthusiastic and loved it. One thing led to another, I traveled and taught English as a second language in various places in Europe and in Israel. Then, I came back and went to graduate school which started my real interest and love for teaching and writing.

Shane to Chris M. Anson: You were in a unique position as a graduate student in the late 1970s and early 1980s when composition was developing new theories and practices. Do you mind talking about that experience? [Episode 25: 01:29–07:48]

I was at Syracuse University doing a master's in creative writing before I got to Indiana. My first semester there, I was working as an administrative assistant in the office of Project Advance, which was one of the first advanced-college dual-credit programs in the country. I was working alongside a newly minted professor out of the University of Chicago named Bob Schwegler. One of our responsibilities was to help shape the writing curriculum so that high school teachers could be trained to teach high-performing high school students in order to earn Syracuse credit while they were seniors in high school.

I was really interested in everything in the English department. I was interested in all the areas of literary study I
was doing, and in creative writing. I was really interested
in Medieval literature and Old English. I kept talking to
Schwegler about what I might do next after this master's, because I knew I wasn't going to probably become
the world's next greatest novelist. He asked, "Well, what
do you want to do?" I said, "I'm interested in Medieval
literature." And he said, "You're probably not going to find
it very easy to get a position when you graduate. There are
not a lot of jobs in Medieval literature. But there's this new
area on the horizon. It goes by various terms, but typically
composition studies, or *rhetoric and composition*. You should
come to a reading group that I'm involved in and start
reading some of the material."

I signed on as a young graduate student, and the faculty were
reading early, early composition work by people like Janet
Emig and James Britton and others. I got really fascinated
in that work. When I explained that to my creative writing
peers, they didn't want anything to do with it. They really
felt that it was not appropriate to dissect the writing process.
This was something that worked by talent and inspiration,
not something that you could scientifically anatomize. So I
kind of fell away from that ideology, and I started reading
more, going to more of these meetings, and getting more
exposed to the literature. I became so interested that, toward
the last months of my M., Schwegler suggested I apply to
PhD programs [in rhetoric and composition].

There were very few at that time. It was 1979. There was
one at UT Austin, there was one at Indiana, and some
other places . . . when I got to Indiana, the director of
composition was Michael Flanigan . . . he became a fast
mentor to me, and eventually a close friend of mine. It was
really Michael who helped me understand student learners
and student writers. I had not really had that much expo-
sure to theories of teaching at Syracuse. I was very teach-
er-centered. I was very concerned about my knowledge,

my projection of knowledge, my appearance even, and not thinking much about what was really happening in the heads of my students. When I got to Indiana all that changed, because Michael soon helped me to understand and put into practice what I had been reading at Syracuse in that reading circle. I learned a great deal from him.

I owe it to Bob Schwegler that I'm in the field, and I owe it to Michael Flanigan that I learned to teach in a responsible, student-centered way. When I think about what I was doing at Syracuse, it was stand in the front of the room and maybe lecture a bit on principles of form or style, or even grammar, and not really think about what was happening with the students, and really not do much that was active. Flanigan changed all that for me. His curriculum was focused on active learning, on student engagement. Teachers didn't spend a whole lot of time in front of the class. They would present some things and get students to work. There would be lots of active discussion, a lot of small group work, a lot of follow up, and that stuck with me ever since.

Shane to Chuck Bazerman: What has surprised you or continues to surprise you the most about teaching writing? What stands out to you about composition studies over the past fifty years? [Episode 13: 01:41–06:39]

I've taught for over fifty years in higher-ed. What surprised me, continues to surprise me, and I've learned more about, is the students: What they know, how they perceive things, how they develop, how individual they are, and how much you have to speak to them to really be of any value. You need to somehow intervene in their own exploration and their own development. So that means you have to get to know them. My early teaching experience was in 1st grade and 3rd grade. The students were a revelation and that's what motivated me and that's what continues to motivate me. Everyone is different. Even if you're teaching the same course for the ninetieth time, they're different students. That's been the big surprise.

All the research and theory has been simply to understand *what is writing* so I can help students explore it and use it better as part of their own development. When I started, there were only a few general folk beliefs about writing: All writing was the same, "good" writing was "good" writing, some people had talent, others didn't. Now, this is like partly true, it's in most expression, you find it in yourself that there are certain favorite forms of writing and they define "real" writing . . . certain literary styles were favored and thought to be worth attention. Everything else was boring, nonfiction, non-creative, right?

As I've come to know writing a lot more alongside many colleagues . . . we've explored writing in different ways, both as the great variety of texts in the world, their role in the world, but also how people produce them and how people develop as readers. That's the thing that's most changed. Students are still students, right? They each come with their own histories and their own motives. But we have a lot more understanding of writing and texts, and how we can use them to help people grow as writers. I've looked into that myself and it's moved from an individual facing the challenges of a particular task. Although, that's important, that's how we experience writing, that's how our students experience writing. You start to see how writing done by many people over many millennia has really worked its way into the heart of society and, in fact, made possible the large forms of cooperation and identity and activity that formed the modern world.

I keep calling it the hidden infrastructure of modernity. It's invisible to most people, the enormous importance it is. People's development as writers and their processes are embedded in that great complexity . . . every role of power involves massive amounts of reading and writing. Writing—different from reading—is more receptive. Writing is having a voice. You don't write, you don't have a voice.

Shane to Beverly J. Moss: What got you interested in studying African American community literacies? How did you see connections between community literacy and teaching writing? [Episode 9: 01:39–04:07]

It's an interesting moment, and this takes me back to when I was in graduate school. My dissertation director, Marcia Farr, is a sociolinguist by training, and so it was interesting to be introduced to composition and literacy studies and rhetoric through thinking about sociolinguistics. We read *Ways with Words* by Shirley Brice Heath. What was interesting to me about *Ways with Words* was not only the introduction to ethnography, because we were getting that in the course, we were getting introduced to the ethnography of literacy, but also that the site for *Ways with Words* was the area that my family grew up in and still lives in. And that I was born in. I kept thinking, "Oh, my goodness, this is sort of about me." So there was a personal connection for me to that work—being from the Piedmont Carolinas—and having that as the site of her work, recognizing moments in that book when she's talking about what happens in those Black church services. I thought, "I've been in those services. I grew up in those settings." And it was that moment where I felt connected to the field in a different way, that I could do this kind of work.

I had gone to graduate school, particularly in composition and rhetoric, because I was interested in the kind of writing and literacies that people do outside of school that have an impact on what happens in the classroom, and here was this study that almost gave me permission to do that, that said, "Oh, yeah, this is actually a way for you to connect."

It gave me a methodology . . . I think about ethnography as a way of thinking. It gave me a way to think about the work I was interested in, and it was also encouragement to really think about and to explore different literacy. Literacy, not only possibilities, but sort of the literacy practices, the rich literacy practices in the communities that I grew up in, which sort of took me back to the Black church. I mean, the way that Heath presented information

opened up all these possibilities, but I thought there were
even richer possibilities, there was more to do, more to see
. . . I tell people I have an agenda. I don't hide that. My
agenda is to document the rich literacy practices that occur
in African American community spaces.

DENOUEMENT

As teachers, we have our own stories to tell. Some might look like
the narratives above. Maybe we were inspired by a high school English teacher. Or we fell in love with a book because we saw ourselves
in it, or we saw our community in it. Or an advisor or mentor told
us to apply to graduate programs and we took a leap of faith. Even
if some of our stories are similar, our pathways are all unique because we come from different places. We have different educational
experiences, different teachers, different mentors. We have different
histories and identities. You see, our pathways are different, but we
share a common bond: we are committed to this work as educators because we understand how important teaching writing is for
ourselves and students, as well as our local and global communities.
Teaching draws us close into lives.

The interviews in this chapter, from teachers who have taught
for a combined 150+ years, demonstrate how teaching is relational
and communal. There is no other profession quite like it where
20 to 25 people with different histories and identities gather in
the same room for months and learn together, read together, write
together, share together. As teachers, we are in an extremely important position. Teaching is an opportunity to encourage and support
students; to walk alongside lived experiences; to listen and share
in learning; to facilitate meaning and knowledge; to advocate for
agency and amplify voices and identities. Like writing, teaching
is a process. Through these interviews, I listened to well-known,
established writing teachers still asking questions and contemplat-
ing their teaching practices. They all understand where they started
and how they are still becoming as writing teachers. How they are
still *in process*. What stood out to me was their enthusiasm when
it came to talking about students, and the childlike glee that came
over them when they talked about their teachers and mentors, and

their unique paths to teaching. To me, teaching is about asking questions, listening, and learning how to ask better ones. It is a lifelong practice of reflection.

My hope is that the following questions will allow teachers and students another chance to talk about what it means to teach writing and the importance of writing itself. These questions give us an opportunity to reflect on our own histories, identities, values, and beliefs about language and writing. We are always adapting and evolving as writing teachers:

- What does it mean to teach composition in the 21st century? How are we defining literacy? What is the purpose of first-year writing?
- What key principles or concepts do you use to help you teach? What are your classroom practices and strategies communicating about what it means to learn, read, write, and compose?
- What assumptions or beliefs do you have about language? How are you addressing the politics of language through your teaching and assessment?
- What kind of classroom culture do you hope to establish with students? What are your outcomes and goals, and what strategies and alternative practices might help students engage with/ in those outcomes?
- How are you meeting the needs of students in your institutional context? What approach to teaching might best support those students? How are you listening and responding to students and their writing?
- What resources are available in and around your institutional context, and how might you draw from those resources to grow as a teacher? How might you collaborate with colleagues and other departments or initiatives across campus?
- How are you embodying your sense of self through your teaching? How are you drawing on your own strengths, knowledges, and experiences? What is informing your teaching, and why?

2

Two-Year Colleges

Two-year colleges, sometimes referred to as community colleges and historically called "junior colleges," are rich sites for teaching, learning, and research. Most two-year colleges have open admission policies, and many are intentionally designed to assist the communities around them. Two-year colleges serve nearly half of undergraduates in the United States. They usually have lower tuition costs compared to four-year universities, and many serve place-based students (e.g., students with families and full-time jobs that are geographically bound to a specific area). For some folks, two-year colleges offer the only path to higher education. As Carolyn Calhoon-Dillahunt (2011) writes, "For many returning—and often place-bound—students, for students who struggled academically in high school, and for low-income students, two-year colleges may be the only means they have for accessing higher education" (p. 119). Two-year colleges have historically been an inclusive space for diverse learners: veterans, low-income students, multilinguals, returning adults, and dual-enrolled high schoolers.

These institutions have distinct missions connected to their students. Two-year colleges are not homogenous. Some are urban, some rural. Some are predominantly White institutions (PWIs), some are Minority-Serving Institutions (MSIs). Some focus on dual-enrollment and transfer, while others develop programs and curriculum around vocations. Writing instruction and writing classes are comprehensive within these contexts given their student populations and unique institutional operations. George B. Vaughan (1982) describes two-year colleges as a "coat of many colors" (p. 7). English faculty often teach a range of classes, including basic or developmental writing and first-year composition courses, and sometimes creative writing and literature courses. This interdisciplinarity requires a great depth of knowledge and skills. Howard Tinberg (1997) writes that it is easier to "say what we don't teach than what we do" (p. 11). Two-year colleges are sites that truly represent diversity and inclusivity and are essential to postsecondary and professional preparation and success.

Two-year colleges were formed from the Morrill Act of 1862 which was signed to grant land to states to establish and support agricultural and technical education. The goal was to develop colleges with curriculum that focused on science and engineering (as opposed to classical liberal arts education) given the demands and manufacturing processes brought on by the Industrial Revolution. Two-year colleges played a significant role through the devastation of World War II and the need of industry workers (Vaughan, 1982). Most two-year college histories center on the importance of the Higher Education for American Democracy in 1947, also known as the Truman Commission Report (Sullivan & Toth, 2016). Even though these institutions have a rich history and tradition in higher education, two-year colleges are usually positioned in the margins of composition studies at large. Holly Hassel and Joanne Baird Giordano (2013) challenge the academic hierarchies and misconceptions about teaching in two-year colleges:

> We press college composition instructors to embrace an open-access mission of higher education . . . we call for a scholarly reimagination that repositions two-year college teaching at the center of our disciplinary discourse. (p. 118)

Like Hassel and Giordano, I agree two-year colleges need to be represented more in professional discourse, including academic journals and national conferences, and should be amplified in conversations on teaching writing. Two-year college instructors offer greater insight on what it means to teach writing to a range of students and these institutions often work closely with K–12 systems and universities (Calhoon-Dillahunt, 2011). Two-year colleges should be positioned at the front of conversations about teaching writing, in my opinion.

I chose to place this chapter at the beginning of this book for that reason and to address one gap in traditional composition anthologies. Most don't include two year-college perspectives and experiences. This affects grad programs in rhetoric and composition and composition studies at large. Since two-year colleges are often situated in the margins of writing theory and research, these contexts are frequently invisible to grad students in traditional rhet/comp programs. English graduate programs "need to reckon with" the lack of attention given to two-year colleges and "change those structures" (see *TYCA Guidelines for Preparing Teachers of English in the Two-Year College*). Graduate programs ought to prepare and develop writing teachers to teach in two-year colleges. The 2020–2021 academic job market is one consideration for the needed increased attention on two-year colleges, but it isn't the *only* reason to reconfigure grad school curriculum. Familiarizing grad students with two-year college opportunities and challenges, as well as reading research from teacher-scholars in these contexts is important and ethical work. It increases equity in our field. There's a real need for programs to explicitly professionalize students for teaching in two-year colleges because, in short, they play an extraordinary role in higher ed and serve diverse students in innovative ways.

Teaching writing in two-year colleges is time consuming and labor intensive in part due to their institutional and administrative missions (see *TYCA Working Paper #2: Two-Year College English Faculty Teaching Adjustments Related to Workload*). Most two-year colleges are teaching intensive, and many depend on non-tenure or part-time and adjunct labor. Instructors teach upward of five to six classes a semester along with other college and departmental service commitments. Professional identities in two-year colleges are unique and complex (Andelora, 2005; Toth et al., 2013), and so are other aspects connected to two-year institutions, such as transfer and placement (see *The Journal of Writing Assessment Special Issue on Two-Year College Writing Placement*, 2019). Having talked with teachers across all kinds of two-year contexts, I noticed a trend: two-year college teachers are passionate about teaching writing and committed to their students. They teach writing in ways that are designed to help students pursue whatever life or career path they want to take.

INTERVIEWS

That trend will resonate through these interviews. In this chapter, I talk with Sharon Mitchler, Carolyn Calhoon-Dillahunt, Jessica Nastal, and Howard Tinberg about teaching in two-year colleges. Mitchler teaches at Centralia College and Calhoon-Dillahunt teaches at Yakima Valley College in the Pacific Northwest; Nastal teaches at Prairie State College outside Chicago; and Tinberg teaches at Bristol Community College in Massachusetts. In these interviews, I ask them to reflect on their institutional contexts as well as their pedagogical practices. Mitchler talks about what it is like to teach at a small rural college between Seattle and Portland. She shares how community is central to her pedagogical approach and describes classroom practices that help her construct this sense of community, such as "safe writing," modeling, and peer response. Calhoon-Dillahunt talks about teaching a wide range of classes, including developmental writing and first-year composition, and offers advice for future two-year college instructors. Nastal reflects on how she teaches first-year composition "as an introduction to writing studies" course, and how she encourages students to think critically about their role in education. Tinberg concludes by talking about the importance of reading, he shares challenges two-year colleges face, and offers future direction for teaching and research in two-year colleges.

Shane to Sharon Mitchler: Do you mind talking about Centralia College in Centralia, Washington, and your approach to teaching writing? [Episode 14: 02:28–06:12]

> Centralia College is halfway between Seattle and Portland. It's a very small rural college, we have about 1,900 full-time enrolled students that's divided between a variety of programs and locations. So, we have academic transfers, those are students who are doing two years with us and then going to another institution . . . they may do a class with us, or they may do a year with us, or they may do a full two years and not complete a degree, or they may do three years and change their mind and then transfer. There's different paths. Then, we have technical programs and certificates and degrees, those range from one-quarter

certificates all the way up to a year certificate or a two-year degree. We also do continuing education classes for adults, pre-college classes, starting with learning the language for second-language students, because again, as a rural entity, if we don't offer it, it doesn't exist . . . we also do GED and high school equivalent, and then we have a number of campuses, and we have two prison sites, students who are at Cedar Creek Correctional Facility . . .

We have a limited number of faculty. We have five full-time faculty in what's called the English department. We don't have a separate WPA because we're so small. We all teach composition and rhetoric, and some of us teach other things as well. I have a master's degree in humanities and a master's degree in English and a PhD in English. So I teach literature and composition and a whole series of humanities courses.

Our comp classes are kept somewhere between 24 and 28 students, depending on how many sections you're teaching . . .we have English 99, then English 101, which is expository writing, and English 102, which is a research class . . . we do technical writing, we do creative writing. The short version is, throw me into a room full of students, I need to know who they are and what their goals are, and then I adjust. If you want to teach in a place where every single section is going to be a little different, the community college is the place for you, because the mix of students and the demographics can be really fascinating even from section to section in the same term. We have a wide range in economic backgrounds, so we have folks who never dreamed they'd becoming to college ever, ever. It wasn't on their list, it wasn't something that they have family connection to . . . we have lots and lots of first-generation students, and then we have lots of people whose life has taken a turn, they've lost a job, a relationship has changed, a whole variety of reasons and they all ended up in a class together. So, facilitating those conversations in that space is eternally exciting.

Shane to Sharon Mitchler: How do you facilitate class conversations? How do you bring that community together? [Episode 14: 06:13–09:44]

> I'll use English 101 as an example because that's the class that most of our students are going to take. It's the place where they're going to see people who are in other areas as well. I've got diesel students, nursing students, someone who's trying to finish high school. They're all together in the same room. So building a community becomes really important. I also know that there are a lot of people who are anxious. They're not excited about this space, they're not sure who else is in the room with them. They may have tremendous amounts of confidence in some aspects of their academic life and not at all in others, and nobody wants to reveal that on the first day of class. We do a lot of safe writing, five minutes at the very beginning of every class.
>
> I have a stack of cards with questions on them and those questions are generated by students at the end of each class . . . at the very beginning of class, one person draws a card, I write the question up on the board and we spend five minutes writing either on that question or something else that they want to write about themselves. They can do whatever they want. It's quiet writing time. I never see it, and I never ask for it. I use that as a stepping stone . . . here's a way that you can start thinking about what you might want to write about . . . they keep a journal or they keep it someplace in their notebook, they do it on a computer. That's how you start writing. You start with the things that you've already got. It starts to help leverage a sense of . . .writing isn't a thing you just sit down and do. It's a prolonged activity, and you handle that in lots of different ways.
>
> Another thing I do an awful lot of is modeling. When we get ready to do something like peer response, we use one of my papers first. I often write right along with students so they can see my reaction to that . . . if I'm getting frustrated, if I'm getting lost, if I'm like, I do not know

what to do with this paragraph . . . they get to see all of that. So, when we do peer response, we'll start with one of my papers and I'll put it up on the screen, and we'll talk our way through, well, what could you say to me about this, and what's helpful, and what's not helpful? It gives them a chance to practice the skills without having it be their work because the sense of identity that's connected to what they're writing is often right below the surface for a lot of these students. And it's really scary to have your work in the hands of other people. This gives them a safe space to see how it works and to try things out and they learn really quickly that you can't hurt my feelings, and that I really do want to know what's not working . . . we do an awful lot of that kind of work, and then when we shift into students doing that work. I'm roaming around the room as they're working in small groups or they're working in pairs, so that they can ask me questions and I can ask them questions as we go. It drops the stakes quite a bit. Again, these are students who have huge time commitments outside of the classroom, and the idea that they are going to go home and spend two hours agonizing over a draft is probably not a useful context when you're thinking about how you're going to develop class time. So, things that you can do in class that give them a chance to practice, that help to encourage them to see that it's a process that it takes longer, those are really helpful.

Shane to Sharon Mitchler: It's important for us to consider how we are ethically assigning and assessing writing. Do you mind sharing how you meet the needs of students who are working 40+ hours a week, who have a family, and who don't necessarily have the same affordance or relationship with time compared to more "traditional" students? [Episode 14: 09:45–11:19]

> I use shorter reading assignments. If we use longer reading assignments, we come back to them multiple times. It's not, "Read 20 pages, come back and let's have a conversation." When we've read something, the first thing that happens in class the next day is everybody gets a highlighter and

I ask them to put the phrase or the word or the section of what they read that meant something to them, or that made sense to them, or that seemed important to them. Then, we develop our conversation based on that. We can come back to that same piece two or three times and delve into the finer points, but that highlights that their knowledge is important. It gets them actively involved in class and helps them see that the class is focused on what they need to accomplish, the goals of the class . . .

With a lot of adult learners, it's important to make that direct connection. They're spending money. They're spending time. There are other things that they're not doing because they're in that classroom. So, you better make sure that the connections between what you're doing and the end goal, and how that attaches to the world that they inhabit when they're not in your room are crystal clear. You don't waste time, and you don't ask people to do things that you don't scaffold well for them to be able to do.

Shane to Carolyn Calhoon-Dillahunt: Do you mind talking about Yakima Valley College and share a bit about what you teach? [Episode 49: 01:02–05:19]

Yakima Valley is a unique context. It's a two-year college and that's a unique context, but we're in a very agricultural area, yet Yakima itself is a city. There's a lot of drug abuse, there's all kinds of health issues that accompany poverty, there's mental health issues. That's our community, so that's who is in the classroom. I'm from this area so I know this community well. Yakima is also heavily Latinx. The city is pretty much bi-cultural and the campus is about 60% Latinx students . . . for the past few years that has been the majority. I've been here for 20 years. Given this context, and given that we're not a college-educated community on the whole, our students are often coming with pretty modest goals in mind, or maybe no goals in mind.

They're coming because it seems like the right thing to do and they're coming to transform their lives. Whatever that means for them. You teach writing with that in mind. It's not really about your content first. It's about your people that you're working with and what they're going to need to be able to move wherever they choose to move. You want to prepare them to move because many times they start with very modest goals and then they realize they have brains and it's like, "Oh, you mean, I could go to a four-year college?" They get really interested . . . because many of them had impoverished K–12 educations. Once they get some really good, challenging education, many of them like it and want to continue. They feel really inspired. You also want to set them up for the career goals they have. If they want to get right out there, you want them to be able to do that and do that effectively, but you also want to kind of keep pathways open for them so that they're able to do things that they hadn't imagined they'd be able to do before.

My college has two developmental writing courses prior to English 101 or first-year writing, and because we're on the quarter system, our writing course is a two-quarter sequence. So the first one is just basically academic writing, introduction to academic writing and using source-based writing. The second one is . . . called argumentation. It's a little bit more research and taking a clear position. So that's kind of the span of composition courses. All of us teach composition primarily. There are very few literature offerings or creative writing offerings or things like that. At most, I probably teach one a year. So really, it's composition and that's the whole department. Even though an increasing number are trained in composition, that's not the majority. Most folks are not coming from writing instruction or writing theory backgrounds.

. . . I generally teach . . . I was going to say about half developmental writing and half college-level writing. I think it's leaning a little bit more towards college level writing at this point because we've changed our placement tool in the past few years . . . more students are placing into 101 as a result, so that's a happy outcome. Though, I am sad because developmental writing are my favorite classes to teach. There's fewer of them, but that's what I teach when I can. I also do some advanced comp courses. I teach research writing pretty regularly. A colleague and I do a collaborative developmental reading and developmental writing course.

Shane to Carolyn Calhoon-Dillahunt: So you teach a wide range of classes from developmental writing to a more argument-centered writing class. What's your approach to teaching these different writing classes? [Episode 49: 05:20–09:38]

It's not that different from developmental to college level. Our entire department has adopted a process-oriented approach, so we see writing as a recursive process and graded writing is always stuff that has gone through revision and feedback processes along the way. In developmental writing courses, I tend to use portfolios to allow more time for the process before grading is involved . . . our developmental writing courses also don't have letter grades, they have "satisfactory" if they're ready to move on to the next level; "credit" if they've completed most of the coursework, but haven't met the course outcomes; and "no credits" would be like if they haven't achieved that. I teach in a quarter system so we don't have a lot of time. Most classes I'm usually doing probably two to three major writing projects and a lot of other writing. I integrate reading in everything I do, though, much more fully when I have that linked reading class where I can actually concentrate on that.

I'm interested in teaching for transfer. I can't say that we've adopted that as a department, but I try to integrate aspects of that where I'm doing a lot of metacognitive work with writing and trying to really make explicit core concepts and the core abilities that they're learning in these areas and the ways that they're applying to other things. I'd say one of the things outside of composition that has really informed my practice in the past three or four years now is our college has adopted an equity agenda, which means different things to different people. I am on that bandwagon and even though administration may not see equity in quite the same way or they're learners on this, I am happy to be there to shape this conversation and to be a part of this conversation.

Part of that is we've received many Title V grants as an Hispanic-Serving Institution. With one of the more recent grants we received, it was devoted to faculty professional development across the disciplines. We adopted a program at the time called ESCALA and it's a consulting organization that does engaged learning for Hispanic-Serving Institutions . . . this program involves going through workshops to kind of learn some key concepts about equity and about teaching minoritized populations. It kind of has a ladder with three prongs and it has the idea of . . . relationships is one of the key aspects of engaging students in learning, building competence is another one, and building trust. That's part of the assessment system, too . . . having a system that's trustworthy. These are things that I felt like I was already practicing, but it's really helped me to be more conscious, more intentional with my planning, more explicit and transparent with students about what I'm meaning. I think it's been a really healthy, positive change for me and for the faculty involved at this point across the discipline.

Shane to Carolyn Calhoon-Dillahunt: How would you prepare someone to teach at a two-year college, or what resources or pedagogical strategies would you recommend? [Pedagogue Bonus: 01:44–07:38]

It's helpful to understand the two-year college space that you're interested in when you go to apply for jobs and make sure you understand the culture, because they're not all the same as is true of any institution. I think they get homogenized more than they really are, and so they vary quite a bit. But in general, the things that are common is most two-year colleges have open admissions. So you do need to understand appropriate practices and effective practices for working with adult learners. I would hope anyone in our field would, but I mean in two-year colleges, particularly, you're working with minoritized populations. You need to not only understand what are effective practices for minoritized populations, but you also need to be invested in that. You need to want to work towards equity and social justice, or we're not really doing anyone a service. You need to understand that your role is not necessarily preparing folks for the university or college. That's certainly an option, and that should be an option available to all students, but you are part of a community that's working with students of all different ilk . . . you might have to be a little bit more pragmatic. I think it's really focusing on learning, and less concerned about your particular content or whatever, and more about what are the learning things that you're trying to get them to do and how can we do that?

I think not only understanding how adults learn but also understanding who your students are. I think 83% . . . at our college, are first-generation. They don't have any language of college, and they don't have any of the support systems. They never did. You can't go in expecting that they know things that they don't . . . you have to teach it. No one else is teaching it. They're not going to get it anywhere else . . . college professors tend to be people who came from privileged, I mean, it might be modestly so, but I mean, you came from literate backgrounds, more often than not; you came because you were a good student, more often than not; you came because the K–12 system served you well, whether you liked it or not. And out there is not you. They're different than you.

So the things that worked for you or the things that you internalized and never knew, are not who your students are. Really understanding how to work with novices. I think for folks at a graduate school, I think you really need to understand that scholarship is going to be on your own time,

Two-Year Colleges / 51

more often than not. That doesn't mean you shouldn't do it, but it's going to be not rewarded in the same way, and certainly not supported in the same way, but there are ways to make it work. So collaborations, thinking about various ways you might publish or put your information out there, thinking about how to focus in on your classroom as a space and use that. Because it's very rich, and there's a lot to do. But you do have to think about scholarship differently if you're at a two-year college.

What other advice would I give? . . . I think a lot of folks in graduate school get pretty honed in on the discipline. There are reasons for that. It was very hard for composition-writing studies to establish itself as a discipline. So we cling to that, and the disciplinary knowledge is important, but at the two-year college, you're going to need to take things from education, you're going to need to take things from developmental studies, you're going to need to take things from disability studies, you're going to need to take things from a lot of spaces. You're also going to be doing kind of this gen ed. You're also going to be working with your colleagues across disciplines more directly . . . I think coming in with that kind of mindset—this is very collaborative. You're not going to get to just sit in your office and work on your stuff. You are always going to be working for the good of the whole. You're always going to need a lot of resources beyond the discipline in order to do that well.

Shane to Jessica Nastal: Can you talk about your approach to teaching writing at Prairie State College, a community college in the south suburbs of Chicago? [Episode 8: 03:25–07:39]

This semester I'm teaching three classes. I have reassigned time . . . I'm department chair this year and I have an overload for a special project I'm doing on student success. Our contract for full-time faculty is five courses a semester. Then, if you teach two composition classes that load gets reduced to four. The online classes are capped at 24 and then English Composition One and Two are capped at 22.

Developmental English classes are capped at 18. So, how all of this affects how I teach writing or my approach is . . . basically, I just want to have fun with my students. I am trying to implement a little bit of a writing about writing approach but I'm not totally there. I like the idea of using this class as an introduction to writing studies. The reason is because it's the best way for me to be able to structure for students a space where I can help them understand how we can use our individual experiences and beliefs to inform whatever kind of work we do and whatever connections we're making with other people.

One of my approaches also is that connection with my students. I grew up on the South Side of Chicago and moved to the suburbs. I grew up in a working-class family. Most of my family before my generation did not go to college. I can relate to some of the concerns that my students have, and I think the thing that they find most fun is that I hated composition as an undergraduate. So, using the experiences that I had growing up and struggles I've had with writing, and then the realization I had—that writing can be something that does something. It can be a force for positive action. Helping my students understand that is a real privilege.

The past couple of years I had a lot of reassigned time for work in assessment and accreditation and I was still doing the work that I loved, but over the summer I had more space to think about how I want to redesign classes. So, in the past I had focused a lot on response to student writing. Students in both Comp One and Comp Two would . . . we'd have some shared readings on controversies in the field of writing assessment, in particular, which is my background. So things like automated writing evaluation, whether to use rubrics and language policies. That was really fun . . . but I always want to challenge myself to do something new and to learn more and apply what I'm learning from colleagues into the classroom. So this year I am teaching a contextualized English 101 class where

I'm trying to bring in some principles of professional and technical writing into English 101, which uses the WPA Outcome Statement and the *Framework for Success in Post-secondary Writing* as the foundation.

In English 102, which is our Comp Two research class, the research parameters I'm using are the submission guidelines for *Queen City Writers*. And so the goal is that some students would continue working on their projects for publication. I was challenged to bring in some of the most recent and exciting scholarship in our field. Some of the things that we're reading this semester are Aja Martinez's work, some scholarship from the *Journal of Young Scholars in Writing* and *Queen City Writers*. It's a challenge for me because I don't really know what I think about some of the stuff . . . I haven't had a lot of time to think about them. But I'm excited to hear what other people are thinking. This makes the class dynamic for me. I think it helps my students because they see my passion for the field and my respect for them and treating them like scholars.

Shane to Jessica Nastal: So it sounds like your composition class takes a different shape than perhaps other first-year writing classes. It sounds like an introduction to writing and rhetoric course or a seminar on composition theory? [Episode 8: 07:40–10:15]

One thing that students do comment on is that they appreciate this scaffolding . . . it's really like a seminar. So in my syllabus for the Composition Two classes this semester, I told them that it will function as a research seminar in rhetoric and composition/writing studies. Even with English 101, there's different modules or different units and everything is related . . . and so, students were able to see how the ideas built on each other within the units and then across the semester or across the session. And in the middle of it, they hated it because it felt redundant, especially for people who are not interested in pursuing this field I just discovered as a graduate student. But by the end it, overwhelmingly, unprompted, too, students will say how they started to see how things fit together and they appreciated that structure. The reason I do it like that is because I think that it provides students with a lot of structure and foundation. I've seen their writing grow tremendously.

I guess the other reason that I said that I chose response to student writing because this is where my research is, and that's true, but it's because of the experiences that I've had as a student and that my students have had. We can all think of some of the best feedback we've ever had and how it made us feel and some of the worst feedback we've had and how that made us feel. I'm trying to encourage students to think critically about that and about their role in their education and how they can change things. That doesn't have to be within the field of education or writing studies. They can be more of an active participant in their own education. If they don't like the way someone makes them feel, they can have a productive conversation about that or they can think about why they felt badly. This is why I think it's such a privilege to teach because it's like, in what other space could I try to suggest a way that I think maybe could help them have a better life? That's presumptuous almost of me to think that way, but I don't know, it's something I really am struggling with.

Shane to Howard Tinberg: You've been at Bristol Community College for 30+ years teaching first-year writing. You wrote a chapter in *Deep Reading: Teaching Reading in the Writing Classroom*, which won the 2019 CCCC Outstanding Book Award, about how students experience reading in a community college first-year composition class. Can you talk about the importance of teaching reading and how teachers can frame reading in their first-year writing classes? [Episode 33: 10:08–14:32]

Sure, I don't want to generalize, but for many community college students, reading is not seen as much as an opportunity as a barrier to their success, their academic success. Of course, many . . . read from the screen and read in a multitasking way. So there's little opportunity, I think, for them to dive deep, or invitation to dive deep into the reading. I think, in some ways, we faculty at community colleges are, I was going to say another word . . . we'll say "facilitate" that assumption or promote that assumption that it's okay for students to come linger on the surfaces. Cynics among us even say, "I will assign my reading, but I'm not assuming the students will do the reading. So here's my PowerPoint demonstration." Students, of course, so often come away from that experience saying, "Well, why did I buy this textbook? What exactly was this textbook doing in this class? I don't have to read. My teacher's going to give me all the bullet points. Why would I bother to read?"

They have very good points . . . I think in some ways, we faculty haven't fully integrated the reading within our own course. It's something we do because when we were students, texts were assigned and the assumption is we went out and read them, not with any help, necessarily. We were on our own. But my students require some assistance, it requires some invitations and requires some skills and strategies to be able to read well, what is in front of them.

I mentioned in the article that historically, reading has been seen as developmental skill. So those folks in the developmental part of the college would be entrusted with the mission of teaching and reading, and that those of us in the English Department, well, what were we doing exactly? We were creating a taste for literature, if that's the way to put it. Or in a writing class, we were inviting self-reflection to the written word, having students get a sense of who they are as individuals.

But it dawned on me for a variety of reasons that reading should be a crucial part of every single course at the college. But I think many of us faculty are assuming that it be done somewhere else, but not in the classroom. I think it was Robert Scholes who said reading is invisible. We have to make it visible to our students. We have to spend time talking about how we read and actually have them read in class. That's something to learn. That's a data point. That's something we have to understand. How well do our students read the work that we're assigning?

Of course, as faculty, we have to ask those questions as we assemble our syllabus: why these readings? Why these and not the others? What's our rationale here, what's our pedagogical explanation? I don't think we do that often enough. I'll say this about the OER movement, the Open Education Resource movement, too, that it's forced many of us to justify the readings that we require, that come at 100, 150, 200 bucks, maybe more. Do we really, from a moral perspective, want to ask students to dish out that money when we don't really understand the role of that textbook in our class, or we're not really spending time walking students through and showing them how to become deep readers of this work? It's a good, good check on our choices because of the situation that our students are facing.

Shane to Howard Tinberg: What are some of the biggest challenges facing two-year colleges? What would you say, maybe even more specifically, are some challenges writing teachers face in two-year colleges? [Episode 33: 19:46–22:43]

Well, I can state the obvious which is the lack of funding, proper funding, for that element of higher ed. Over the years that I've been at Bristol and Mass, Bristol is part of the Massachusetts Community College system, the state has withdrawn support in staggering amounts over the years. We used to be almost like a 60% public institution funded by the public. Now, gosh, it must be closer to 30%. Over the years, I've thought about this question of what holds us back. When I say, "hold us," I mean our students, as well as those of us who work at the community colleges. I've come to believe that it's in some ways psychological. We do not—meaning those of us who've committed ourselves to two-year college or community college—see the possibilities. I've written about this a lot, that while our students sometimes have difficulty seeing the horizon and seeing how they may succeed down the road, I think we faculty also tend to limit our vision as to what we can do in the classroom, how we personally can succeed as professionals. So we don't learn as much. We don't review our curriculum as often. We're not as open to change.

Yeah, I know I'm generalizing here, but I've considered it an important part of my work to reach out to faculty, both in my college and elsewhere to two-year colleges to mentor them, to maybe even be a kind of example of someone, of a teacher scholar who can . . . so we could teach five sections, but also write for publication. It's still a kind of rare thing. It's a rare bird, because we do teach so much at the community college. But as I said, we have no choice but to reflect on our teaching if we want to improve it. If we want to continue to learn our craft and to be able to make our courses interesting to our students and stimulating, we need to innovate as best we can.

But it's a scary thing to do that. It means essentially subjecting your teaching on an ongoing basis to research, to reflection. I'm really into classroom research, still am. Trying to figure out how my students are responding to the tasks that I give them. I've always used student voices within my writing because I feel that they have something to teach me about the work. When we shut down, we don't draw upon students' work in our publications, I think that that's a real void.

Shane to Howard Tinberg: What future direction for research and teaching might you suggest others think about and study moving forward in two-year colleges? [Episode 33: 22:44–27:45]

I've been amazed at the crop of teacher-scholars and activists, Patrick Sullivan is one of them. When I first started writing about the two-year college experience, most people were not writing for publication. They may have been scholars, but they weren't necessarily exchanging their ideas with others. Right now, it's huge. Such significant numbers and you've named them early before our conversation here, people who can do all that, who can teach and share what they've learned in teaching and write eloquently passionately about their work. So I hope that that continues. There are pressures. Most definitely pressures on all of us who teach community college, to be productive and to be accountable for the teaching that we do.

There are a lot of demands on our work, but I hope . . . I dearly hope that each community college system will support and nurture teacher-scholars to see the teaching at the community college, teaching anywhere, requires constant reflection, and that we allow some space for colleagues to do that. Sabbaticals, obviously being one of them. But even space within a semester, a typical semester. Obviously it's crass to say, but compensate folks in order to do so. I worry about younger faculty not necessarily making a great deal of money because of the economics of teaching at a community college. So they have to load on the courses and load on the online courses, especially. They may burn out sooner than later. Burnout was often cited for me, as one of the seemingly inevitable byproducts of teaching in community college.

At some point you stop, you begin to lack energy. You're not curious anymore. As far as I can see that's public enemy number one for faculty who teach at community colleges. I think we have to hopefully create the conditions for people to continue to want to learn, to be curious, to tackle difficult questions, teaching questions. By the way, the scholarship doesn't necessarily have to be classroom research. It could be more traditional conventional scholarship, maybe even a lab-based research. I still think that's a possibility. I do worry about two-year colleges morphing into cheaper four-year baccalaureate program. Obviously, many colleges have done that. There's a unique community mission at open access public two-year colleges, community colleges, that needs to be maintained. But there will be lots of pressures. There are already lots of pressures to, in some way, become that affordable four-year school and make it less accountable to the community. That would be a shame if that were to happen.

Within our own professional organizations, I think those of us who teach at open access institutions need to keep our voices loud and insistent. I know that colleagues mean well, definitely in composition and rhetoric, we are thoroughly committed to teaching, but we're not immune and they're not immune to the privileges of academe, shall we put it. So sometimes the voices of folks who teach at teaching-intensive institutions are not always heard at our professional meetings. I think we have to speak up for ourselves. We have to be good scholars. We have to demand that we be let into our flagship journals to share what we know about teaching, at same time, keeping our feet firmly on the ground.

DENOUEMENT

These interviews bring attention to some practices and strategies two-year college teachers use in writing classes, and show how different teachers approach writing given their pedagogical values and institutional missions. My hope is that this conversation illuminates the range of two-year college contexts and the diverse students they serve, and that this chapter is just a springboard for graduate programs and the field to resist placing two-year colleges in the margins. I think this conversation speaks to the labor, teaching, and research activity happening in two-year colleges, and that this work demands increased visibility to create a more equitable and sustainable future in composition studies. These interviews provide a glimpse into the nuanced nature of two-year colleges and the range of knowledge needed to teach effectively within these contexts. Teaching in two-year colleges takes a reimagination of best approaches to teaching writing.

I would encourage others to read *Teaching Composition at the Two-Year College* (Sullivan & Toth, 2016), a collection of essays and the first critical sourcebook of its kind dedicated to teaching writing at two-year colleges. I would also recommend *Sixteen*

Teachers Teaching: Two-Year College Perspectives (Sullivan, 2020) and the flagship journal for the Two-Year College English Association (TYCA), *Teaching English in the Two-Year College*. These texts provide even greater inquiry into two-year college contexts and are terrific resources that amplify the work of two-year college writing instructors. Mitchler, Calhoon-Dillahunt, Nastal, and Tinberg reminded me of the importance of knowing our students and institutional contexts, and building curriculum in meaningful ways as a response to these needs. I offer the following questions based on our conversation:

- What historical and current conversations about teaching writing are happening in two-year college contexts? How are two-year college perspectives being centered in your English program (undergraduate and graduate)?
- How are you considering your student populations through your approach to teaching? How are you designing and developing writing curriculum to be more accessible, inclusive, and diverse?
- How are you supporting first-year students in ways that move beyond transferring knowledge to other academic contexts? How are first-year writing classes sites for community engagement and activism?
- How are you teaching reading in first-year writing? How are you considering the costs and ethics of asking students to purchase textbooks? What are the affordances of using open access materials in first-year writing?
- What kinds of relationships and collaborations do four-year universities and two-year colleges have, and how can these bonds be strengthened in your local/regional context?

3

Historically Black Colleges and Universities

The Higher Education Act of 1965 defines Historically Black Colleges and Universities (HBCUs) as "any historically black college or university that was established prior to 1964, whose principal mission was, and is, the education of black Americans" (1965). HBCUs are diverse and dynamic sites for learning and teaching writing. Most are in the south/southeastern parts of the United States. HBCUs are private, public, religiously affiliated, undergraduate-serving, graduate-serving, four-year, and two-year institutions. Some have enrollments of 10,000+ (e.g., North Carolina A&T State University), while others have fewer than 1,000 students (e.g., Rust College). HBCUs have a rich legacy of supporting Black students and are driven by institutional missions designed to celebrate Black lived experiences. HBCUs ultimately are places that honor Black epistemologies, histories, and traditions. As of 2021, there are 107 HBCUs that serve over 220,000 students (US Department of Education).

HBCUs have a unique history within higher education. Schools like Alabama A&M University (in Alabama), North Carolina A&T State University (in North Carolina), Central State University (in Ohio), and Fort Valley State (in Georgia) emerged from the Second Morrill Act in 1890, which was created to support land grant colleges. The Second Morrill Act was also formed to address racial discrimination in college admission policies and standards. States were required to establish colleges and universities for Black students who were being denied admission to other land grant institutions. The Civil Rights movement in the 1950s–1960s, of course, brought about other significant changes to education. For instance, the US Supreme Court decision of Brown v. Board of Education of Topeka (1954) established that racial segregation in public schools was unconstitutional. After this decision, the Civil Rights Act of

1964, Title IV (1964) passed, which enforced the desegregation of public schools. Then, the Higher Education Act of 1965 was established to distribute grants to support teaching and learning at HBCUs. Here it should be noted that HBCUs have had to (and continue to) endure through inequitable funding from federal and state governments.

HBCU first-year writing classes are sites that explore culture and language. In her award-winning dissertation, Temptaous Mckoy (2019) writes, "HBCUs allow for Black lived experiences and epistemologies to become a part of the classroom and not a specialized interest" (p. 25). David F. Green Jr. (2016) adds that "HBCUs are places that highlight the complex entanglements of language, culture, and legacy with dominant institutional objectives" (p. 156). Some HBCU writing programs were established by foundational feminist thinkers and scholars (Spencer-Maor & Randolph, 2016). HBCUs are often innovators in writing pedagogies and practices. Critical hip-hop pedagogies (Stone & Stewart, 2016), critical race theory, cultural rhetorics, feminist frameworks, and linguistic justice are natural byproducts of teaching first-year writing at an HBCU. Kedra Laverne James (2013) writes in her dissertation on writing programs and HBCUs, "Writing instruction should mirror the goals and founding principles of the institution so that the university and its curriculum coincide rather than contradict each other" (p. 5).

Since HBCUs serve students from diverse socioeconomic and cultural backgrounds, including other minoritized populations (e.g., Native Americans, Asian Americans and Pacific Islanders), first-year writing programs and curriculum are often unique. Some HBCU writing classes expose students to cultural contexts and empower students to think critically about the ways in which language works within societal and professional contexts, and across disciplines. For example, in her first-year writing class at Howard University, Teresa M. Redd (2014) talks about the importance of developing "students' rhetorical knowledge and sense of authorship so that they can adapt writing to different purposes, audiences, and contexts" (p. 147). In a multicultural environment like an HBCU, there are a lot of opportunities to investigate how knowledges and languages circulate.

HBCU writing classrooms and programs also face challenges. Faye Spencer-Maor and Robert E. Randolph Jr. (2016) describe how writing teachers and classes "struggle to reconcile traditionally entrenched attitudes and approaches . . . [and] faculty often have little expertise in writing theories or pedagogies" (p. 179). Spencer-Maor and Randolph Jr. explain how some HBCU teachers focus on identifying "error" in student writing, and thus overemphasize grammar and mechanics. These traditional approaches and entrenched attitudes aren't exclusive to HBCUs. Though, they often contradict HBCU missions—to amplify Black lived experiences and traditions—and make visible a much larger problem across institutions in higher education. Traditional approaches that focus on grammar are problematic because they emphasize Standard Edited American English (SEAE), and associate SEAE with "quality" and/or "good" writing. SEAE is "often a racial marker, a marker of whiteness" (Inoue, 2015a, p. 23). Thus, a grammar and mechanics-based approach to teaching that promotes SEAE ultimately diminishes the value of other linguistic variations and Englishes (e.g., Black English).

As a field, composition studies needs to pay closer attention to the work being done by teacher-scholars at HBCUs, especially those who are cultivating cultural literacies and linguistic differences and critical language awareness in writing classrooms. HBCUs have largely been excluded from conversations about teaching writing in scholarship. Which presents another problem: a whitewashing of where teaching writing happens, who teaches writing, how teaching occurs, and who receives writing instruction. Twenty-two years ago Keith Gilyard (1999) wrote that HBCUs "may not have always been in the house of mainstream composition studies, but we were always knocking on the door" (pp. 642–643). Jimisha Relerford wrote in 2012 that "there has yet to be a comprehensive, meaningful treatment of composition instruction at HBCUs" (p. 117). In 2016, Green reiterated this lack of presence: "Scholarship on HBCUs and composition studies remains on the fringes of the field, which is a disservice to the field and to those compositionists working in HBCUs" (p. 162). One step forward would be for composition studies at large to listen, acknowledge, recognize, and amplify HBCU teacher-scholars through publications, citations, and other forms of circulation. HBCUs center conversations on diversity, inclusivity, culture, community, and language, which are core tenets of our field.

Through the interviews in this chapter, I think you will pick up on the complex nature of HBCUs, including their missions and institutional differences, and how teachers approach teaching writing within these contexts. Moreover, you will hear teacher-scholars talk about the turbulent relationship between HBCUs and writing studies at large, or the absent presence of HBCU perspectives in rhetoric and composition.

INTERVIEWS

I was fortunate to sit down and talk with four teacher-scholars at different HBCUs: North Carolina Central University, Howard University, Bowie State University, and Spelman College. Karen Keaton Jackson, David F. Green Jr., Temptaous Mckoy, and Alexandria Lockett share their experiences teaching at HBCUs and talk about how their institutional contexts inform their writing pedagogies and practices. Jackson starts by addressing commonplace assumptions and misconceptions about HBCUs, and explains how HBCUs are complex institutions with nuanced missions. She also talks about the role of mentorship in her writing classes. Green talks about Howard University and his responsibilities as a writing program administrator (WPA). He describes Howard as a place that "emboldens and kind of bolsters students to really cultivate and think about their identities in relationship to their learning and in relationship to the curriculum." Mckoy reflects on her experiences as a student and teacher at an HBCU, and she shares how she draws on students' lived experiences to foster engagement. She offers her vision for HBCUs in writing studies scholarship and challenges teachers to "stop acting like we ain't here." Lockett adds, "The field owes a huge debt to HBCUs." She describes her approach to teaching writing and how she draws on Black feminist thinkers to encourage students to examine their own histories and rich literacy practices.

Shane to Karen Keaton Jackson: You teach at North Carolina Central University, a public Historically Black College and University (HBCU) in Durham, North Carolina. A lot of your research is in on HBCUs, too. What are some commonplace assumptions or misconceptions about HBCUs? [Episode 34: 01:47–04:53]

One of the common ones is that we're homogeneous. HBCUs are so complex. Our student populations are so heterogeneous. I think because we're not included in the conversations as much, and you may have one person presenting, then, you know, you get this one perspective of HBCUs. But you know, we're public and we're private; we are big and we're small; some have grown out of religious institutions versus state institutions. I mean, yeah, like you name it, it's there. We just haven't been in as many conversations. So the fact of how complex we are is one of the biggest misconceptions.

Then, the other thing that comes with that is who makes up our student populations. I think overall, for most HBCUs, the general number is about 70% of our students are African American. The other 30% can be international students, White, Hispanic . . . we have a growing Hispanic student population [at North Carolina Central University] and are purposely recruiting students because of the population in North Carolina. So you have the racial demographics. I think the other thing is in terms of the student preparation level. We have a wide range of student competencies, which makes teaching very interesting and exciting and challenging. I think because of the mission of most HBCUs, you may have students in our classrooms who may not get a shot at another institution. You know, and part of that is our mission.

We're serving underrepresented groups. I call them our diamonds in the rough. Students who have all the potential, but often because of the communities in which they grew up, the school systems they were in, the lack of access to college preparatory classes, honors, AP . . . you know, a lot of the school systems didn't have that.

They come to us, you know, "not prepared," right? We have those students who kind of just barely made it in, but they are here and they are ours and we will love them. Then, we have the students who could have gone to Harvard or MIT or Duke . . . but maybe for financial reasons or family legacy, wanting to be at an HBCU, they've chosen to be in our classrooms as well. So it makes it interesting compared to some institutions where the admissions requirements are a bit more strict, you know, educationally, you might be able to generalize a little bit more about your student population versus at an HBCU. It's very hard to generalize in terms of their level of preparation and kind of what exactly they look like.

Shane to Karen Keaton Jackson: In "We Belong in the Discussion," you talk about the absence of HBCU perspectives in composition scholarship and how HBCUs have been silenced when they should be leading conversations about race and writing. You ask, "How and why can the field of composition benefit from the perspectives and experiences of HBCU compositionists, and more particularly HBCU African American female compositionists?" Do you mind spending some time talking about the motivations behind this article and also the importance of hearing HBCU perspectives, particularly African American female compositionists in conversations around race and writing? [Episode 34: 05:00–10:15]

My coauthors, Dawn and Hope, they are amazing. We spent a lot of years on this article. We had some rejections on this article. It was not an easy path and there were times I wanted to give up on it. I realized as we went through the writing process how much we had to lay out to justify your very question that "No, this voice is needed." Because what I felt like some of the comments were as we were going through the process, and rightfully so when I can step out of my own feelings, was just really having to justify, "But what is so different about your context that we need to learn something from you?" I felt like that was, overall, kind of this question: "What are you doing that's so different from what we're doing?"

So part of it was my first answer, laying out our student populations. That's very different than a lot of schools. I think about just the ways that our institutions are set up. Those at Research I (R1) schools have teaching assistants and a lower teaching load. I mean tenure is based on you having to publish a far higher load than what I would have to do at a teaching institution. Just justifying the difference in the context was a really big piece. I kept looking at a lot of research that talked about teaching African American students. It won't fit for all my students . . . I think about my first-generation college students, and HBCUs have a higher percentage of them generally speaking than predominantly White institutions (PWIs). There's just a difference there in terms of how to approach students. What's going to engage them? . . . Normally you might think, "Oh, a student should know this coming into a college classroom. I can assume that a student has this baseline level of writing experience or writing competencies." I don't ever go into my classroom with that assumption. Some students do, and then some students don't.

A lot of that goes back to access and the school systems. That's a whole different conversation. I think those baseline assumptions that we could often make at other institutions, we can't necessarily make at all HBCUs . . .

I mean, there's a lot of time, like on a regular basis spent really stepping into this kind of mothering role—a mentoring role that's totally outside of academics. It's a normal part of the day. I mean, it's just like teaching class, so it's not like this one off . . . it's pretty consistent that students are searching for that kind of mentoring but with a little love mixed in there as well. So in this other mothering kind of space where we're constantly weaving in the academics with this affective component of learning, that's just naturally woven into HBCUs just like any other part of your syllabus or class.

Shane to David F. Green Jr.: Howard University is a private HBCU in Washington, DC, with over 9,000 students and a notable list of alumni, including Toni Morrison and Thurgood Marshall. Talk to me about what it's like to teach at Howard University? In what ways do the traditions at Howard impact the writing classroom, and how does this also affect your work as a writing program administrator (WPA)? [Episode 31: 02:16–06:54]

> There's this long legacy, this strong Black intellectual traditional at Howard. You can really feel it when you come on campus, and when you're in the classrooms. I teach in Alain Locke Hall, the first African American Rhodes Scholar, and one of the major stalwarts of the Harlem Renaissance. Sterling Brown is one of the main architects for my English department. He's often cited. His work is shared around the classes and what we do, and it's also integrated into a lot of the programs. So the tradition is kind of always there in ways that I find very refreshing, in part, because it gives it a different model of how we might think about some of these disciplines.
>
> When I begin to think about what should a writing class look like in this space at this institution for these students that want that kind of tradition, I often begin with what conversations are relevant to these students who are predominantly Black, but also for these students who come from a variety of walks of life. We have a large international population. Students come from Ethiopia and Egypt. They come from Nigeria. We have a large population of Caribbean students, students from Jamaica and Trinidad. So you have this international mix of students as well as . . . White students, Hispanic students. You have this very, very diverse population in which whiteness is not necessarily centered. When we begin to talk about tradition and we talk about even just certain rhetorical practices in the classroom, students come to expect something extra or something that connects them or connects us to that lineage. So even on our syllabi, when we talk about the program, you'll see those kinds of references and those kinds of scholars. Toni Morrison is always present in many of the works we do, as well as a host of other writers, and thinkers, and intellectuals working in that tradition.

I find it very fun, especially when I first got to Howard, because it allowed me to be flexible in ways that I hadn't thought about before, meaning moving beyond just focusing on the text. Bringing music into class is understood as vital and important—it's a part of many of our ceremonial traditions, it's a part of many of our intellectual talks that occur on campus. Students are geared for it. It allows us to think and work in multimodal ways . . . working as a WPA has been interesting as well because of this tradition. Faculty have been very receptive to some of the changes that I've made or argued for. They've been very receptive to rethinking stances on Black English or other language practices, even terms like *translingualism* or *linguistic difference* have been central to how we've started to think about what our program should be for today's student, or for the modern university. So it's been exciting.

Outside of the WPA work and the writing program itself, we have a host of other kinds of programs, like the Sterling Brown Society, and students have writing cyphers and other kinds of programs in which they come to display their writing in various forms, whether it's poetry, reflective memoir writing, rap, or even just essay or traditional essayist writing. They've come to see it much more dynamically as a part of their lives. I appreciate and enjoy that.

Shane to David F. Green Jr.: In your article, "Expanding the Dialogue on Writing Assessment at HBCUs," you write, "Even at HBCUs where Black English traditions flow through ceremonies, social events, and sports culture (see any HBCU homecoming), classroom discourse focuses on normative standards for writing. In other words, HBCUs push students toward social justice goals within the institutional context while also pulling them toward certain dominant, White language norms within classrooms." I want to hear more about this dynamic relationship, this kind of push and pull that you're talking about here. How do students at Howard respond to this tension between social justice and White discourse? [Episode 31: 06:57–11:31]

That has been one of the more interesting questions, in part, because the students themselves are pretty much free. Howard is a place that emboldens and kind of bolsters students to really cultivate and think about their identities in relationship to their learning and in relationship to the curriculum. So students are always having a kind of push/pull relationship with the curriculum itself, as they should, and as we all do. We pick up certain things that we find valuable, and hopefully we can put down certain things that do damage to our expressive identities, to how we think about ourselves, to any insecurities we may have about our language practices.

I've been very proud of how students have pushed back on some of the invisible . . . I use the word traditional, or normative practices that go along with a writing program. Say maybe an outsized emphasis on certain grammatical learning practices, or as other scholars in the field refer to it, "skill and drill" . . . I think it was the work of the teachers. We needed to begin to rethink some of these invisible assumptions and some of these entrenched beliefs about what is "good" writing or what it takes to produce "good" writing. What are we doing to our students' linguistic identities? For the most part, students have been dynamic, resilient, energized, and they've energized me. I think you'll find them kind of putting pressure on some of this tension in classes. Students will ask questions about certain readings. Students will begin to question certain grammatical formations and certain linguistic performances.

For example, when I first got here, the idea of "shade" and how shade was being used. [Shade] is an African American term that meant throwing critique or providing a subliminal critique or subliminal diss of an idea. But you find it in their work. They're referencing how W. E. B. Du Bois was throwing "shade" at Booker T. Washington, or how in this essay, I see the author throwing shade on this idea or this concept. Well, what do you do with that? It's not like they're linguistically wrong. So we've had to readjust our

thinking to that norm. If students want to express themselves in this way, and in a way that is critical and critically
rich, how do we help them do that in a way that supports
their identities, but also the rhetorical choices they will
have to make out in the real world?

Shane to David F. Green Jr.: This makes me think about how we can
reimagine traditional assessment practices (e.g., rubrics) that might
emphasize "grammar" and replace those standardized notions of
English with concepts that are more elastic, such as rhythm, tempo,
or cadence. These concepts might give new meaning to assessing
and responding to writing, and valuing linguistic diversity. I know
you incorporate hip hop into your writing classes. Can you talk
more about what that looks like? [Episode 31: 15:23–19:05]

So for me, hip hop comes out of African American rhetoric. It's become a global phenomenon. Many people from
various rhetorical traditions can lay claim to hip hop because of the forms, because of rap, because of production,
because of dance style and dress. But its beginning and its
roots really comes out of the African American rhetorical
tradition. The idea of signifying, playing with language,
the way folks have employed call and response in a variety of ways, how we even begin to think about communities and collectives, and the cyphers that form out of
that. What I do different, where my research diverges from
maybe traditional hip-hop studies work, is that I'm very
invested in what hip hop offers us in how we think about
composing. How does it offer new concepts that are fresh
that allow us to think about terms that we use? Like multimodal, and begin to think about multi-medium writing in
very dynamic and different ways. Adam Banks mentioned
this in his book, *Digital Griots*. What does it mean if we
think about our students as DJs of a tradition, or if we
think about ourselves, as scholars, as DJs of a tradition?

If we're always pulling on these various discourses to help
people either understand or interpret different types of
information, we're really architects. What does it mean

to move back and forth between the past and the present in dynamic ways? For me, in terms of the classroom, this often takes a variety of different forms. I don't just teach a particular rap artist or particular rap songs, although I find that work valuable—getting a deeper understanding of how certain rappers perform the tradition. But I'm always interested in the conversation in placing maybe older texts or older questions, right up against newer questions or newer texts. How does the work of Black Thought speak to the work of Ernest Gaines? Or how might we rethink a CCCC Chair's Address by Victor Villanueva or Gwen Pough in relation to what Lauryn Hill says, or more recently, Megan Thee Stallion? How do we place these folks in conversations in ways that are productive for students? Not just so they can engage or talk about their favorite artists, but how does this create a substantive conversation that we can build on and that can help students gather a new understanding about how rhetoric functions, and how they might rethink their own compositions in relation to what they've seen, or heard, or discussed in class.

Shane to Temptaous Mckoy: Your teaching centers on students' embodiment and lived experiences. You went to Elizabeth City State University, a public HBCU in North Carolina, as an undergraduate. How does your own experiences as a student at an HBCU inform your embodiment as a teacher at Bowie State University, a public HBCU in Maryland with about 3,000 students? [Episode 38: 14:33–21:30]

Those little miniature communities that you create at the HBCU space is one of the most beautiful things I think that could have worked in my favor at Elizabeth City . . . there are a lot of life lessons, friendship lessons, lessons on being "professional," right? I spoke about this in the article I did with Brittany Hull and Cecilia Shelton titled "Dressed but Not Tryin' to Impress." I discussed how at the HBCU I was "professionalized." Right? *Professionalized.* You wear your suit, you put your stockings on, you do all of these things to be professional, and then it wasn't until I got out of it that I realized like, "This is coded for whiteness. Y'all trippin." I didn't have the ethos to push back against that until I got the PhD behind my name. I couldn't do that as just regular old Temp. So now that I am a faculty member at an HBCU, those same lessons show up in my classroom.

For example, when we're teaching the damn resume assignment, because you got to teach the resume assignment in technical writing . . . what I'm running into at Bowie State is I'm working with students who have ethnic names just like me. I can say to a student, "Look, my name is Temptaous, and I go by Temptaous. But there was a time in my life when I only went by 'Shawn' on professional documents." It was the reason I decided to go and get my PhD because I applied to a job with "Temptaous" and "Shawn." Two applications back-to-back . . . and Shawn got a call back. Shawn is a cut-down version of my middle name Ta'Shawn. If you leave the "Ta'," you still know I'm Black.

I was like, "If I do Shawn, you ain't going to know if I'm Black, boy, girl, it ain't going to matter." Shawn got the call back. When I finally called them, they told me I lied on my application. They rejected anything else after that. That was the push I needed to go get my PhD . . . when I'm in my class and I'm teaching my students . . . I realized the power that I had, and not in a dictator way, right? That representation matters moment. Because now my students see in front of them, a Black woman named Temptaous that understands when they're saying, "I don't know what name I want to put on my resume. I'm not sure what I want to do here." I'm also in a sorority. My sorority is a racial identity, Sigma Gamma Rho Sorority Incorporated. That is also a racial identity marker. You look at my address, there's a lot of things that I have and a lot of people know these things that are racial identity markers on our technical documents.

It's always this conversation with my students . . . I never tell a student to not place their government name on the document. But I do have an honest conversation with them about it. "Hey, just letting you know, this is what you up against. Is this what you want to do? Okay, cool. Let me help you do it the right way."

I think going to an HBCU provided me that opportunity to come back and do that. I think of all the things I could not say at East Carolina University that I can say now at Bowie State, mainly because at East Carolina I may have had two or three Black kids in each class. Maybe. There were a lot of things that I had to be careful saying because I knew those kids wouldn't get it. It's not because I think they were bad students, they just didn't get the cultural references. They may not understand why it would matter to not go by a certain name. Those types of things don't show up in the class with White students, nor do they really understand how they themselves reject racial-sounding names. So it becomes a teaching moment at East Carolina, but then at Bowie State, it becomes a moment for my students to be uplifted. Right? I feel if nothing else, I went to Bowie State to be the teacher that I needed.

Shane to Temptaous Mckoy: What is your vision for HBCUs in rhetoric and composition? [Episode 38: 21:31–28:16]

Like keeping it all the way one hundred, it would be honestly for people to stop acting like we ain't here. That's probably my big overarching thing. People don't rock with HBCUs 'til they see themselves wanting to benefit from diversity, or it's some other buzzword thing they feel they want to tap into. I really hate that sometimes HBCUs are overlooked for being great places for learning, and even more so, which is a whole 'nother book I'm going to get out of my head one day, HBCU elitism is a real thing. A lot of people really don't see how that happens. They only know of the Howard's, the Spelman's, the Morehouse's, the Clark Atlanta's. Those are the things they know about, but they forget about your Bowie's, Elizabeth City State University, Shaw University, Livingstone's. All these smaller HBCUs are just as important. I don't say the HBCU elitism flight to knock my other people, because first of all, they already heard my rant about that in the beginning. I think it's important that we honor those major HBCUs.

My overall vision for the field would be that HBCUs really are being brought into conversations. I'm tired of HBCUs having to be a special topic. That really bothers me. I'm tired of it having to be, "Oh, we got this special panel on HBCUs." Why can't HBCU panels be a part of the party? Don't get it twisted, I'm down for the recognition, but it's always HBCUs are a "but" or a supplemental. That really bothers me to my core . . . I went to the CPTSC (Council for Programs in Technical and Scientific Communication) conference, I realized you can count the number of Black folks in there on two hands. Maybe just one, if we're being completely honest. But in two hands I can count the amount of Black people that were in there . . . so just imagine if HBCUs were looked at and appreciated the same way that we do many of these PWIs, and what would it look like in these conference spaces? If I was able to bring in ten of my Black kids from Bowie State to this next conference, what does that mean overall to the organization? Because you're no longer talking about buzzwords, right? . . .

I appreciate and love my HBCUs. I feel that they're definitely a sacred space for learning Black community. It's the one space in the world that I think back to . . . and I know people always say it sounds dramatic, but it's the honest to God truth—that's the one space that I can forget that I'm Black. Some people really don't understand the power in that . . . I'm not walking around campus thinking about who am I going to walk into? Do I got to deal with this racist instructor? Am I going to have to be . . . sitting in a class, reading a book based on race to only hear a White student telling me it doesn't exist?

I hate how some people get the game twisted . . . if anyone ever does any research or archival research, and I've learned this, North Carolina A&T is literally the Black version of North Carolina State University. If you look at these founding documents, what these schools came out of, they're literally the same damn school. Just one is a HBCU and one isn't. But when you look at it historically and what that meant, North Carolina got all that funding. NC State got the funding as an R1 whoop-de-doo. But A&T got left behind. So what if we really stopped to peel back these layers and histories about what's happening and how our HBCUs are forgotten?

Once we pull back those histories, then we can start to shoot forward about what it means to include HBCUs in the field of rhet/comp and technical communication. That's something that I'm really big on. Telling people like, "No, check yourself. Look at the history." The sense of ideal community is embedded in HBCU. It's there, it's in the threading of an HBCU . . . when I look at PWIs and the conversations that's happening, and I look at how we're trying to bring it together, that same sense of community is not embedded in PWIs. I don't want to say it's a free for all, but it's a way that I think PWIs really could learn from HBCUs. I'm saying, literally, just take the time to see what's happening in that HBCU space and what has happened historically to keep that HBCU going afloat.

Shane to Alexandria Lockett: What is your sense of how HBCUs and scholarship from HBCU teacher-scholars is situated in rhetoric and composition? [Episode 60: 16:57–24:33]

Well, we have been continuously producing scholarship, but it's very marginalized and it's very little if you look at the scope of production. I think there's a lot of reasons for this. Number one, just sheer segregation in terms of, how should I put it? I think we have to come back to the National Education Defense Act and really the growth of sort of English programs. We have to also look at the increase of your bureaucratic institutions that happened at the turn of the century. We have to look into democratization of higher education. Then, we have to look at the desegregation of higher education. All these major factors, legislatively and socially and culturally and technologically, led to a place where the writing program emerged. And by the writing program, we're talking about whether it was the required mandated writing course because literally Harvard men couldn't write in the nineteenth century.

. . . they're lettered, cultured men, failed miserably on basic standard tests. Even as we will attribute that failure to people of color entering White schools. I would say that the history of the emergence of writing programs and its connection to racial segregation and desegregation mandates, you won't see that in Berlin's history. You won't see that in Harris's history. You won't see that in a lot of people's history of the field, because the scholars who came to write the histories of the field . . . the writing course as a requirement has been a consistent thing since the nineteenth century across all institutions, first of all. But suddenly remedial education and how that was supposed to make up for the deficient students who were coming to college, I'm looking particularly at the '60s.

They were built off the backs of these Black students who were just trying to get ahead and try to get a chance. A lot of these White scholars who participated in that unknowingly, who literally saw an opportunity, they professionalized composition studies off of this context. Writing wasn't something that they learned in a class. Hell, writing wasn't something I learned in a class. I was one of those people who didn't have to do it and look at me teaching it. I have to always confront that, too. I didn't go through what they're going through. I'm building a class that I never had to take. How many of us practitioners are in that situation, Shane? And imagine the ones who started this shit in the '60s and the '70s. You know they were in that position.

. . . it's interesting to note that the best thing about rhetoric and composition is that we are one of the only disciplines I know of that historicizes itself. That's pretty fucking cool. On the other hand, it is also, when I talk about the scam of rhetoric and composition, there is a kind of competition in this field to be recognized and there's an insecurity about visibility and recognition that leads to the coinage of terms and the barring and appropriation of knowledges from other disciplines without an acknowledgement of interdisciplinarity. That then leads to a kind of reproduction of a discipline that is really empty and shallow because let's be clear, the people who professionalized composition in the '70s, there was no composition studies, so these people were making it as they were going along as an administrative duty to run writing programs. The democratization of education led the institutions to see writing programs as a stop gap for that average student to acclimate and assimilate into the college because college and universities have still failed to define themselves after desegregation.

HBCUs all the while have been doing what HBCUs do: Educating our people the best way that we know how. We definitely can say that the programming in our institutions is diverse, and when we start trying to borrow from the "mainstream institutions," it doesn't quite work as well because our students are very much about that practical education. They want to know what is going to help me in this next class? What is going to help me get into grad school? What is going to help me? Now, I'm not saying the way it's taught is always as progressive as the field would imagine. It's no surprise that we're marginalized within the field. But it's kind of surprising when you see this marginalization alongside this sort of social justice in the classroom, antiracists, let's teach our students to be woke citizens.

That's really hard to do when a lot of your Black scholars, if you have any Black scholars, because as you noticed our conferences are White, White, White-ity, White, White, White. Why would Black people want to be part of a profession that has little opportunity for growth, very little pay, very little recognition, a reproduction of White supremacy with little financial reward and no power for you anywhere? My sense of HBCUs is that we are marginalized, but with everybody's attention on race, with everything hitting a fever pitch, with racial violence, and it being very apparent that education has to change fundamentally if it's going to serve diverse students, now, people are more interested in, "Well damn, all this history of composition everywhere, where were the HBCUs? What were the HBCUs doing?" Oh, you guys weren't publishing their work is what it was. I think that the field owes a huge debt to HBCUs.

Shane to Alexandria Lockett: Spelman College is a small, private, liberal arts HBCU for women in Atlanta, Georgia. It's the oldest one of only two HBCU women's colleges in the US. Talk to me about Spelman College and what it's like to teach there? [Episode 60: 01:21–06:25]

. . . I want to start off by saying it's quite an honor to be at Spelman because the history of writing at Spelman is really quite fascinating. Jacqueline Jones Royster, who's one of the vets and OGs in the field, she started our program as a writing across the curriculum (WAC) program. What's really fascinating about the history of our program at Spelman and why it is so interesting to teach here is because it started off in . . . Dr. Beverly Guy-Sheftall, she's one of the formidable Black feminist thinkers of our time and historian of Black women's work, and she's done numerous anthologies with Black woman writers of all kinds, whether they were critics or whether they were creative writers or whatever, she's cataloged exhaustively. She also runs our women's research and research center here at Spelman. The program actually started in her office.

The writing program started in a women's research and resource space. It's kind of intriguing to kind of imagine that our writing program could emerge from that situation as opposed to say a lot of writing programs, which emerged from desegregation mandates for remedial writing programs to get Black people "acculturated" into White institutions. That's the first thing, I think having that history of writing at Spelman is kind of cool because we are a small college. We do have a comp requirement. It's one semester, it used to be two, but they eliminated the stretch component because we also have a course here at Spelman called ADW, African Diaspora in the World, which is a two-semester sequence, which is intended to be a kind of decolonial historic . . . it's kind of like instead of Western Civ, we have ADW, which sort of destroys the idea of having Western Civ.

. . . I think in an HBCU space writing instruction becomes very peculiar and interesting because your students are overwhelmingly . . . Elaine Richardson's "To Protect and Serve" is a great article that I actually assign to my students as a way to get them to start thinking about their own literacies. If they're at Spelman College, they're not there because they were some kind of fist-in-the-air resistant student, they're there because they are the best of the best. They followed all the rules, they did everything right and now they want you to help them keep doing everything right. Okay, I'm a Black woman. They're a Black woman. I always ask them the same question I asked my students at PWIs, am I the first, not even am I the first I don't frame it that way, I say, "Have you ever had a Black teacher at any grade level, regardless of gender?" The overwhelming answer, 95.5% of the time is "No, you are the first. I came to Spelman because I have a legacy of parents who said, 'This is where I would learn my Black history.'"

The problem with the marginalization of HBCU scholars in the field is there's a lot of assumptions about who this Black student is that we're teaching. And a Black student that I'm teaching at Spelman College is not going to be a Black student I'm teaching at Penn State or OU [University of Oklahoma]. The joy of being in an HBCU is the pedagogical challenge of not being in a situation where I'm trying to model my students to be a particular citizen, but that I'm actually in a position where I can help somebody retrace their literacy and their ownership of literacy and say, "What kind of freedom do you want to have for yourself?" And as a Black woman, the most radical thing I can teach you is how to say "no."

Shane to Alexandria Lockett: What do you teach, and how do students respond to this kind of approach? [Episode 60: 06:26–11:50]

Well, I teach honors composition, and some semesters it's just fantastic and then some semesters it's terrible. Like any institution, I don't care what kind of institution it is, honors students tend to come into that classroom having felt like they've arrived and they're ready to do the work, which is a great frame, except when you're saying, "Hey, the way that you think about writing is not really going to help you." And they panic real quick or they realize they don't have experience with writing they thought they had or their attitude towards communication is they realize how inherently performative and White it is. And it's what they do with that realization that will make or break my class.

Let me tell you about my class and let me tell you a little bit about the structure. I've developed a structure for honors composition after much tinkering and here's what works for me. I spend the first half of the class talking to them about what does being an intellectual mean? What does it mean that we don't associate Black women with the term *intellectual*? We start off with Toni Morrison's *The Site of Memory* where she talks about how her composition process is informed by this kind of absence. She tends to be categorized as a fiction writer, but clearly she's drawing on an autobiographical writing tradition which she traces to the slave narrative. And she says, "Well, the formerly enslaved, when they were writing their narratives, they had to leave out certain things, the sordid details of slavery, we really don't get a lot from the slave narratives and imagine how much sort of detail we do get."

But Morrison calls that a veil. She says these writers had to write with a veil because they had a very particular rhetorical purpose . . . it was to get these White readers, predominantly White readership to see them in their humanity using Christian appeals overwhelmingly. But for Morrison as a writer, it's that veil that she wants to pull back as a writer to say, "What kinds of creative resources in the world did these people have to make these narratives in that time and to own their literacy and to wield their literacy in such a way that the writing could be as impactful as it is?" When they see Morrison talking about her process in such a clear way, it's a great piece because they start to wonder, what is a Black literary tradition? How do we write? What is the purpose of writing? And what is truth? What are facts?

Because Morrison goes into all the philosophical quarries . . . and then we read Jacqueline Jones Royster's perspectives on the intellectual tradition of Black women. Royster, of course, in her very incisive writing style just sort of schools you. You don't think about Black women when you think about being intellectual. You don't even know who Black women writers are. She of course introduces us to this scope of Black women writers. They also read the introduction to Shirley Wilson Logan's *With Pen and Voice* and the introduction to the 18 volumes of nineteenth-century Black women writers in the Schomburg's Collection of *The Pen is Ours*, written by Gates.

My students start to realize quickly, they don't know nothing about Black women writers and they're at Spelman College and they're Black women. It's kind of like, I don't have to teach, they get to see it for themselves when they're reading about it for themselves. That starts to motivate them to start thinking about their literacy. I give them writing prompts. Some of them are simple and could be applied to any classroom space. Tell me about the text in your home because I'm trying to introduce them to narrative writing. Not that narrative is . . . because they do associate narrative with fiction and creative writing only, and then there's academic writing only. I need to disrupt that for them just like Morrison disrupts the boundaries of being an autobiographical or fiction writer . . .

Where we go with that is I ask them the question, I say, "Tell me, describe a scene," to get them into showing and not telling. Tell me about the text in your home that you grew up around. Did you have bookcases? Magazines? Whatever that means. Then they start to kind of realize, "Huh, we only had this one little bookcase" or "We had a whole, my parents are professors, so we had tons of books, but I didn't like those books." . . . Second part to that question: when was the first time you ever independently, not in a classroom, not by your parents, when's the first time you independently pursued and read a text written by a Black woman? When they answer those two questions, something kind of happens.

DENOUEMENT

As I reflect on these interviews, two words stand out to me: *agency* and *voice*. Who has agency in our classes and in our field, and who doesn't? How are teachers helping support student agency by drawing on diverse cultural knowledges and encouraging students to reflect on their previous experiences with language and literacy? Whose voices are heard through our curriculum and in our scholarship? In what ways are we critically investigating rhetoric and composition history, and how should we retell and rewrite that history? HBCUs are models for what it means to develop programs, initiatives, and classes that celebrate diverse student populations. As the field continues to problematize notions of "standardized" English and works to embrace language diversity and linguistic justice (Baker-Bell, 2020), we would do well to pay more attention to HBCUs and investigate our problematic history as a field (see Royster & Williams, 1999).

I think we see from these interviews that writing classes and programs, and composition studies at large, still has a way to go in listening to HBCU teacher-scholars and amplifying perspectives and experiences from HBCUs. So as we push toward equity and inclusivity in our classes and field, I offer the following questions about agency and voice:

- In what ways are your pedagogies and practices valuing your students' rich language habits and the communities they come from? How are you pursuing linguistic justice?
- What diverse histories and perspectives are being heard and circulated in your writing classes and program? Whose histories and stories are being told?
- How are you supporting your students' lived experiences, and how is that being complemented through your curriculum and assessment?
- How are you judging and assessing writing (e.g., language)? In what ways does writing assessment reproduce White language supremacy and Standard Edited American English or emphasize grammatical errors? How might you reconsider traditional writing assessment practices and incorporate more socially just ones?
- How are you responsibly preparing language users, and in what ways are you emphasizing diverse cultural and linguistic practices, rhetorical knowledges, and ways of making meaning?

4

Hispanic-Serving Institutions

Hispanic-Serving Institutions (HSIs) are defined as any eligible higher education institution that "has an enrollment of undergraduate full-time equivalent students that is at least 25 percent Hispanic students at the end of the award year immediately preceding the date of application" (US Department of Education). The United States Department of Education offers three grants (Title V, Part A; Title V, Part B; and Title III) to assist with educational opportunities and build sustainable programs to improve learning at HSIs. HSIs enroll two-thirds of Hispanic college students, and these institutions range from private to public, four-year universities to two-year colleges (Hispanic Association of Colleges and Universities). Teaching writing at an HSI provides unique opportunities to analyze and promote diverse sociocultural contexts and perspectives. Many HSIs enroll first-generation college students with a range of socioeconomic and linguistic backgrounds and whose access to education has been limited by financial and sociocultural constraints and circumstances (Newman, 2007).

There are over 500 colleges and universities that meet the Higher Education Act of 1965 criteria for being defined as a "Hispanic-Serving Institution" (1965). Effective writing instruction at an HSI means developing pedagogies that value Hispanic (e.g., Chicanx, Mexican American, Latinx) cultural practices, histories, knowledges, and traditions. This might look like adopting culturally sustaining pedagogies (Paris & Alim, 2017). Beatrice Mendez Newman (2007) writes, "Compositionists at HSIs should have some understanding of how cultural and familial expectations shape the Hispanic student's classroom experience . . . [and] the compositionist at an HSI needs to learn to hear student voices and respond to the *message* rather than to what appears to be errors in writing" (pp. 20, 25–26). Culturally responsive teaching (Hammond, 2014; Ladson-Billings, 1994) and funds of knowledge (Rodriguez, 2013; Vélez-Ibáñez & Greenberg, 1992) are educational frameworks frequently cited and used in multicultural environments, like HSIs. Both frameworks emphasize cultural and linguistic diversity as an *asset* and advocate for cultural and linguistic awareness.

These approaches to teaching often empower students to take ownership of their learning. This means establishing a student-centered environment where students feel a strong sense of belonging in the writing classroom and where their literacies are affirmed. Moreover, this usually involves confronting previous negative experiences in English classrooms. For some linguistically diverse students, the writing classroom has been an unsafe space, a site where their own languages have been critiqued, removed, and replaced by notions of *standardized English* reinforced through prescriptive approaches to grammar, writing assessment and grading, and unfair outcomes. In short, it has been a site of distress for many students at HSIs. Culturally responsive teaching intervenes and taps into cultural knowledge. This approach seeks to build curriculum around students' languages and lived experiences, thus flips traditional, mainstream education that is top-down or hierarchical. Culturally responsive teaching engages students in more meaningful ways and embraces cultural identities, which presents dynamic opportunities for teaching at HSIs.

The funds of knowledge concept is a powerful tool in HSI contexts, too. Funds of knowledge are "the historically accumulated and culturally developed bodies of knowledge and skills essential for household or individual help, individual functioning and well-being" (Moll et al., 2001, p. 133). It works from the exigence that teaching and learning should be about knowing students' cultures and households. The more teachers know their students and their families and histories, and advantageously use social and cultural resources, the more engaged students will become and the more agency they will have in their learning. It challenges teachers to make connections between school and family, for example, a Chicanx student's caregiving responsibilities at home or religious beliefs or their relationship to regional and/or familial activities, like cooking or farming, and the knowledge that comes with these practices.

This approach to teaching bridges the gap between culture and making meaning in the writing classroom. While many HSI teachers draw from innovative pedagogies and practices (e.g., culturally relevant and sustaining pedagogy), there remains an underrepresentation of perspectives and lack of critical engagement on what teaching writing looks like in HSIs in composition studies at large. Much like the previous chapters (see Two-Year Colleges and Historically Black Colleges and Universities), this chapter amplifies where teaching writing happens and calls for the field to listen to teacher-scholars at HSIs. The absence of HSI teacher-scholar perspectives in scholarship is surprising since Hispanic populations are the second largest demographic and one of the fastest-growing minority groups in the US. The silencing of native Spanish speakers in the US has a long, violent history (e.g., the English-only movement). As Michelle Hall Kells (2007) writes, "Linguistic terrorism insidiously silences students in the classroom, workers in the field, and voters at the poll" (pp. x-xi).

Kells calls on rhetoric and composition to establish effective mentoring programs for Latinx students and suggests graduate program reform: "We need graduate programs reimagined and revisioned for the kind of work we are doing in HSIs" (2007, p. ix). Newman (2007) adds that traditional training inadequately addresses the "impact of many Hispanic students' sociocultural, socioeconomic, and ethnolinguistic makeup on performance in the writing class" (p. 17). As a field, we need more multi- and transcultural theory and praxis, more multi- and translingual frameworks, more crossdisciplinarity, more decolonial approaches to composition, and more attention to race and language. And of course, in the writing classroom, we need to listen to marginalized students' histories and literacies. Newman writes, "New understandings, new pedagogies, and specialized training in rhetoric and composition are necessary to keep both faculty and students at HSIs from becoming casualties in the contact zone of the college composition classroom" (2007, p. 17).

INTERVIEWS

In this chapter, I sit down and talk with Ginny Crisco, Beatrice Mendez Newman, Steven J. Corbett, and Cody Hoover about teaching writing at different HSIs: California State University, Fresno; the University of Texas Rio Grande Valley; Texas A&M University, Kingsville; and Clovis Community College. Crisco talks about teaching at a four-year university in central California, and she explains how she draws on culturally sustaining pedagogies and practices, as well as the funds of knowledge concept, to help frame her writing class. Crisco also reminds us of the pedagogical innovation and research that happens at teaching-intensive institutions. Newman shares her experiences teaching at one of the largest HSIs in the nation, serving 30,000 students—90% Hispanic students—on the border of Texas and Mexico. She discusses common misconceptions about HSIs, how students are "marked" in "pejorative ways," and describes how she integrates students' linguistic identities through her teaching. Corbett offers his first-year writing assignment sequence and talks about his approach to teaching near Corpus Christi in southern Texas. He challenges teachers to be "careful in assuming who our students are, what they know, what they do, and what their home life is like." Hoover shares his experiences at an HSI two-year college, and he encourages institutions to reconsider their aims and missions: "We need to do more reflection about what that [HSI] designation means, and also if it means anything to our students."

Shane to Ginny Crisco: Do you mind talking about teaching at California State University, Fresno, a public Hispanic-Serving Institution with about 25,000 students? [Episode 62: 01:07–03:39]

> Fresno State is part of the California State University system, and it's one of 23 campuses. It's one of the larger campuses in the system. So, often we're looked at from other campuses as a kind of a model. We have a very diverse student population. In fact, White students are the minority at Fresno State. Hispanics, like Latinx students, are the majority. Most of them are local. We do get some from other areas such as the Bay Area or Southern California. It is very rewarding to work at Fresno State. The students I work with is one of the most rewarding pieces of working at Fresno State because those students, and this is a huge generalization because there is a lot of diversity in our

Latinx student population, but the most rewarding experiences are those students who have really come from very poor backgrounds, who don't speak English as their first language, whose parents work and work and work, and are not educated themselves. They come to college because they see hope for the future.

Seeing that diversity and supporting students is one of the great things about working here . . . I work with teachers a lot now and help teachers think about the ways that they can cultivate culturally sustaining pedagogies in their classrooms . . . and that's really a term from education. But it's this idea, like if you've ever read Moll and Gonzalez, about accessing our students' funds of knowledge and building on that and using that as a resource in our classrooms. Our field has been talking about that for a long time. I'm not sure that we always do that, but we want to do that and that's a good thing.

Shane to Ginny Crisco: What does it look like to embrace culturally sustaining pedagogies or what practices help foster students' success among diverse student populations in your local context? [Episode 62: 03:40–08:08]

What people have been talking about for a long time is to incorporate a diverse reading list, pulling together readings from scholars of color or writers of color and women. To me, that's a very basic one. I think one of the ways, particularly in our first-year writing program, but also in the work that I do with teachers, is I've been really trying to think about the idea of how we integrate code meshing and how we make that something part of our pedagogy and how to support new teachers in making that happen. I think it's more challenging in secondary institutions because of the state standards that they have to follow. Administration doesn't quite understand all those different things.

. . . and also I think our field is really new at those pedagogies and what that looks like, even though there is conversation about that and there's really good conversation about that, I think we're still thinking through how best to teach code meshing. So using model texts is one way of doing that, right? There are different kinds of code meshing. There is the code meshing that's more of a Black English approach, right? Where you're integrating Black English. But then there's also, what's really more common at the Hispanic-Serving Institution is the Spanglish or in our case Hmonglish, because we have a Hmong student population as well. Trying to find readings that model that kind of code meshing for different audiences because that's part of the issue.

Like Gloria Anzaldúa's "How to Tame a Wild Tongue" is an example of code meshing, but it's written for a White academic audience and you can kind of tell just by analyzing it. So I'm trying to find those readings that will model the ways that professional writers are doing that, and I'm trying to help students understand the idea of audience because audience is a very abstract term. Right? If you start thinking about audience, who's your audience? "Oh, it's everybody." That's the kind of the default with students. But once you start saying like, "Okay, well, what if your audience was your friends. Are you going to speak this formal language?" Then . . . in that kind of language teaching, trying to, first of all, talk about power dynamics of language.

Second, talking about the choices that we have, right? So even just saying something like, "What's the difference between a formal tone and an informal tone?" To sort of help students see that there are choices as far as that goes when they shape their sentences and their language and do those kinds of things. Then, helping teachers to think about the way that they respond. This is something that Asao B. Inoue brought to our writing program. He did research with some graduate students several years back when he was here, and part of what they found was that the students who were second-language speakers, or that spoke English as another language, they got more comments about their language. We might say like, "Oh, well, that makes sense because maybe they're still learning how to speak English in a formal way." But his point was to say maybe we need to look into that because maybe we're targeting those students too much. Maybe we are not making a space for diversity in our language practices. That's one of the things that I've continued to do even after he left: Let's look at the ways that we are encouraging our students, supporting them, helping them to use the variety of language practices that they have in their lives. Part of first-year writing is getting students ready for the rest of the university. But it's also cultivating public intellectuals.

Shane to Ginny Crisco: You have taught at Fresno State for fifteen years. Is there anything that sticks out to you about teaching there? What has surprised you the most about teaching at a Hispanic-Serving Institution? [Episode 62: 16:24–22:11]

I think one of the things that has surprised me, and one of the things that I continue to talk to my junior colleagues about, is that there is a lot of opportunity for innovation at the California State Universities. I mean, we are a teaching institution, we're not a Research I (R1). So you kind of think like, well, it's the Research I universities that really have the opportunities for innovation because people have course releases and they're expected to publish. There are more resources often because there are more opportunities for grants or different kinds of fellowships and those kinds of things. But in fact, we have a lot of administrators on campus who are open to our ideas, who will listen to us, who want to innovate, who want what's best for our students, and who are really grateful for our work.

It doesn't always happen right away. Sometimes it takes a long time for it to happen, but if we continue to persist . . . for example, one of the things that we have been working on since I came in fifteen years ago is trying to create a writing across the curriculum (WAC) program . . . the CSU has a graduate writing assessment requirement. They call it the GWAR requirement. It means that when you graduate, either with a bachelor's degree or a master's degree, that you have to demonstrate proficiency in writing. And the way that we do that, and the way that many CSUs have done it, is through a deficit model. Which is, you take a test and if you don't pass it, then you can take the test again. And if you don't pass it then, you have to take a course. So that's really saying, "Hey, we got to remediate you." We are trying to move into a writing in the disciplines (WID) approach where students are learning about their literacy practices in different disciplines. But professors, and often it's lecturers who teach those courses, need to have guidance on best practices in writing instruction. Particularly language instruction, too.

. . . I think it's good to provide support for students as far as giving them classes and resources, but I think sometimes we might get a little paternalistic and think, "Oh, you got to take a lot of classes in order for you to be up to par or whatever." That's just as dangerous and damaging to students as well. We really need to be mindful about how we support students and what kind of requirements we put on them. I mean, this is really coming out of universal design for learning (UDL), too. One of the things that UDL says is, okay, well students with disabilities, they get accommodations, right? . . . but what the UDL folks have found is that some of the modifications or the approaches that universal design for learning takes actually work for a lot of different people, including second-language learners, including high-performing students. Their research, while not integrated with culturally sustaining pedagogies, really focuses on this idea that all learners that come into the classroom are diverse. So we need to be aware of those diversities . . .

We can't just say, "Oh, we need to load them up with more classes." Instead, we need to have those targeted interventions that are not just good for our most vulnerable students but can also be good for all students.

Shane to Beatrice Mendez Newman: You teach at the University of Texas Rio Grande Valley, which is a research university that has multiple campuses in the southernmost part of Texas. Student enrollment is around 30,000, and 90% of students are Hispanic. UT Rio Grande Valley is the second or third largest HSI in the nation. Can you talk about your institutional context and your approach to teaching writing? [Episode 41: 01:22–06:11]

> I would say that we focus a lot on the power of literacy. We have a program that is made up of a lot of different lecturers . . . even the first-year writing coordinator is a lecturer. We have what I would consider a constructed pedagogy that I'm going to define by inclusion, access, and innovation because of the lecturers. They are not traditional rhet/comp specialists with that huge background that goes all the way back to Aristotle . . . they basically have to invent the pedagogy, which I think is a good thing. So there's a lot of idiosyncrasy but I'm using that in a very positive way. It allows each lecturer to participate from where they're coming from in terms of getting students to recognize their literacy, and what they can do with it.

> The first-year writing coordinator draws heavily on the work of Chip Heath and Dan Heath, specifically their ideas about the power of moments. He's been using that to drive the way he talks to the lecturers . . . he likes the idea of stickiness and gravity, so he uses those terms a lot to try to define what goes on in the classroom. While some of those things are accidental, he wants us to try to figure out, "Well, what is it that happened? What led up to those moments of learning, and moments of connectivity, and moments of empowerment of literacy?" He talks a lot about that.

> My personal pedagogy is driven by the concept and construct of space. Going all the way back to the idea of third space. I try to create a situation in the face-to-face classroom

and online where students can find their voices. I am deeply influenced by Steven Johnson's *Where Good Ideas Come From* . . . I'm trying to get students to recognize how they can use their cultural background and make a difference and find their voice . . . I start with narrative like a school memoir. They go back and talk about how they learn and what conscious decisions they make when learning?

We also use a lot of film in my class because it's a great way to analyze text that is not traditional. As they would put it, "a dull and boring book." So, we have analyzed *Dead Poets Society* and *The Ron Clark Story*. You know, how can you create change in yourselves in order to create change . . . in the world? We also do a lot of revision. Everything that they do, whether it's a discussion board or an essay, we revise. I draw heavily on James Paul Gee and his ideas about discourse and literacy. It is not just knowing how to read and write, but knowing how to use your abilities in order to make things happen—the agency that you have with literacy.

Shane to Beatrice Mendez Newman: How do you integrate your students' rich cultural, racial, and linguistic histories and identities through your teaching? How do you resist traditional standards and norms associated with language/writing in order to foster linguistic diversity? [Episode 41: 07:16–12:39]

That is the most salient characteristic that our students come to this university with. I mean, if you were to enter the space of one of our classrooms, you would notice that everybody, just about everybody, is Hispanic. We're not 100% Hispanic, but the reality in the classroom is that almost everybody is. That's the first thing. People who come from other states that have been in more traditional classrooms, that's one of the things they say . . . and then, the other thing is most of our students come from our area, so the four-county area that is the Rio Grande Valley. Because of the way that second-language learning is handled in Texas, many of them have been marked throughout their school careers in some very pejorative ways.

You know, LEP [Limited English Proficiency] is a term that's used nationally. It is in our actual state documents. LEP sounds like such a negative term: *Limited English Proficiency.* Also, ESL students, and EL or English learners. They've been marked in this way. They come to the university and they've got that sense of deficiency because of the way that they are tested. The first thing that we discover is we have to make sure that they don't feel that way. We give them opportunities to use their language in creative ways. That their language is not a deficiency. That it is nothing but a positive because of the great things that happen in your brain when you have multiple languages.

The other thing is that, again because of the fact that the kids come mostly from this area, family is a priority. That is a Hispanic given. Your family is there. It's nonnegotiable. You never say, "Well, here's what I have to do with my family or for my family. Here's what I have to do for school." If there's a clash, family always supersedes. Because it's a commuter campus, many of the students live with their family . . . family is really involved. That creates a lot of trauma and a lot of drama as well. A lot of the kids have jobs . . . and interestingly, a lot of our students have spouses. They are married. I had an 18-year-old freshman in a class and she had two children. They were all living with her family. There's a real integrated sense of family . . . then there's also the "crossings." I've had students who've said, "I came by myself as a teenager. I left my family in Mexico because I wanted the opportunities in America." That is amazing. Twelve-year-olds or 13-year-olds. They left their family. The bravery is just amazing.

Some of them are not citizens, they've written stories of acquiring citizenship or helping family members acquire citizenship. I think the most harrowing story I've read is a boy who wrote about his family, what you see on TV, crossing in the dark. Then, the issues that he faced when he had to decide, "Do I tell the school that I am illegal and lose my scholarship, what do I do?" You know, that sort of thing is just a given in our classes. As English professors, we see the students much more closely than like an engineering class or a history class where there's 250 people in the class. So that means they feel really comfortable and safe, safe in a good way, in our classes.

Being bilingual or translingual, whatever word you want to use, multilingual, is a definite positive. It creates hybrid language possibilities that you don't have if you're a monolingual speaker of English. I resist "error" hunting. I teach a lot of prospective teachers and graduate students that is not the way to approach language learning or literacy. You don't focus on that. I resist traditional standards in the sense that it exacerbates the deficiency model. I don't like that. We value our students' backgrounds tremendously.

Shane to Beatrice Mendez Newman: What are some commonplace misconceptions about teaching at an HSI? How would you train and develop instructors to teach writing at an HSI? [Episode 41: 12:55–16:53]

Oh my, I discovered this when I started going to conferences. They're like, "Your students all speak Spanish? They write in Spanish?" I want to say that's probably the most common misconception, that students speak Spanish *only* and cannot speak English. Or when they speak English, they speak it incompetently. That's a huge misconception. And that they write in Spanish . . . I mean, they might integrate words here or there when they're appropriate for the context . . . but very, very few. So the other misconception is that everybody is an ESL student. Well, you know, they're not. I mean, some kids actually don't speak Spanish, and they talk about that, "Yeah, I'm Hispanic, but I just never really learned Spanish for whatever reason."

[To train instructors] I would start with a background in traditional ESL theory, where you learn great stuff about interlanguages and about . . . how everybody who is learning a second language is not all in the same spot at that point. That it's a transition. I would also depart from ESL theory to explain that the concept of translingualism is really innovative because it doesn't see the traditional trajectory from L1 to the target language, L2. Instead, translingualism allows for a merging of rhetorics and constructs from the two languages to create a new way of presenting yourself rhetorically and your literacy.

So that would be one thing, you know, use the traditional discussions of ESL with the big names like [Rosalie] Porter and [Stephen] Krashen. I would also point out that "error" is a good thing. A must read in classes like this one is Bartholomae's "The Study of Error." I think everybody should read that. Error is a way of showing what you know, not of showing what you don't know.

I would spend some time on funds of knowledge, especially if you are dealing with a population of students that so richly depends on their background and culture to understand and shape their perception of the world. Also, the idea that literacy is multifaceted. Deborah Brandt's idea of the way that literacy is kind of like a commodity that we use, the economies of literacy. The sense that every single student has so many stories to tell. Students, many times, come to our institutions thinking that they don't have stories to tell . . . I actually had a high school teacher say, "My students can't do those prompts on the mandated exams because they've never had any *experiences*." I was like, "What?" They come with these ideas, so we have to understand that they have so many stories to tell. Then, we shape the spaces that they are in physically or pedagogically to encourage them to feel good about their contributions to the community of learners—and the contributions that they're making toward their own development as users and agents of language.

Shane to Steven J. Corbett: Do you mind talking about Texas A&M University, Kingsville, and how your institutional context shapes your approach to teaching? [Episode 58: 01:02–04:14]

We're down here in South Texas, we're very close to Corpus Christi, which is a beach/resort town. We're about a half hour south of that. You know what's really interesting is I had listened to Beatrice Mendez Newman . . . and I just thought we had some interesting similarities. Now, we're not quite as far south as they are, and you see that, I think, in the student population that we have. So where they're about 90% Hispanic, we're more about 70%. Even still, we're the fifth largest Hispanic-Serving Institution in the country, so it's very interesting. We're technically an R1 university, even though we're a smaller school of about 8,000 students. We have such a heavy agriculture school, such heavy engineering down here . . . I want to get back to what Professor Newman was talking about that really struck me when I heard her talking about it in terms of our context and students . . .

I very much assumed, "Wow, there's going to be a lot of bilingual students. There's going to be a lot of students that are speaking Spanish and maybe struggling with their English because they don't speak it at home and all these kinds of things." But what's really interesting, and it parallels with what Dr. Newman was saying, "No, that's not actually the case here." Similar to the case with her institution. I run a writing center with twenty tutors and technically, right this moment, I only have one bilingual tutor. I have eighteen Hispanic tutors, but only one that's actually a bilingual tutor.

I think you got to be careful and I think you'll hear this theme running through the things I talk about, we have to be careful in assuming who our students are, what they know, what they do, and what their home life is like. There's so many variables that go into a person's identity. You can't just look at somebody and start making assumptions about who they are.

Shane to Steven J. Corbett: So I'm interested in hearing more about the kinds of texts or assignments you use in your writing classes and how they complement your larger pedagogical goals or aims and support the multiplicity of identities in your classes. [Episode 58: 04:15–10:42]

Students will actually start with a syllabus analysis. So they're coming at the genre of the syllabus in a way that they've never maybe quite done before. They're going to go in there and they're going to read it, but then they're also going to do a couple of other readings. They're going to read an old Donald Murray piece talking about process. They're going to read a Rachel Toor talking about the habits of writers and . . . how it's not easy for anybody to write. Then, this sounds odd, but they're going to research me. They're going to Google "Steven J. Corbett and writing," and they're going to be like, "Who is this? Who is this person?" They're going to write a brief paper. I make sure they understand that whatever they write, they get full credit for as long as they do it. They get full credit for it.

I use a portfolio system, actually a guaranteed B system. I'm doing a lot of stuff early on to try to make them feel comfortable, make them feel like, "Hey, okay, this might not be my typical English course where I've struggled in the past and I wasn't getting a lot of support." So they find out a lot about me. After that, the first thing we do is a peer review activity, right, where they literally just pull up their papers, either hard copy or on the screen, and we just bounce from chair to chair, or from screen to screen if it's virtual, and they read every single paper that everybody else wrote. They don't give *any* comments. I talk about this in terms of just reading. "You're reading, you're listening to each other." But in the meantime, "What are you really doing? Oh, you're judging . . . and hopefully, you're absorbing strategies, right?" You're listening to what everybody else has to offer. You're looking at their titles, you're looking at their intros, you're looking at all these different things, and you're saying, "Hey, okay, if I didn't do it the first time, if I didn't make the moves that I thought would be great the first time, could I do it in a subsequent draft?"

Then we go into an assignment where they write about their major. The whole course, this freshman composition course, is about, "Why are you here? What are you interested in majoring in? What do you want to pursue? What do you know about it?" Let's just see if we can't figure some of that out together, right? They're writing a paper about their major, why they're interested in it, why they want to do it, what's interesting about it to them, and that's a short assignment . . . they're actually going to exchange the short assignments that they wrote about their majors, they're going to read each other's papers, and then they're going to write a comparative paper about that, about their major and their point of view on it and compare it and contrast it against these other folks. Now, because we're in a portfolio system, they've got the entire term to try to produce the best paper that they can do.

. . . so everything up to this point has been practiced for, it's been getting them comfortable with me, getting comfortable with your peer group members, so that they can really try to write the best stuff they've ever written . . . and then of course, since they're doing an e-portfolio, they're doing lots of reflections and reflective writing on their processes and everything that got them to be able to produce these things that they've produced, including a final conclusion . . . lots and tons and tons of writing, Shane, and then their final conclusion to their digital e-portfolio book and what it took to get there and all the processes and everything . . . and then they tell me what grade they believe they earned for the course.

Shane to Cody Hoover: Clovis Community College is an HSI in central California. Can you talk more about your approach to teaching writing? What are some values or practices that help you build a community of learners in the two-year college writing classroom? [Episode 52: 02:00–05:29]

I'll talk a little bit about Clovis Community College. It's a newer community college. It was established fully as a college in 2015 . . . they say we have 13,000 students now, but I think that's between all the extension campuses and dual enrollment and things like that. So it's a pretty small campus—we have three buildings on campus. We're teaching a lot of students and enrollment is always going up. It's small, which is good for building a community of learners. Having a small campus really helps with that. A lot of the students in my classes are taking other classes with each other just because the way their schedules work out.

. . . I do a lot of group work and projects in class. I guess my philosophy, in general, I'm trying to train them and give them a set of tools to question and problematize their identities and their communities. So that not only can they share them within the classroom community, but they can then actually point to issues that exist within those communities or with identities that they bring to the classroom. Overall, that's the culture I'm trying to instill in the classroom.

We're talking about HSIs . . . I'm not going to have this *specific issue* that has to do with the Latinx community in my class as part of the theme that we're working with or whatever. That is artificial to me and also doesn't invite students to really share their actual experiences because you're giving it to them already or telling them, "This is what it is." Because for me, I'm half Latinx, so my experience growing up is way different than other people's experiences. So it's interesting, because I've been in a lot of classes as a student where it's like, "Come on guys, you all have this experience." But most people don't. Giving students a set of tools to think through different issues that they're bringing or different problems that they're bringing to the table, that's my approach.

Shane to Cody Hoover: You've taught at various HSIs: Fresno State, UC Riverside, Moreno Valley College, Fresno City College, West Hills College Lemoore, and now Clovis Community College. How have these contexts helped shape your teaching? [Episode 52: 11:28–15:28]

I guess first maybe we can talk a little bit about the context of HSIs because I feel a lot of schools in California, almost all of them, would be an HSI. I was poking around and reading about it a little bit. I was reading their bylaws and I was just curious about like what does it actually take to be designated as an HSI? Apparently only 25% of your student population needs to be Hispanic and that can be full-time or part-time students. I think it really just depends on if the college actually wants to apply for the HSI designation, apparently you just do that and have to have that certain percentage of students who are Hispanic and then you pay the yearly dues or whatever.

There's a lot of federal grants that colleges can get through being designated as an HSI. It seems like a very top-down thing. It's something that maybe administrators are concerned about. I'm generally cynical about this stuff . . . it seems like a marketing thing or just something admin care about to get grant money. I don't know, because on like a student or faculty level, I feel there isn't anything that's really different.

Maybe those of us who teach at these institutions, especially in somewhere like California or Texas or something like that, maybe we need to do more reflection about what that designation means, and also if it means anything to our students. Because for me, someone who was a student and a teacher at only these kinds of institutions, it isn't something that I've thought much about or has even really been anything I've been aware of. So doing a little bit of reading or research about it was the most I've ever learned about it. It is weird to think about that it has to meet that 25% threshold *only*. I feel it's like a line in a brochure or something like that, especially in California, I feel there's a large tendency for different institutions to do this where it's like, "Oh, we're an HSI. That checks off our diversity box. So we're all good because we have this one thing that we can cling on." I think, especially in California, which is such a liberal state, you have to think about how much of a neo-liberal state it is, how it constantly is continuing these different modes of oppression of non-white students, or students of color.

Maybe it's a cynical thing, but you could almost see that HSI designation is perhaps another tool of systemic oppression where it's like, "Well, we got the HSI thing, we're all good, that's all we need to do."

Shane to Cody Hoover: In what ways can HSIs better support students? [Episode 52: 15:29–18:26]

Maybe this is partly a community college situation, but being a student and also teaching at Fresno State and UC Riverside, which are four-year universities, there were definitely a lot more ethnic studies courses like Latinx culture and history. At Clovis Community College, we don't really have any of those courses. When I was thinking about this last night, I went back and looked through the catalog to make sure that I wasn't just talking out of my ass with this, but it's just a handful of courses, there's like a Latinx literature course and I think a class in sociology, but we don't have an ethnic studies department or specifically ethnic studies professors or anything like universities that are HSIs might have.

So I feel it's so much about running certain classes that will actually have enrollment, which is true everywhere, but our classes have to fulfill, most of the time, some other requirement, especially if students choose to transfer. From teaching and being a student at Fresno State and UCR, something I've learned is how important those courses are. Like I've been saying, I'm not even quite sure of how important the HSI label is as much as, is the institution fully supporting and funding these courses, like Latinx culture and history? It doesn't surprise me that Clovis Community College is an HSI because it fulfills 25% barrier or whatever, because of the funding we have and the courses that we offer to fulfill transfer requirements. We don't have any of those courses. That's a pretty big hole. I taught at Fresno City College, which has a long history of offering those courses. To answer your question, a lesson that I've learned is that I think it's most important to offer ethnic studies courses regularly.

DENOUEMENT

One responsibility all writing teachers have is to recognize and promote students' linguistic and cultural resources and identities. It is important to listen to students' past experiences with English and consider students' needs, which means inviting students to participate and examine their communities and identities. This work also happens when we disrupt Western rhetorical traditions, histories, and ways of thinking and making meaning. It means adopting culturally responsive and sustaining teaching practices and frameworks, such as funds of knowledge, that take an asset-based approach to education. How are teachers creating spaces that are equitable to a range of students? How are writing classes valuing multiculturalism and multilingualism? This, quite possibly, could require a reorientation of pedagogies to fully accommodate students' rich literacies in writing classrooms. It might mean embracing multimodal practices and assignments.

For more good work on teaching writing at HSIs and/or scholarship centering cultural literacies, I suggest reading *Bordered Writers: Latinx Identities and Literacy Practices at Hispanic-Serving Institutions* (Baca et al., 2019), *Community Literacies* en Confianza: *Learning from Bilingual After-School Programs* (Alvarez, 2017), *Teaching Writing with Latino/a Students: Lessons Learned at Hispanic-Serving Institutions* (Kirklighter et al., 2007), *Latino/a Discourses: On Language, Identity, and Literacy Education* (Kells et al., 2004), as well as the journal *Latinx Writing and Rhetoric Studies* from the NCTE/Latinx Caucus. I would also recommend Victor Villanueva's (1993) *Bootstraps: From an American Academic of Color. Bootstraps* is a narrative that critically explores the relationship between language and race, cultural biases and inequities, and English education. In addition to the aforementioned works, Iris D. Ruiz's (2016) *Reclaiming Composition for Chicano/as and Other Ethnic Minorities: A Critical History and Pedagogy* diverges from traditional composition histories, recovers excluded stories, and offers more inclusive pedagogies and practices for teaching writing.

As we continue to investigate our responsibilities as language instructors, here are some questions that might help guide us based on the interviews:

- What strategies are you using to support multilingual writers? How are you inviting students to play with/in languages and modalities to make meaning?

- How are you making visible students' linguistic and cultural resources, and how are you integrating these resources into your practices and curriculum? How does your teaching draw from students' cultural knowledge and communities?

- In what ways are you exploring connections between language, race, class, and identity? And how are you incorporating diverse perspectives?

- How are you addressing issues with monolingual ideologies and standardized English, or issues concerning immigration policies and discrimination?

PART II. PEDAGOGIES

5

Classroom Writing Assessment

> We never used to think much about the assessment of writing.
> We resented all the grading of papers and sorting of students
> but went about it as a grim duty . . . but those attitudes belong
> in the past, along with grammar drills and orthography.
>
> −Edward M. White, "The Changing
> Face of Writing Assessment"

> How do we teach English so people stop killing each other? Per-
> haps, we might ask, how do we judge language so that people
> stop killing each other? That, I think, is the real question.
>
> −Asao B. Inoue, *Labor-Based Grading Contracts*

Classroom writing assessment always has values and beliefs attached
to it and implications for teaching writing. Asao B. Inoue (2015)
says, "Classroom writing assessment is more important than pedagogy because it always trumps what you say or what you attempt
to do with your students" (p. 9). The first third of this book talks
about where teaching writing happens, such as two-year colleges
(TYCs), Historically Black Colleges and Universities (HBCUs),
and Hispanic-Serving Institutions (HSIs). This section is about
what happens in writing classrooms. Each chapter, then, offers
conversations about different practices and approaches to teaching
writing. I start with classroom writing assessment because assessment should be informed by where we are and what pedagogies we
use to teach writing. Writing assessment research asks teachers to
consider how assessments are affecting students in local contexts:
"Are our assessments affecting students differently? What kinds of
changes might we make to existing practices to ensure that all students are assessed in a fair and culturally sensitive manner that is

also context based?" (Inoue & Poe, 2012, p. 1). This localization of writing assessment to institutions and programs and students, and attention to fairness is extremely important for writing teachers. Just because one classroom writing assessment model works in one context, doesn't mean that it will work as effectively in another.

Writing assessment is theory and practice. It's multivariate and fraught with attitudes and beliefs that guide and place value on language and student writing. Our focus as writing teachers should be on how assessment can "aid the learning environment for both teachers and students" (Huot, 2002, p. 8). Writing assessment should complement pedagogies and support student learning. Edward M. White (2004) writes that scholarship on assessment is "arguably the most creative and varied in the entire area of composition studies" and adds that it's impossible to teach writing and be uninformed about writing assessment (p. 110). Research focuses mainly on program assessment (e.g., placement testing, exit testing, portfolios) and classroom assessment (e.g., rubrics, feedback, grading contracts). Program and classroom writing assessment, while separate, should be viewed as interconnected with an understanding that program assessment should help inform classroom writing instruction.

Maybe "grading" is the first thing that comes to mind when we hear about classroom assessment. Grades, though, can be taken up through different systems of assessment. The process of producing and distributing grades is complex. For instance, some teachers might use the A–F scale, points or percentages, while others might use portfolios or grading contracts.[2] Each form of assessment has its own values and beliefs about learning—and each has its own flexibilities and affordances. When we talk about classroom writing assessment, then, we are referring to the ways in which we are facilitating and measuring learning in our classes. What habits or practices or outcomes do we want to cultivate and promote through our teaching? What resources and means are available to assess student learning? In what ways can assessment reflect our values associated with literacy and learning? All this is to say, classroom writing

---

2   Portfolios and grading contracts take different forms, too. Which is another reason why it's important to understand classroom assessment models and variations.

assessment ought to be grounded in theory and should be contextualized to help students ultimately engage in learning. Teacher response takes different forms, too. A teacher might respond in the margins to offer specific comments to student writing, like about an idea that needs developed more in the writing or a claim that needs supported by evidence. Or a writing teacher might use an end comment to summarize their thoughts and suggest a plan for action and revision. There are different types of feedback: informal (e.g., more conversational), formal (e.g., more direct), constructive, formative, summative, peer-to-peer, teacher-to-student, and self-reflective. As writing teachers, we use different kinds of response on any given assignment, and our feedback comes at various stages of the writing process. For example, response on an earlier draft might ask for substantial content-based revisions, whereas feedback on a later draft might be more concerned with stylistic elements of writing. When writing teachers see grading and response in more nuanced ways, we can explore what classroom writing assessment practices are doing and how students might perceive them in relation to learning.

Writing assessment is a process that occurs across different times, through different modes and mediums, and for different purposes to invite students to participate in learning. The Conference on College Composition and Communication (CCCC) position statement on Writing Assessment says:

> Assessments of written literacy should be designed and evaluated by well-informed current or future teachers of the students being assessed, for purposes clearly understood by all the participants; should elicit from student writers a variety of pieces, preferably over a substantial period of time; should encourage and reinforce good teaching practices; and should be solidly grounded in the latest research on language learning as well as accepted best assessment practices. (National Council of Teachers of English, 2009, Introduction, para. 2)

Research on best practices for assessment has grown a lot over the last fifty years. There was a wave of books and articles in the 1980s that informed how teachers used writing assessment, such as Peter L. Cooper's (1984) *The Assessment of Writing Ability*, Edward M. White's

(1985) *Teaching and Assessing Writing*, Peter Elbow and Pat Belanoff's (1986) "Portfolios as a Substitute for Proficiency Examinations," and Lester Faigley's (1989) "Judging Writers, Judging Selves." Concepts on validity (Cronbach, 1988; Messick, 1989) and reliability (Moss, 1994; White, 1993) became prominent features in writing assessment scholarship. In the 1990s and early 2000s, teachers began reconsidering classroom grading (Elbow, 1997) and reimagining theory and practice (Huot, 2003), including rubrics (Broad, 2003). In the late 2000s and early 2010s, grading contracts increased in visibility (Danielewicz & Elbow, 2009) and there was greater attention to how assessment should change to account for race and diversity (Inoue & Poe, 2012). Over the last several years, teachers have been investigating and challenging traditional frameworks and implementing alternative assessment practices.[3] This includes conversations on "ungrading," which critically decenters the act of grading itself.

INTERVIEWS

The interviews in this chapter are a small representation of the threads in classroom writing assessment research over the years, specifically teacher response and grading practices. The focus of these interviews and questions is designed to capture the nuances of response, the emergence of technologies that help guide assessments, and reflections on grading practices and values. Noticeably absent are conversations on scores and/or tests which are often associated with institutional admissions and program placement. The interviews indicate how significantly important response is to teaching writing and how teacher and student communication, including making transparent grading practices and values, are the heart of the writing classroom. Through this, we see that response can be used to reflect pedagogical and classroom values, listening to students' perception on feedback is necessary to teaching writing, technologies can help facilitate and provide new directions for research on assessment, and fairness should be at the center of classroom grading practices.

In this chapter, I talk with Nancy Sommers, Chris M. Anson, Jennifer Grouling, and Asao B. Inoue about responding to writing

---

3   See *The Journal of Writing Assessment* special issue on contract grading (2020).

and attitudes, beliefs, and values associated with classroom writing assessment. For example, Sommers reflects on how she has grown as a teacher in recognizing and understanding the differences between "writing comments to the writer versus writing comments to the writing." Anson shares how the field continues to evolve by focusing on "student response to teacher response," and he talks about the tonality and attitude of response through technology-mediated devices, like cassette tapes and screencasting technologies. Grouling shares her research studying the differences between hard-copy and iPad collected papers and response and explains how assessment should reflect the teacher while keeping in mind the institutional context. And finally, Inoue problematizes traditional standards for judging writing and talks about how "labor" is a more equitable measure for classroom assessment: "The labor of the classroom is really the engine for learning."

Shane to Nancy Sommers: You've been a pioneer in research on teacher response. I'm thinking about three articles in particular: "Revision Strategies of Student and Experienced Writers" (1980), "Responding to Student Writing" (1982), and "Between the Drafts" (1992). In "Responding to Student Writing," you write, "We comment on student writing to dramatize the presence of a reader to help our students to become that questioning reader themselves, because ultimately we believe that becoming such a reader will help them to evaluate what they have written and develop control over their writing. Even more specifically, however, we comment on student writing, because we believe that it is necessary for us to offer assistance to student writers when they are in the process of composing a text, rather than after the text has been completed." Could you talk more about what got you interested in studying response, and how your thinking has changed since that landmark essay in 1982? [Episode 6: 06:12–11:47]

> I started studying commenting as a result of the work I did on revision because it was quite clear that students revised, or their sense of why they should revise, was in response to the comments they receive. So it seemed that I needed to do a companion study about commenting. And as you say, I did the first one, that was a long time ago, and since then

I've done lots of other smaller studies. I did a small study on commenting with Bunker Hill students, and of course, I did the longitudinal study at Harvard to understand the role of comments in student's undergraduate education.

I think it's important to think about comments because when we think about all the time we spend teaching writing, commenting and responding to our students' work is really what we spend the most amount of time doing. It takes a lot of time to write comments, and it takes a lot of time to write a good comment. I think how my thinking has changed is to realize how important comments are to students in ways that I didn't realize before. The first piece I did was looking at comments through the perspective of teachers, much more than students. But when we did the longitudinal study, we started to see comments through the eyes of students. It helped me to see how important our comments are in a deeper way than I understood before.

The way that my thinking has changed is understanding the difference between writing comments to the *writer* versus writing comments to the *writing*. What I mean by that is, that it's very easy when we're reading a student's paper to just circle the things that aren't working, or to say a sentence is confusing, or we're responding to the writing. But when we step back and say, "Well, how would a student use this comment?" Or, "What would the students do with this comment that would make the next draft better?" Or, "How could a student use this comment to expand thinking, or to do something specific, a specific skill?" Then, we're thinking about the writer. We think about it as an act of communication, a dialogue between a teacher and a student, between a reader and a writer.

I deepened my thinking. I've also realized through all the studying and through all the comments I write, how complex it is. It's not simple. One of the things I learned was to start a semester by talking about commenting, and not wait until the first time students received comments to talk about comments, but to say right from the very beginning that, "I will be giving them comments, and their peers will be giving them comments, and I would like them to use the writing center to work with writing center tutors, so that they can enlarge their world of receiving comments and feedback." I want them to see the way we learn and that . . . nobody writes in isolation, we write in community. I ask students a couple of questions. One is, why do you think teachers comment on papers? And also, what kinds of comments will help them the most? I want to get students from the first week engaged with the process of commenting. I think it's really important to think of commenting as part of a pedagogy, and not just that thing you do when students turn in papers.

Shane to Nancy Sommers: I like the idea of commenting as part of a pedagogy. So you're really talking about responding to student writing as being foundational to teaching—as a primary guide, so to speak, for the class throughout the semester. We all have different pedagogies and teaching styles and values, and we also respond in different ways. What types of comments best complement your values as a teacher? [Episode 6: 11:48–16:00]

I really like that question, Shane. I really like the idea of thinking about how comments reflect values as a teacher . . . that has a lot to teach us in our profession. We could learn a lot by thinking about the ways in which our comments reflect our values. I like that idea a lot. I think that my comments reflect my values because I want to bring a spirit of generosity into the classroom . . . I want students to feel that the voice they hear in my comments is the same voice they hear in the classroom. That it's not as if I become this other person when I comment. It's my voice, and it's the voice they know and trust from the classroom. I try very much always to respond with generosity and compassion.

For instance, a common thing is a student who has written a paper has a scattershot of ideas. So instead of saying, "There are just too many ideas here," I might start with positive statements such as, "You have an abundance of good ideas in this paper. Think about which one means the most to you, and pick one, and develop that idea." You know, any comment we want to write can be phrased in a generous way.

I think also that I want my comments to reflect the classroom. So one of the things that's always important to me in teaching is that there's a common language in the classroom, that students and I have a shorthand when we talk about a thesis, for instance. We always talk about the "so what" of the thesis. Why does this thesis have to be argued? Or when we look at a reading, an argument, we always talk about, why does this argument need to be made? So we have this shorthand language of "so what." I want my comments to reflect the language of the classroom. In fact, I think about commenting as something that begins on the first day of class. So how can I use that language from the classroom in my comments?

I think also, the comments reflect my values, because I think a lot about how students develop as writers. I wouldn't want to write a comment that a student would just look at and say, "Huh? What am I supposed to do with that?" I want my comments to match where students are developmentally, and I want my comments to say to a student, "You can do this. This is something you know how to do." So that means that I'm always thinking about where students are in a developmental perspective, and what they can do and can't do, and I would never overwhelm them. I would never give them 15 things to do between the drafts. I would focus on, "Well, what are the two or three things that would make a difference in the next draft?" That's where I would want to put students at attention.

Shane to Chris M. Anson: Teacher response has always been a thread through your research. I'm thinking about your article "What Good Is It? The Effects of Teacher Response on Students' Development" (2012). I'm also thinking about your contribution to *Twelve Readers Reading* in 1995, which became a foundational collection to teacher response research. Can you talk about how you became interested in feedback, and how you saw a need to focus on students' attitudes and perceptions on teacher response? [Episode 25: 09:16–14:03]

> I became interested in teacher response way back as a graduate student. The material that was being published at that time, the research literature, was focused primarily on what teachers were doing, I think in an attempt to theorize, or create models or approaches to teacher response that would be most effective, without really testing out whether they were effective. We saw a number of different articles and research studies looking at what kinds of marginal comments teachers wrote, what kinds end comments they wrote, studies categorizing teacher comments, and the different kinds and so on. There wasn't really much interest in what was happening in the minds of students. There wasn't much interest in the reception of that commentary until more recently. Now, I think we're seeing considerable new research that's looking at student response to teacher response.
>
> I became interested in the student perspective when I started using cassette tapes to respond to my students' writing. I inherited that from my mentor, Michael Flanagan, who was doing that in the graduate courses that I was taking with him. He would record on a cassette tape long analyses of our projects. I started doing that with my own first year writing students. I would ask them to bring in a cassette tape that they didn't want. Many of them would bring in a music cassette tape that they'd popped the little tab out of so it would actually record, there's a protection tab on those. I learned a lot about my students from what they were giving up, what they didn't want to listen to anymore, so that was kind of interesting.
>
> But I would get these tapes—I had bought a little cassette tape holder with a handle on it at Kmart—and I would

go in and collect all the tapes and put them in this little satchel, and then take it back home and read their paper, turn on the tape recorder and record sometimes 20, 30 minutes at a stretch, whole weekends of just me mumbling in my study. I've always done surveys on specific methodologies that I'm experimenting with in the classroom. Not student evaluation surveys, but additional ones. I asked my students to comment on the use of cassette tapes and they really loved it. I learned a lot about what they liked or didn't like about the cassette tapes and how I could refine those a little bit.

I started doing that with almost every class I was teaching until, over the years, cassette tapes started to disappear from use. At that time, because computer technology was replacing things like cassette tapes, there wasn't enough bandwidth to do much with oral recorded response. The flash drives of the time were so small in terms of memory that you couldn't put anything on them just to swap them in class. We didn't have the bandwidth, we didn't have a cloud to be able to send oral comments, so for a few years they just fell by the wayside. I stopped doing oral responses.

And then, obviously, with computer technology getting more and more enhanced and more memory and so forth, when those capacities increased, I went back to doing first oral recordings using computer technology. And then eventually, when I discovered screencasting, I thought this is fabulous. Because not only can I speak to the students, but I can have their paper on screen, and I can refer to certain passages or paragraphs, and highlight things as I scroll, as I'm talking, and that turns into kind of a miniature video that the students can then watch and hear me speaking. I was absolutely enthralled by screencasting, and I did more surveys with my students who said they loved it.

Shane to Jennifer Grouling: In your article, "The Genre of Teacher Comments from Hard Copy to iPad," you talk about how technology allows writing teachers opportunities to comment in different ways, and how there's not much research that focuses on what that looks like or there's not much that studies the differences in response practices between hard copy and iPad collected papers. What did you notice between traditional, handwritten response practices and comments mediated by technology? And what other directions should we go in research on response and technology? [Episode 18: 06:36–09:32]

> So it wasn't real student papers. I actually had a ton of fun writing fake student papers . . . I was trying to do that to kind of control and get high, medium, and low ones in each set. I had five different teachers—TAs and the contract faculty—grade these. Five on hard copy . . . and five on the iPad.

> When teachers used the iPad, they used Notability so they could type on student papers, they could highlight, they could write with a stylist in the margins. I thought that was particularly interesting because some teachers who favored handwriting could still take that sort of approach. Really, what I found was there was not that big of a difference in their feedback—length wise, it was similar. I adapted the coding that Straub and Lunsford in *Twelve Readers Reading* used where they code for focus and mode. Is it posed as an imperative or a question, or how is it framed? But also is it about an idea, is it about organization, global organization, sentence structure? What type of things? I coded like that and had a bunch of people code with me and then I got the help of someone who knew actual statistics to run the numbers of the codes. The only thing of statistical significance was there were more imperative comments with the iPad, which was interesting, so more command-driven comments.

> Then, when I looked at it for individual participants, because I also did interviews with these people about their process in both modes, what really stood out were the teachers that did not like the iPad. I'm not so sure that the iPad, or that any kind of technology, leads towards a

different type of commenting, but I think if you're less familiar or less comfortable with the technology, it leads you to potentially be harsher with students or frame your comments in a way that maybe is different than what you would in a technology you're more comfortable with.

Shane to Jennifer Grouling: So it sounds like you saw how teachers' attitudes might change depending upon the technology they're using to respond to student writing or how their familiarity or lack thereof with technology affects their response. I'm curious about what sort of future directions you see response mediated through technology taking. What kind of work do you feel like needs to happen so that writing teachers can have a better grasp on the advantages and disadvantages of technology or using technology to respond? [Episode 18: 09:33–12:14]

> I think we need to know a lot more about course management systems and how they constrain us . . . I think we make a lot of assumptions about even how students navigate those systems, whether they even know where to look for our feedback, what they see, how they work with it. And then, of course, all the issues with surveillance. I've noticed now we can just track [data], like how many times have they been on the site, how many times have they downloaded this or looked at this page?

> You can build rubrics with course management systems. I'm really curious how that's affecting the way teachers or will affect in the future how teachers respond to students, particularly if they're required to use those for assessment. Like when we were using Blackboard, we pulled artifacts from Blackboard through Blackboard Outcomes and that means students weren't even aware that we were pulling their writing for assessment. So, then there's a push that like, "Well, if you aren't using Blackboard, you aren't compliant with the university. So you need to be collecting their papers on Blackboard so we can pull them for assessment. And then we can assess them using Blackboard outcomes." So the technology drives the response in the

assessment in ways that I think we need to really question and look into.

I mean there's probably some advantages, too. You can do audio feedback right on Canvas. I think it's not all bad, but I think it would be interesting to see more how that constrains and changes our feedback. I know one of the reasons I wanted to study the Blackboard feedback, and then was frustrated that they changed up the system in the middle of my study, is that I found myself, when I respond now, not giving as much in the way of marginal feedback. I think that can be good, but part of it is the difficulty of leaving marginal feedback on something like a course management system.

Shane to Asao B. Inoue: One thing that has changed for you over the years is your understanding of classroom assessment and who assessment privileges. You have problematized judging language based on writing "quality," which you say reproduces White language supremacy because those standards have historical roots that privilege whiteness. Could you talk about what led you to question traditional assessment practices and how you came to value labor? [Episode 12: 01:50–05:11]

Classroom assessment is typically yoked to grades and a grading system that's hierarchical. That's point based. That usually judges every student by the same standard, or by the same metric, and then strings them onto a linear line and says, "You are better than this person," or "You get 10, you get 20, etc." I started rethinking classroom assessment by having problems with the products of a system that's hierarchical and that puts everyone on the same line, so to speak. I found that there was no way . . . no matter how I crafted assignments or rubrics or collaborated with my students to talk about my feedback and the grading system, there was no way to account for how much labor they did. And in any classroom, no matter what, every student is going to labor differently. There's going to be different amounts of labor and different kinds or quality of labor.

That is what students do when you ask them to write an essay or to produce an outline or read something and respond to it.

When I really sit down and think about it, the labor of the classroom is really the engine for learning. It's what students take away; it's the experiential thing they remember; it's a bodily thing that they have. I wanted to find a system that would agree better with what I think most literacy and writing teachers understand about the practice of writing which is—it takes time, it takes labor. Ultimately, when we give an assignment, for instance, we're asking students to spend time and to labor. I thought, "Why should I try to grade a product of that just because that's all I have to grade?" I think there might be other things we can establish grades from and that could be labor. For me, the problematic part of the system was that there are a diverse range of students in any classroom and they come to labor differently. I think conventional grading systems don't match up very well.

Shane to Asao B. Inoue: So you started thinking about alternative classroom assessment models (e.g., grading contracts), and you chose to construct a system where "labor" was at the center. You use labor-based grading contracts as a means for complementing anti-racist, social justice-based pedagogies. What are some values embedded in labor-based grading practices that you feel like complement writing pedagogies more broadly? [Episode 12: 13:27–16:14]

It certainly does one thing that I think all writing teachers want to accomplish in their writing classroom: It doesn't punish students for embodying the literacies that they are and that they come from. It doesn't say how you have languaged up to this point is "not right," "bad," "inappropriate," or whatever. I think those are the wrong messages that we want to send. Like [Kenneth] Burke has talked about, human beings are symbol using, symbol misusing animals . . . I think we forget that when we were really young, when we were babies, when we were toddlers, language was a fun enterprise, but when we get to high school and get to college, often times, it becomes this thing that was so stigmatized and so punished for doing things "wrong," and you can't play around with it and you can't do any of the things that come natural to us as human beings. It becomes this thing we stay away from and that you have these negative associations with. All of that comes from grading based on "quality" and it's really based on a particular standard—a standard that is not natural or inherent to any group outside of academia.

A lot of students aren't trying to be academics so why do I want to reproduce that? I want to reproduce language users that use language, that love using language and can play with it and can be critical about it. That doesn't mean they got to be academics. It just means that they're going to do it in a different way for us for their own uses. That's what I care most about. Part of my job in my classes is helping students re-acclimate to a labor-based system. English studies and English classrooms, we give a lot of lip service to this, I think, in different ways, we might not say "labor," but we care what students do and what they're reading and how they're writing. When it comes down to it, if we're still grading them on the products using a particular standard, they're going to get another message that's going to conflict, and they may not know how to understand that conflict, or that paradox.

Shane to Asao B. Inoue: In *Labor-Based Grading Contracts* you write, "Trying not to be unfair is the only way one can ensure equitable and inclusive practices and inherently unfair systems." So you mention how traditional assessment systems are inherently unfair, how they are exclusive, and how they disadvantage students of color in particular. You suggest labor-based grading contracts as an opportunity to do antiracist and social justice work through classroom assessment. Can you talk about how "labor" is a more equitable measure than traditional standards for judging language? [Episode 12: 08:24–13:26]

When we look at the research on what students say about grading contracts, Spidell and Thelin's (2006) early study on that several years back . . . students were ambiguous about it. But they never described exactly what that contract was. What was the ecology that was set up in the classroom? What are students really responding to? My argument is that it is likely they're not responding to a pure labor-based system. They're responding to a system that trying to do both. It's what [Peter] Elbow and I call a "hybrid" system, or a hybrid contract. Which is up to a B it's based on labor, and after that it's based on judgments of quality.

In mine, in labor-based grading contracts, it's all based on labor. The more work you do in the class, the more time you spend on the labor, the higher your grade. This still is a problematic. The problematic just shifts. It shifts away from the politics of language and the politics of identity in the ways that we've talked about it in literacy circles to the politics of economics and how much time do I have. Am I a working student? Am I a mother and a student? How much time do I have to spend on this class? It doesn't levitate me or the classroom from having a system that is still problematic in some way.

But I think it does offer a fairer system to work from. Labor-based grading contracts takes the one thing that I know everyone can offer in the classroom, or at least that we can try to agree upon, which is how much time do we feel is appropriate for the B? That's the default for us. Then, how much more do we think will require to get a higher grade than that? We determine all those things and then we renegotiate at mid-point because we've had six or 10 weeks or whatever it is to live in the contract for awhile, see how it works on us, see how we work with it, and then we make another decision. My question . . . at that midpoint is simple, "Is this contract still fair enough for all of us? And if it's not, what needs to change?" Then, the contract is set in stone at that point.

Life is so damn short. We've only got so much time on this earth. I am so thankful that over the years I've been able to cultivate a stance in the classroom and classrooms that continually challenge me. I've said it for years: To make a system fair, there's no magic to it like it's a certain method or it's a certain practice. It's all about participation. The more one participates in the system, the fairer they will feel that system is. Fairness doesn't exist in objective systems. There are no objective systems. There are only subjective ones. Fairness isn't really about equality in a system. It's a feeling that we have as people who exist within systems. My job is to help everyone feel that it is fair. I think that is the best, most honest way we can approach assessment . . . "Do this work, you get this grade."

DENOUEMENT

Writing teachers should use classroom writing assessment to support students and complement pedagogical values (e.g., feminist rhetorics, multimodality, antiracist practices). Through investigating how writing assessment functions to promote beliefs about language, and by reimagining what assessment does and can do to better support learning, teachers and students can address larger societal issues on race, gender, linguistics, socioeconomics, disability, and power. As Staci Perryman-Clark (2016) writes:

> Decisions about writing assessment are rooted in racial and linguistic identity; the consequences for many writing assessment decisions are often reflective of the judgments made about who does and does not deserve opportunities for success, opportunities historically denied to students of color and linguistically diverse writers. Put simply, assessment creates or denies opportunity structures. (pp. 206)

Teachers and students can critically examine writing assessment to uncover implicit and explicit judgments made on language and identity, and to investigate who does and does not have opportunities for success in classrooms and programs.

These reflections often reveal a lot about teaching writing. For instance, if a writing teacher values translingualism and encourages students to embrace linguistic variations in their writing, then classroom assessment ought to coexist with these pedagogical values. Teacher response should support these values, too (Wood, 2020). It is important for writing teachers and programs to consider how writing assessment is accounting for all students—the full range of diverse learners in writing classrooms. Therefore, teachers and administrators need to pay close attention to fairness, equity, and social justice in writing assessment practices (García de Müeller & Ruiz, 2017; Perryman-Clark & Craig, 2019; Poe et al., 2018), alongside more traditional concepts of validity and reliability.

I suggest reading journals such as *Assessing Writing* (est. 1994), *The Journal of Writing Assessment* (est. 2003), and *Journal of Response to Writing* (est. 2015) for research on writing assessment and response. Additionally, Norbert Elliot's (2005) *On a Scale: A Social History of Writing Assessment in America* provides a comprehensive history on writing assessment, while Richard Haswell and Elliot's (2019) *Early Holistic Scoring* takes a good look at the history of holistic essay assessment. I also recommend reading *Reframing Writing Assessment to Improve Teaching and Learning* (Adler-Kassner & O'Neill, 2010), *Writing Assessment in the 21st Century* (Elliot & Perelman, 2012), *Race and Writing Assessment* (Inoue & Poe, 2012), and Mya Poe, Asao B. Inoue, and Elliot's (2018) *Writing Assessment, Social Justice, and the Advancement of Opportunity* because it offers future considerations for writing assessment and social justice. For research on two-year college writing placement, read *The Journal of Writing Assessment*'s 2019 special issue (vol. 12, issue 1). And for teachers interested in labor-based contract grading, I suggest reading Inoue's (2019) *Labor-Based Grading Contracts*. Teachers and students can use the following questions to examine classroom writing assessment standards, policies, and practices:

- How can we ensure writing assessment is meaningful and is being used to complement program and classroom goals and outcomes within our local contexts? How are our assessments helping democratize learning?
- How are writing assessment practices valuing diverse students? How is writing assessment and teacher response advocating for linguistic justice and diversity?

- How are assessments being used to shift and/or resist traditional power structures and hierarchies? And what are some issues with current and/or emerging classroom assessment models?
- What systemic issues circulate in and through writing assessment ecologies that impact how student writing is being perceived, valued, and thus assessed?
- What are students saying about assessment, and how might we better listen to them when it comes to grading and assessing their writing?

6

Multimodality

> Teaching multimodally and teaching multimodality are *not* the same as simply adding a "digital assignment." A multimodal pedagogy is not just additive; rather, it is a stance, an orientation, and a privileging of the many ways of making and receiving meaning.
>
> —Rick Wysocki et al., "On Multimodality: A Manifesto"

"All writing is multimodal," write Cheryl Ball and Colin Charlton (2015). Multimodality means using multiple modes to make meaning, and it also means understanding how each mode of communication (e.g., visual, aural, linguistic, spatial, gestural) privileges a particular audience to act, move, respond, or react in a certain way. Communication is dependent on the tools and resources available for us to compose, and an awareness of which mode would most effectively transmit the appropriate message to the intended recipient or audience. A multimodal approach to teaching writing moves beyond alphabetic text and challenges teachers and students to consider how different modes have different affordances that can reach different audiences. This approach to teaching pays close attention to how individuals are situated within contexts and culture (Arola & Wysocki, 2012).

The call to integrate multimodal assignments has increased in response to rapid technological changes over the last twenty years. Multimodal researchers and theorists like Jason Palmeri (2012) have traced the history of multimodal writing pedagogy back to the 1960s, 1970s, and 1980s. Palmeri writes that writing teachers "have a substantial history of engaging analog technologies for composing moving images and sounds—a history that predates the rise of the personal computer" (2012, p. 6). Since the early 2000s, though, multimodality has been extensively theorized in composition studies, given the rise of digital technologies. Research on multimodality usually bridges theory and practice and offers strategies for teaching writing through multimodal orientations (Khadka & Lee, 2019). This idea stems from The New London Group, a group of educators who met in the mid-1990s to discuss the "state of literacy pedagogy" after having concerns with traditional approaches that were too restrictive (e.g., monolingual, monocultural, rule-governed) and disconnected from social and cultural realities and futures. The New London Group proposed an approach to teaching called "multiliteracies" pedagogy[4] that embraced the changing social environments in public and private life. Multimodality as a framework for teaching utilizes tools, technologies, and practices to engage with/in communities. This approach considers how images, videos, sounds, gestures, speech, and texts are all used to make meaning.

A multimodal approach to teaching writing invites students to explore various literacies: "Composition classrooms can provide a context not only for talking about *different* literacies, but also for *practicing* different literacies" (Selfe, 2009, p. 643). Multimodality asks us to practice and engage in different experiences that increase critical thinking of texts and technologies and that bring attention to rhetorical awareness and genre knowledge. Thus, a multimodal approach gives students opportunities to make choices about what modes and mediums are available to communicate most effectively given a specific rhetorical situation. Multimodal assignments include brochures, advertisements, memes, podcasts, infographics, videos, posters, websites, zines, and scrapbooks.

A multimodal approach to teaching writing also focuses on materiality, production, circulation, and reception. Which brings greater attention to how knowledge is produced and circulated within communities (Luther et al., 2017). For example, teachers might consider DIY culture and self-publishing, or the remaking of old media with new, or the relationship between writing and technology. In first-year writing, this might look like asking students to research alternative cultures (e.g., punk rock bands) and the genres these communities use to communicate. This inquiry could then be used to examine

---

4   "A Pedagogy of Multiliteracies: Designing Social Futures" (1996)

cultural values embodied within genres. For instance, students can analyze zines as rhetorical activism, how zines work to resist norms and hierarchies. Zines can be used to talk about power and privilege and resistance. Or teachers and students could focus on the materiality of zines, the combination of alphabetic texts and images held on by glue and coated with glitter. The first-year writing class becomes a site to study [counter]cultural histories and how zines make [counter]cultural arguments that circulate in underground scenes and that are influenced by feminist rhetorics.

Additionally, a multimodal approach might invite students to investigate specific meaning-making practices. A teacher can encourage students to think about the nuances of multimodality through the ways in which they experience different mediums, like *sound*. Steph Ceraso (2014) writes, "Sound is an especially ideal medium for better understanding multimodal experiences because unlike visual or tactile experiences, interactions between sound and the body depend on vibrations" (p. 104). She offers *multimodal listening* to "expand how we think about and practice listening as a situated, full-bodied act . . . [which] can help students develop a deeper understanding of how sound is manipulating their feelings or behaviors in different situations" (p. 103). A multimodal approach to teaching brings awareness to the interconnected nature of composing, circulation, interpretation, and meaning-making. It offers opportunities for self-reflection on how different modes and mediums are felt and experienced.

INTERVIEWS

The following interviews attempt to capture some of the complexities of multimodality and how different teachers embrace multimodal pedagogies and practices. Many of these conversations will reveal how multimodal approaches overlap with other pedagogies, too. Jody Shipka starts by offering a brief definition that suggests teachers see multimodality as including but "not limited to the digital." Shipka offers multimodal assignments like composing on clay tablets, making scrapbooks, and macarons. Meanwhile, Laura Gonzales and Stephanie Vie talk about incorporating digital technologies and spaces (e.g., social media) in writing classes. Gonzales defines digital rhetorics and says that "tools and technologies are not neutral." Christina V. Cedillo talks about how she intersects disability studies with multimodality. She offers "critical multimodality" as one way to examine how multimodality privileges some bodies over others. Vie concludes by talking about how writing teachers can intentionally and ethically incorporate technology.

Shane to Jody Shipka: How would you define a multimodal approach to composition? [Episode 30: 12:44–15:07]

> For me what's been really important is to remind people to advocate for the position that a multimodal approach to writing, or to composing, includes but is not limited to the digital. So I think beyond the square or rectangle of the paper or the screen. There are so many other modes and senses that we can draw on to make meaning, to tell our stories, to move people to some kind of action or emotion. I've been really clear about that and bothered by the ongoing conflation of multimodality as digital media or new media.
>
> The other thing that I think is really important . . . is thinking about new media in a historical context and to recognize, as Jason Palmeri and other people have talked about, that all media at one point in time was new and came with its own struggles and baggage. I'm mindful of that, that old analog forms of communication or media can be new to the user or new to the user's purpose.
>
> I've been really, really mindful of that. When we talk about *new media*, it's not just digital . . . I routinely have students compose on clay tablets. This is new to them and comes with a whole lot of questions about, "How do I use this? What do I use it for? How does it cause my body to work?" Right? I think in both cases we need to be mindful that multimodality includes but is not limited to the digital, and we need to think about the newness of media, not only historically, but in the biography or lifespan of the user.

Shane to Jody Shipka: What multimodal assignments do you use, and what is the biggest source of resistance for students in terms of perceiving and interacting with these types of assignments? [Episode 30: 15:08–19:44]

A lot of the assignments that I did in first-year comp have been ones that I've modified for courses I teach now. One of my approaches to multimodality privileges choice . . . I think early on people misunderstood my work as demonizing print linear forms. I've really tried to underscore, even though a lot of students choose to do things other than a standard-looking research paper, that it is always an option for them to pursue. It's always been about, what is it that you want to accomplish? What do you want your work to do? What choices do you have, right? What are the final forms that would allow you to do that? If you want to inform, you want to persuade, you want to humor, what are the ways of doing that, right?

Part of my approach to multimodality has been about privileging choice, but . . . there'll always be non-negotiable elements to an assignment. But there's a lot of choice there. I think more than anything else there's the resistance that students tend to be more comfortable with or used to being given an assignment that says, "You must do this, this, this, and this," and my assignments tend to be, "Here's a situation. How can you respond to that? What work are you doing?"

If my goal is to tell you something about my life, what options do I have to do that? A memoir, a scrapbook, a home movie, a diary. Students see right away that it's not about privileging the final form, but about that work that you want or need to do. Then, it becomes, "What ways could we accomplish that?" Not all of those ways are going to be socially acceptable. Not all of those ways are going to get you the job, or the A, or whatever the goal is. I want students to always think about, "I did this, but I could have done this, this, and this," and then it becomes, "What's the difference?"

An example I use is there's no reason why, if you go for a job interview, that you couldn't go into the building and write your resume in lipstick on a mirror, right? And then you sit down for the interview and they say, "Can I have your resume?" "Well, it's in the bathroom," right? This is probably not going to get you the job, but it could be done if you're communicating that information. So it becomes a discussion of "Here are all the ways we could solve this communicative task, but which ones are socially acceptable?" I think this gets to genre. How much can you push up against genres? How much bagginess or elasticities does it have?

Shane to Jody Shipka: What would you say to someone interested in adopting a multimodal approach to teaching writing, and are there other texts and/or resources you would recommend? [Episode 30: 22:44–29:19]

The answer is different depending on how you see your approach, right? Is the multimodal going to be mostly digital? If so, are you going to tell students what they need to make? Is it going to be more open-ended and choice-based? I think part of what that requires, just as a kind of mindset, is a willingness and the ability to communicate to students that you're learning with them. Not everybody can do that in the same way . . . I think it's a risk to be able to foreground "I'm a student in this class, too," particularly for students who expect you to know the answer and to know what's right. It's that willingness to learn a privileging of flexibility, being willing, both for the student and the teacher to continue to question, to linger in the uncertainty, to not privilege efficiency.

I would say to my students, "Inquiry ends with judgment and our job is to put off judgment as long as we possibly can and to continue to think about how could this be different. If we do things in this way, who does that privilege? Who does that silence?" I think that for this kind of approach that is beyond the digital, that is choice-based, there needs to be a willingness to trust that students will make good decisions and that is always really, really scary.

I've had to say, "But not this, but not that," in terms of what students can work with or how they can work with it.

The other thing is to see yourself as an expert in something. Like if I were to teach a course on designing macarons, I pretty much have an idea of what that's supposed to look like. If I had students all doing that, I could see myself going, "Oh, no, aesthetically, that doesn't work," or, "Why is it just one color? Why isn't it . . . ?" So I think it really helped me that I never felt like an expert in writing . . . I think students have helped me become more of an expert. Now, I've seen so many things in my time of teaching. Students will now say, "Well, I was kind of thinking about doing an object argument." "Oh, well, let me tell you about these other ones that I've seen." Right? The projects I get often take more time to grade. So again, with a mind toward people who don't have an office space, who might be freeway fliers, who are dealing with 120 students—I understand my privilege having smaller classes and being able to do this.

Shane to Laura Gonzales: Emphasizing digital rhetorics is another application of multimodality. You teach technical communication which allows you to do this work in dynamic ways. Can you talk about the intersections between digital rhetoric and technical communication? [Episode 21: 01:40–05:31]

A lot of people consider digital rhetorics related specifically to digital technologies and multimedia and making meaning or making arguments through different media, but I like to embrace a more expansive definition of digital rhetoric. Drawing on Angela Haas's work and her idea that digital rhetoric starts with our digits, our fingers, the way that we see the world. In addition, through our eyes and our bodies. Taking that approach has also helped me make connections between digital rhetoric and technical communication. Obviously technical communication has many different perspectives and definitions, but my orientation to technical communication is helping students understand how complex information can be adapted, repurposed, remixed, and shared with a wide range of audiences both professionally and in the community, as well as academic audiences.

I think at the core of this is the idea that all tools and technologies, whether they're behind a screen or not, are always infused with cultural values. A lot of times we don't see these values because we assume they are just neutral, but as a lot of technical communication and digital rhetoric scholars have taught us, tools and technologies are not neutral. Things are designed for some people and inherently exclude some people. I use digital rhetoric as a way to teach my technical communication students that anything that they design is excluding and including certain people. That's okay because you can't design something for everybody, right? There's no general audience. But I try to help my students be more honest and aware of who they're excluding in their designs and who they're purposely including and what the implications of that are.

Digital rhetoric is a way for me to help my technical communication students understand that as it applies to the design of technical documentation . . . specifically we look at how different tools and technologies have been designed. It can be anything from like a form to sign up for a lease or a patient medical history form to a social media campaign or an ad. We use digital rhetoric to understand the implications of that design, and then apply that to our work as technical communicators.

One of the things that I really like about teaching technical communication is that I get to tell my students we don't just analyze things and look at them and critique them. We do that, but we're also builders of things. We're also designers ourselves. Technical communication lets me, and this is just how I perceive it, take digital rhetoric to the next level because it's not just analyzing different tools and technologies, but also building different tools and technologies. That's what I try to help my technical communication

students see . . . they have the power to make design decisions, make recommendations for designs based on their
own experiences. Digital rhetoric is a way to do that ethically and responsibly.

Shane to Laura Gonzales: Your approach to teaching through digital rhetorics and multimodality also connects to language and culture. What does it mean to teach and use technology through a
translingual framework? [Episode 21: 11:40–15:43]

What I think is really useful about the translingual framework is that it moves us away from this idea of languages
as static things that can just be transported wholesale from
one expression to another. So in our brains, we don't have
containers labeled English and Spanish, for example . . .
like that doesn't exist, right? All of our linguistic practices
are always in our brain all the time. They're always interacting, they're always making connections to these things that
we see and hear. So the way that we speak is not based on
one single container of a language that we just decided to
go into that day or for that expression and transport out.
Whatever we say out loud is based on all of our language
practices interacting all the time and interacting with other
people as well.

That's the thing that I find really valuable in a translingual
approach is this move away from understanding that there's
one standard English, one standard Spanish . . . but that
languages are always changing. Languages are always in motion. Dictionaries are always growing, right? So language is
always changing and being adopted by people because language is a tool that people use to communicate. I would say
the same with technology . . . technology is always changing. There's not one right way to make a visual design or
one right way to make a video that's always changing. So
how can we take this translingual approach understanding
communicative practices as fluid and always changing and
apply it to all the different options that we have when we
compose in digital environments? . . . this expands students'

approaches or what they see as viable options for making an argument, or saying something in their writing.

It doesn't have to be standardized. It doesn't have to look like a five-paragraph essay. It can be drawing on multiple language practices and multiple technologies at once. It doesn't have to be a formal film. It can include some video and also some visual texts and also sounds. It doesn't have to be a polished podcast necessarily, but it can include some podcast elements that also have a transcript. Whatever students find to be most appropriate in a specific context. The translingual approach is nice because I can ground it in language. I can say, "How has language changed just in your lifetime to students or just in one context, or how do you change the way you speak based on who you're talking to? Like if you're talking to your parents or talking to someone at school, how do you change your language?" "Okay, well then how do you change the way that you communicate through technology?"

They'll tell me about different platforms they use to talk to different people . . . I open up that conversation for students so that we can say, "Okay, well what about us? Like we're talking to each other. How are we going to talk to each other in this class? How are you going to talk to me when you do your assignments? How are you going to talk to your peers? How are we going to talk to your community partners? If we're doing like a sort of service-learning project." There's a lot of options available to make those conversations be as dynamic as possible. What are we going to select and why?

Shane to Christina V. Cedillo: Your approach to teaching engages in multimodality and disability studies. Can you talk about a disability studies framework to multimodality and technology, potentially even what that means for teaching online? [Episode 29: 17:03–20:54]

Well, there's the really practical aspects. For example, how to design a PowerPoint with disabled audiences in mind

where you use alt-texts if you're going to upload that on-line. People on the CDICC (Committee on Disability Issues) and the disability SIG (Special Interest Group) in the Conference on College Composition and Communication have really been active in trying to get people to think through these things. So for example, providing conference copies in regular and large print. For most people they tend to think of that as a courtesy—and it's not. It's an appeal to multimodality because the person is there and you may be seeing them or listening to them and you also have access to the paper. As someone with ADHD, neurodivergent people can often use the paper to follow along
. . .

It's like a recursive process. It's definitely an approach that has to be conditioned over time, right? Where people might not think about certain things, but then as you start trying to become much more open, inclusive, generous, you're like, "Oh, what about *this* group of people? What about *this* group of people?"

For me, I think that disability studies and also thinking about things like race and culture really opened the door to what I call a critical multimodality. Critical multimodality is when we think through multimodality from the perspective that automatically is going to center what has been construed as difference. Also, thinking through what difference itself allows to be an affordance. Just because we all have access to the same technology or media doesn't necessarily mean that those modes are going to mean the same depending on who we're talking to. Certain cultures are going to prefer certain things.

Disability studies . . . allows for us to really start considering what it could be to remix multimodality itself. Because for a long time, and this is my common argument, we've tended to privilege the digital . . . some students . . . might not have access to internet. What does that look like? When [Gunther] Kress is talking about limitations and affordances, I think for a long time we've really taken those terms for granted without necessarily interrogating what it means to be an affordance. For example, now we can throw in a YouTube video and people can see what you're talking about . . . but that affordance isn't an affordance if you're talking about an audience that has visual impairment, right? Your reliance on that particular mode is actually a limitation.

Shane to Stephanie Vie: I know you incorporate social media (e.g., Twitter) in the writing classroom to help build collaboration and a sense of community. How do students respond to those technology-driven, social media-based assignments? How does multimodality help us better understand teaching writing? [Episode 3: 04:02–08:41]

So one of the things I've seen in my own teaching is that the majority of students are very open and are positive to the use of social media when/if pedagogically appropriate. But there is a small contingent of students who will have concerns, who don't want to put themselves out there. I want to honor that. Because I do research around privacy policies and around terms of service. I'm a very careful person in thinking about my own engagement in social media spaces, so I never want to have students . . . using technologies that make them feel uncomfortable from a privacy or an engagement kind of standpoint. That means I need to do some additional work at the beginning of a semester to consider alternatives, different assignments. If a student says, "You know, I don't feel comfortable creating a social media account." Now what? I think, for me at least, and this is going to be for every instructor to kind of think through, "What are your boundaries and what is your comfort level?"—I don't want to insist and say, "You know what, too bad, you're in this class and this is what you're going to do. If you don't like it, drop the class."

I would rather try to think about what was my learning goal; what were my outcomes; what did I want the student to try to do; is there an alternative way that they could try to meet those goals that asks them to use a different social media tool, a different technological tool altogether? So that does mean that there is some additional learning that needs to happen in terms of scaffolding. But that to me, aligns with things kind of along the lines of universal design and learning. I'm going to try to make this class accessible to everybody . . . whether they're going to be having some privacy concerns or having engagement concerns, or whether they're pro social media . . .

From the studies I've done, we've found the majority of students find that social media use has some kind of positive correlation to their writing. In other words . . . we've talked with about 88 to 89 different students about the effects of social media use on their writing. A little less than half of them—47%—said I think it has a positive effect, only 2% of them said that I think using social media in my writing classes has some kind of negative effect on my writing. The interesting category I think is that 24% of them are unsure. When I look at the kind of responses about "Why are you unsure?" it points to a potential area for growth in social media with a pedagogical focus. That is, if you are not making a connection for the students, and if you're not scaffolding it throughout the semester . . . if you're not making it clear to them what is the purpose and what this has to do with writing and rhetoric, then it's going to seem like it's just an *add on*.

People in our field, Cindy Selfe especially, have been talking about you're not going to throw technology in as an add on. It needs to be something that's thoughtfully incorporated from the get-go. Students are savvy to that. What bothers them the most, at least from the responses to the survey and the follow-up interviews with undergraduate students and graduate students across the nation, they hate when they have to teach their teachers about technology . . . students want us to scaffold our classes really effectively.

Shane to Stephanie Vie: I'm hoping you could talk about our responsibilities as teachers to use emerging technologies in the writing classroom, and to do so responsibly and ethically? [Episode 3: 08:42–13:28]

There's a couple of different approaches that people tend to take. One is, "I'm not going to use these in my teaching because it takes a lot of time and there's a lot of concerns and there's a lot of challenges so I'm not going to use them." I don't think that confronts the reality of 21st century literacies and the world we live in where it doesn't matter if you are a student or a teacher, like we are using these technologies to compose and to communicate. So to sort of push it aside and ignore it because they are a problem seems itself problematic. Then, there's the other side which says, "I'm going to use these things, it's all going to be great, it's all going to be wonderful, my students are going to benefit," that doesn't think critically about the possible challenges and it doesn't think about the "what-ifs." This is also problematic because that's assuming that none of these challenges about privacy, surveillance, data mining, who has access to my data and where is it being shared, that those just don't exist and that technology in a class will always be positive.

One of the kinds of narrative threads that has always run through my research that I harp on continually because it is so important is this kind of critical approach to technology. If you are going to compose with and incorporate technology in your classroom, or into your life, I think it behooves you to be really critical about that: "What am I gaining? What am I giving up? What are some of the possibilities? What are some of the perils?"

So what should we do as teachers? I think that we have a responsibility to think about any technology we're going to incorporate in the classroom and think about what we need to do to incorporate this effectively and responsibly. What kind of conversations do we have to have with students ahead of time?

Maybe that means we're having some big picture conversations rather than just skills-based conversations. You know, "Here's how you use this tool, here's how we're going to use it in this class." But also, we may need to have some conversations about privacy and about data mining. In one class where we were using social media, we even had some real uncomfortable conversations, but generative conversations, about what happens with your social media accounts after you die. That's not something a lot of us want to confront or think about, but it's something more and more necessary these days. If I asked you to create a blog, or create a Wiki, or create webpage, you know, am I contributing to the mess that is abandoned web spaces online? Am I asking students to create something that's not going to have a life outside of the semester or this quarter that's just going to be out there cluttering it up, but it's part of your digital identity and digital footprint? So what activities am I asking my students to do that contributes to their digital footprint that's very hard to erase once established? I think we need to be thinking about that.

DENOUEMENT

Multimodal pedagogies are attuned to social, cultural, and historical contexts, and require an awareness of how multiple modes and mediums act and are acted upon by different kinds of audiences. As can be seen and heard through the interviews, a multimodal approach to teaching is often interconnected with other theories and practices (e.g., digital rhetorics, translingualism, disability studies, cultural rhetorics), and thus can be used as a framework for examining language and culture. Adam Banks (2010) writes, "Black rhetorical traditions can form crucial links between oral, print, and digital communication and digitized, rhetoricized conceptions of access for African American users" (p. 12). Multimodality provides opportunities to investigate accessibility and other cultural issues and ideologies. As Selfe (1999) has argued, we can't ignore technology. Writing teachers must pay attention to how technologies embody assumptions, biases, values, and beliefs. Tools and technologies aren't neutral. Selfe adds that writing teachers should consider how these tools can be used to help students become "better humanists" (p. 435).

I also think writing teachers can investigate how these tools and technologies can help complement core principles in our field, such as process-based orientations to teaching writing, accessibility, inclusivity, and universal design for learning, and how multimodality can work to reconceptualize traditional frameworks for assessment (Wood, 2018). A multimodal approach to teaching privileges choice and values accessibility, and it creates new pathways for student engagement and new possibilities to meet program outcomes and goals. I offer the following questions to help teachers think more about incorporating a multimodal approach to teaching:

- What kinds of modes and mediums complement writing classroom objectives (e.g., critical thinking, rhetorical awareness)? What multimodal texts can be used to support these learning outcomes? How would a multimodal assignment be assessed?
- How are multimodal texts produced, circulated, and received within communities?
- What are the affordances of inviting students to use different modes to compose? What are the advantages and disadvantages? And how might traditional assignments be modified and made more accessible to the widest range of students?
- What kinds of literacies are valued in my writing classroom? Does this include digital literacies? How am I going to address issues (e.g., privacy, surveillance, ethics) surrounding technology with students?
- What pedagogies (e.g., genre, cultural rhetorics) might help center multimodality?

7

Social Justice

> The way Black language is devalued in schools reflects how Black lives are devalued in the world . . . the anti-Black linguistic racism that is used to diminish Black Language and Black students in classrooms is not separate from the rampant and deliberate anti-Black racism and violence inflicted upon Black people in society.
>
> –April Baker-Bell, *Linguistic Justice*

> Let us demand of ourselves and encourage one another to do more than mouth our commitments: to make our actions match our words; to transform our classrooms, our departments, and our institutions as well as our communities; and to learn from one another as allies who possess the courage to effect change.
>
> –Frankie Condon and Vershawn Ashanti Young,
> *Performing Antiracist Pedagogy in*
> *Rhetoric, Writing, and Communication*

Composition pedagogies and practices centered on social justice, antiracism, and linguistic justice as theories and frameworks for teaching writing have become increasingly more visible in composition studies over the last decade. Composition has been marked by turns, or waves in theory and practice. For example, the writing-as-process movement in the 1960s and 1970s (Murray, 1972), the cognitive turn in the early 1980s (Flower & Hayes, 1981), the social turn in the 1980s and 1990s (Berlin, 1988; Trimbur, 1994), the public turn in the 1990s and early 2000s (Mathieu, 2005), and the multimodal and digital turn in the 2000s and 2010s (Selfe, 2007; Shipka, 2011; Yancey, 2004). I think a case could be made that we now find ourselves in a social justice-based orientation to teaching writing or a "social justice" turn (2010s and 2020s).

Race, gender, class, language, privilege, and power have been themes in composition studies throughout its history, yet many first-year composition anthologies (e.g., *Naming What We Know*, Adler-Kassner & Wardle, 2015; *A Guide to Composition Pedagogies*, Tate et al., 2014; *Cross-Talk in Comp Theory*, Villanueva & Arola, 2011) that take as their purview theories and practices in the field have yet to include a standalone chapter that offers social justice as a pedagogical approach to teaching writing. Often, social justice is linked with other pedagogies and theories like critical pedagogies, queer theory and rhetorics, feminist rhetorics, and translingual approaches to writing instruction. Given the substantial research on social justice practices over the last ten years, I include this chapter for teachers interested in taking a more explicit social justice approach to teaching that focuses on race and language[5].

A basic keyword search for "social justice" in CompPile[6] results in 117 citations (as of September 2020) with the majority occurring in the last decade. A narrower search for "social justice pedagogy" or "social justice-based pedagogy" returns zero results. That said, there's been a lot of recent theory and practice in composition studies intersecting race and language through justice-oriented frameworks. Here is a brief, noncomprehensive sketch of this work:

- 2013: Frankie Condon and Vershawn Ashanti Young coedit a special issue in *Across the Discipline* called "Anti-Racist Activism: Teaching Rhetoric and Composition."
- 2013: Carmen Kynard publishes *Vernacular Insurrections: Race, Black Protest, and the New Century in Composition-Literacies Studies.*
- 2015: Lisa King, Rose Gubele, and Joyce Rain Anderson coedit *Survivance, Sovereignty, and Story: Teaching American Indian Rhetorics.*
- 2015: Asao B. Inoue publishes *Antiracist Writing Assessment Ecologies*, which provides a framework for social justice writing assessment practices.

---

5   There are many social justice frameworks, aims, and initiatives writing teachers can take up, including disability justice, criminal justice reform, and LGBTQIA+ rights, to name a few.

6   https://wac.colostate.edu/comppile/

- 2015: Christie Toth and Holly Hassel circulate a CFP for "Race, Social Justice, and the Work of the Two-Year College English."
- 2017: Condon and Young coedit *Performing Antiracist Pedagogy in Rhetoric, Writing, and Communication,* which offers reflective practices and strategies for embracing antiracism.
- 2018: Laura Gonzales publishes *Sites of Translation: What Multilinguals Can Teach Us about Digital Writing and Rhetoric,* which intersects language diversity and technology.
- 2018: Mya Poe, Asao B. Inoue, and Norbert Elliot coedit *Writing Assessment, Social Justice, and the Advancement of Opportunity,* which adopts social justice theory as a means for investigating "the deeply rooted concern for the ways we are bound together, the nature of justified constraint, and the extent of individual freedom" (p. 9).
- 2019: Romeo García and Damián Baca coedit *Rhetorics Elsewhere and Otherwise: Contested Modernities, Decolonial Visions.*
- 2019: Staci Perryman-Clark and Collin Lamont Craig coedit *Black Perspectives in Writing Program Administration: From the Margins to the Center.*
- 2019: *Spark: A 4C4Equality Journal* launches as an "open-access journal committed to activism in writing, rhetoric, and literacy studies."[7]
- 2020: Aja Y. Martinez publishes *Counterstory: The Rhetoric and Writing of Critical Race Theory.*
- 2020: April Baker-Bell publishes *Linguistic Justice: Black Language, Literacy, Identity, and Pedagogy.*
- 2020: The Conference on College Composition and Communication (CCCC) releases a demand for Black linguistic justice in response to the anti-Black racist violence and police brutality against Black people and communities in the US.
- 2020: Louis M. Maraj publishes *Black or Right: Anti/Racist Campus Rhetorics.*

Social justice pedagogies, practices, and rhetorics have increased in visibility over the last ten years in composition scholarship, but

---

7   In July 2020, Volume 2 honored/celebrated Black studies, social movements, and activism.

I would be remiss to not acknowledge that the roots of this work are tied to earlier texts that helped pave the way for us as a field: "Students' Rights to Their Own Language" (CCCC, 1974); *Talkin and Testifyin: The Language of Black America* (Smitherman, 1977); *Lives on the Boundary* (Rose, 1989); *Bootstraps: From an American Academic of Color* (Villanueva, 1993), to name a few.

This chapter is dedicated to social justice because I see this as the present and future of rhetoric and composition in the 21st century. Teaching writing should be about investigating how language is perceived, how language is valued, what biases are attached to language, what attitudes are associated with language, and what systems and structures are privileging some linguistic variations/habits and disadvantaging others. Writing pedagogies and classrooms can embolden the value of *all languages and dialects*.

INTERVIEWS

The interviews in this chapter offer different orientations to social justice through teaching writing. I talk with Frankie Condon, Asao B. Inoue, John Duffy, Cruz Medina, and Cecilia Shelton about how they incorporate social justice practices in their classes. These teacher-scholars frame teaching around race, language, ethics, and multicultural rhetoric. The overarching theme here is how it takes an intentional effort and critical consciousness to embody social justice values and aims. Condon describes how her writing assignments focus on antiracism and how she asks students to think critically about their histories and experiences with language. Inoue problematizes traditional assessment standards attached to judging language and assessing writing. Duffy talks about reimagining traditions and classroom values and practices. He asks, "What do our practices tell us about ethics?" and he talks about how teaching writing is always connected to rhetorical ethics. Medina shares how he intersects digital and multicultural rhetorics to frame social justice, and how technology and social media platforms maintain cultural norms that privilege some and oppress others. Shelton concludes by offering a Black feminist pedagogical framework for disrupting traditional norms and expectations for teaching writing.

Shane to Frankie Condon: How does social justice and antiracism play out in your classroom practices, for example, your writing assignments? [Episode 28: 17:37–22:53]

I'll talk about a couple assignments, and I'll offer the caveat that none of this is perfect. None of it works perfectly all the time, or I fail at it all the time, right? I'm just always on the quest to learn how to do it better next time. This semester, for example, I'm teaching a first-year writing class. It's an introduction to academic writing and all of the students in my class are math or computer science majors. The first assignment that we're doing, I actually have adapted from an assignment I found in a book called *What Makes Writing Good?* This is a really old, edited collection. In this edited collection, Jim Sledd . . . included a piece in this book with permission he had taken from a friend who was teaching at Claflin College.

The assignment was to write four dialogues. Each dialogue should reveal something new about the writer, some new aspect that they would want people to know about them, right? So the first dialogue would be with a police officer, the second with a perspective employer, the third with a best friend, and the fourth with a small child. The writing sample that Jim Sledd includes with this assignment is one that's written in African American English or an African American English. Oftentimes, if I've used that in a writing center theory and practice course, the first response of prospective tutors is to fix and change that writing. To talk about how they would tutor that person in order to make that and to straighten up that prose. Right?

But of course that's a problem because the assignment asks the student to reveal things about themselves. What this particular writing sample shows about this writer is that when confronted by the police, he is inclined to call out the racism of the police rather than capitulate to it, and to do it in a fierce kind of street way. He shifts his mode of address in talking with the perspective employer but does so without trying to step out of who he is. He's just performing it in a different way, right? You can see this happening in each of the dialogues that this student writer has produced. The first assignment for my class this semester is to write that set of dialogues for themselves.

My prediction is that they're going to write these dialogues and as best as they can, they're going to make them all the same and try and wipe out all of those differences in discourse that they would in fact use if they were talking to their best friend, or they were talking to a small child. So then we're going to work on putting those things back in. How do you do that thing where you recognize this is how I would actually talk to a police officer, this is how it's different than how I would talk to my best friend, and this is what those differences reveal about me that I want an audience to know of who I am, how I represent myself, who my audience is and what I want them to know and my agency in revealing or withholding?

Then, the last assignment is called the funk it up assignment. They read Vershawn Young's "Should Writers Use They Own English?" and we investigate the debate between Young and Stanley Fish. Then they can choose one of the pieces of writing they've done throughout the term and their job is to learn how to code-mesh, which of course requires that you understand how sentences work much more deeply than if you simply write correct White sentences, or standard academic English sentences. You can't fake it. You have to actually learn how to do it. To write in an academic context or to write in a professional context should never mean that you leave yourself and your home language and home discourses at home. Those should come with you. The question is how to use them in ways that are fun, creative and smart.

Shane to Frankie Condon: So obviously this work goes a lot deeper than assignments. I'm interested in the conversations you have with students about language and languaging because I know that has to be a central part of antiracist work in the writing classroom. [Episode 28: 22:54–25:06]

> It seems to me students come to my classroom having already deeply internalized the notion their home languages or home discourses diverged from what they've been taught as standard academic English, or a normative English, a White English. That those home languages are *wrong*. So in order to make some determination about the use value of their work, they have to contend with that and unlearn that notion that what they have to say and how they have to say it is always inevitably wrong, and relearn how to engage with the work of writing in ways that have meaning and value to them that are useful to them. Where they have agency and get to define the terms for what counts as good writing. In some way, I think that to begin with the *What Makes Writing Good?* assignment—the dialogues, and to end with the funk it up assignment requires the in-between.

> We talk about how it is that we have learned such a dysfunctional notion: That what we have to say and how we have to say it is inevitably wrong. Not only is it inevitably invariably wrong, it's wrong because we are not the people that we should be. We're not performing our subject position in a way that's dutiful and obedient. What they've been taught to think of their own writing and their agency with regard to their writing is invested with sticky stories about who they are, who they're capable of being, and who they should be, that are dysfunctional maybe at best, and at worst, oppressive. Right?

Shane to Frankie Condon: What's the most entrenched resistance that you've experienced as a teacher-scholar who is doing antiracist work? [Episode 28: 14:24–17:36]

> The most entrenched resistance has seemed to me to be driven by the fear of White folks. That fear from my

perspective had in large part to do with a worst-case-scenario thinking. So if I do this work from my position as a writing center director, I'll get fired. Or the provost won't like me anymore. Or the teachers won't send their students to the writing center anymore. Or people won't like me anymore. This was many years ago, Beth Godbee and Moira Ozias and I did an antiracism workshop before a Midwest Writing Centers Association conference. They had a workshop day, like CCCC does, and we did a half day antiracism workshop. What was really interesting to me about that workshop was a moment when we asked participants to reflect on, "What prevents you from starting antiracism work? What prevents you from trying?"

To the best of my recollection, I think there were two women of color in that workshop and all the rest were White women. All of the White women talked about these fears: "People won't like me. My writing center is already marginalized in my institution. What if it gets more marginalized?" Two women of color in the workshop talked about fears for the safety of their children, experiences with lynchings, both literal and metaphorical. I often think that White people don't start or they resist because they're living a failure of their imagination to see a world beyond the impossible. I think the problem of, "What if I lose what little power I have?" is an extraordinary piece of resistance, and a place where people really get stuck.

Shane to Asao B. Inoue: You approach writing assessment through a social justice-based framework by problematizing traditional standards and values on judging language. Can you talk about this work? [Episode 12: 05:15–08:23]

At least in the contemporary university setting, traditional writing assessment standards and values were created around the late nineteenth century. In that time, there was really only one demographic going to college: White males. In the United States, and again . . . we're talking about the United States university system that was migrated from

Europe, the German university system. There is one group of homogenous students . . . all we have to do is look at some of the really good histories written in our field about the origins of literacy assessments that get students into college. I'm thinking about the origins of the SAT, for instance. What were they looking for at the turn of the century? They were looking for students who had read the kind of books that those Harvard and Yale college professors had read and felt were important to know. Why would they think it's important to know? Not because it offered them some way to think or whatever. It offered them certain dispositions in life. Certain ways to be distinguished as a human being.

We can have all the social critiques we want of that. But ultimately, when you're grading student performances, literacy performances, based on something like that or based on "Here's what I think the quality of that is and I'm going to rank it," you're doing a similar thing as they did before. You're saying how close are you to me, the teacher and my background. I don't think most of the time when I walk into a classroom that my students come remotely from the places that I came from and from the kinds of background that I came from. A few do, but most of them don't. That's good for them and good for me. So we need to find ways and grading systems that help us get away from just simply reproducing ourselves.

I think *problematic* is the right word. I'm thinking about [Paulo] Freire's notion of a problematic—that which is both social and idiosyncratic. Meaning it's of the individual. It's a system that is problematic because it's necessarily part of my biases. I make judgments based on my biases. But it's also where do I get those from? Where are the boundaries and limits that give me those, the history? It's the social aspects of my life in history and in education and in my classrooms that I gather from that give me the boundaries to let me make certain kinds of judgments and have certain kinds of biases. It's truly problematic. I like to

replace problematic or put a slash over that and say problematic is also a *paradox*. Yeah, that's true. It's also not true.
Or there's elements of those things that are good or bad in
this given situation. It's *probabilistic*, if you will.

Shane to John Duffy: How does ethics inform your approach to
teaching writing? [Episode 11: 01:59–04:55]

> We have a sort of grand tradition, the rhetorical inheri-
> tance, and we work towards citizenship and the good com-
> munity and so forth. I just began asking myself, given the
> work we do, we seem so disconnected from the reality of
> public discourse, even though we're teaching things that
> should be influencing public discourse. So that was one
> question. Why was that true? Then, the other question was
> what might we be doing that we're not doing now? I want
> to stress that that's a hard question to answer because I
> think that the work that we're doing now is so good. I
> mean, I really do. You look from program to program and
> you look at the scholarship and it's so impressive. But it
> did seem to me that the more I read, the more I started to
> think about the role of ethics in the teaching of writing.

> Not that we should be teaching ethics, but it seemed to
> me that we were already teaching ethics. We were teaching
> practices of ethical discourse but we weren't naming those
> practices. They were implicit in what we were doing. Now,
> I don't mean that there wasn't a single person or teacher
> or program doing that. I mean, in general, if you look at
> our scholarship, there's not a lot of attention paid to eth-
> ics. We've embraced Aristotle's rhetoric and we've mostly
> ignored Aristotle's ethics. So I started to look into that,
> and to see how that might inform my work here at Notre
> Dame as a writing program administrator, but also what it
> might have to say in the field.

Shane to John Duffy: In "The Good Writer," you write, "As teachers of writing, we are always already engaged in the teaching of
rhetorical ethics, and that the teaching of writing necessarily and

inevitably moves us into ethical reflections and decision-making." Can you talk more about what you mean by rhetorical ethics, and how teachers are always inevitably teaching practices of ethical communication? [Episode 11: 04:56–10:25]

> Typically, when we talk about ethics, there are two traditions in the West that have been dominant, the so-called Big Two. One is deontology, which is the ethics of obligation, the idea that there are certain things that are categorically and indisputably right and indisputably wrong. So for example, torture. We might say that that is categorically wrong and should never be done. The most famous practitioner of this is Immanuel Kant, who talked about the categorical imperative, which was the sort of thing like if you would will it for everybody under all conditions, then it is categorically imperative. The other tradition is consequentialism of the ethics of outcomes, where you try to base moral decisions on what is going to promote the greatest good or happiness for the greatest number of people. And I have argued that both of those traditions have influenced the way we teach writing.
>
> When we teach students, historically, when we've taught students about grammar, when we've taught students about usage rules, that's often framed categorically, right? These are the rules, and if you break them, if you violate them, you are doing something wrong. You're an error. We've also been influenced, I think, by consequentialist ethics, in the sense that we rank students, we grade their papers, we create consequences, and we base the goodness of a writing assignment or a task or product on how well it promotes a good consequence. So those traditions have been prevalent in our classrooms, again, mostly implicitly. But it seemed to me that neither of those really captured the ethical dimensions of our work. I started to think in terms of practices, like what do our practices tell us about ethics?
>
> The example that I've used many times is, in an argument, when we teach students to write a claim, we are presuming

or there is an assumption that in making that claim the students are going to be truthful. That they're not going to make claims that are knowingly dishonest. Because if they do, their arguments won't be successful, for the most part. I mean, you can always think of exceptions. But similarly, when we teach students all the things we teach about evidence, about its sufficiency, its adequacy, its relevancy, we are in a sense teaching them to be accountable. We're saying that you have to be able to stand up and defend the claims you make or substantiate the claims you make.

The final example that I use is when we teach students that they need to look at alternative points of view, if only to address those points of view, we're teaching practices of intellectual open-mindedness, intellectual generosity, and intellectual courage. Because it's hard to read people you fundamentally disagree with and read them to the end and try to really think about their arguments. But this is what we're asking students to do. So those things: truthfulness, accountability, open-mindedness, courage, they're part of another ethical tradition. That's tradition of the virtues. When I talk about ethics, I'm talking about the kind of ethics that moral philosophers call *virtue ethics*. It's rooted in Aristotle, it's rooted in Confucius before Aristotle. We are teaching practices. In those practices, inherent in those practices, are what I would call *rhetorical virtues*. When I say rhetorical virtues, I simply mean the discursive enactment of virtue.

Shane to Cruz Medina: Your teaching intersects digital writing and multicultural rhetoric. Can you talk about how social justice and digital writing and multicultural rhetoric come together in your classroom? [Episode 24: 02:12–05:49]

Sure, so I think the connection between digital writing and multicultural rhetoric for me goes back to James Berlin and thinking about the idea of the social epistemic and thinking always how when we're writing we're never really disconnected from the cultural influences or the knowledge in a specific geographic space that we're writing in. Even when we're composing in digital spaces, they're still informed by this cultural knowledge or traditions that are happening.

I'm someone who's used a blog for more than ten years. What I found was, there was certain *traditions* . . . it was Natalie Martinez's video she created that really inspired me for the idea of the *digital testimonio*. I could kind of see that tradition she was borrowing from. As much as we want to say there's a certain neutrality for some of these digital platforms, we can definitely see that how we're using them is informed by rhetorical traditions that we come from or that we value. I've really been pushing for students to think a lot more about bringing in their own images or video or things that they're creating. There's a very tangible way for them to be thinking about these multimodal projects. So it's a lot to always say how are we going to teach multicultural rhetoric because you're including a lot of different traditions in that. I think if they can come away with at least a few bits of those kinds of ways of approaching their critical thinking and writing, that's all I can hope for.

Shane to Cruz Medina: In *Racial Shorthand*, you write about the importance of examining online spaces and media because "racist discourse about, and threats against, non-whites continue to circulate in social media due to the fact that users believe they are hidden (or hooded) by cyber-anonymity." Can you talk about this complex relationship between social media and social justice? [Episode 24: 10:58–15:31]

I think in the collection Miriam F. Williams . . . does the best job in thinking about the use of the hashtag #BlackLivesMatter and how that created its own sort of platform or connective space. That once folks were using the hashtag they were able to connect. I think going back to the mind space I was probably in working on that years ago, there was a lot of hope in terms of thinking about how a lot of these social media platforms felt maybe a little more neutral, or felt just like these writing tools. I think it kind of went with that same hope at the time when like Yancey and Andrea Lunsford in *Writing Matters*, that we're writing more and writing in all these different places and students are texting, and this is great. I think in part of that message is like, "No, this is good. We can leverage these platforms in a way that they can really be just like any other kind of writing in their own sort of . . . how we're deciding to use them."

That's kind of the double-edged sword a little bit. I think what was really encouraging was they provided these spaces for writing and reflection, critical thinking, and then, of course, action. When you're thinking about it, I think a lot of people who might be isolated activists in terms of rights for different groups, and they don't feel like they're around those groups in different places, social media gives them that opportunity to connect with others. So that they're not feeling isolated necessarily. Or they can see maybe when they're gaslighted in their own communities in terms of telling people that these are issues, and other people just kind of dismissing them away.

Then a couple years ago when Safiya Noble's *Algorithms of Oppression* came out, she sort of drew attention to a lot less of the neutrality in these online spaces. Raising the question of, "Why is it that we're getting these certain search results?" That really raised a question as we went through the election in 2016. We started to see the influence of things like bots and realizing that these spaces weren't as neutral or protected or altruistic or democratic that we thought. These certain algorithms rank and promote certain kinds of tweets or videos on YouTube that can very much work against social justice practices by spreading misinformation and sort of continuing the wrong dominant narratives.

Shane to Cecilia Shelton: In your article "Shifting Out of Neutral," you talk about using Black feminist pedagogy as a means for equity and social justice in technical and professional communication.

Can you talk more about how this framework disrupts traditional norms and genre expectations? [Episode 39: 05:50–08:23]

> It takes a different stance than a traditional Eurocentric masculinist kind of approach to pedagogy where lived experience isn't a valuable kind of evidence, where it's necessary to feign this distance between your emotion and the object, or the topic of your inquiry. A Black Feminist epistemology and pedagogy invites students to value lived experience, to think about their personal expressiveness, to think about personal accountability, to think about ethics, think about people. It's important to ask students not to only think about the business context and the objects and the topics that we typically discuss when we're talking about business and technical communication, but to also think about who are the people in these environments? Who are our colleagues? Who are the publics that we're serving? Who are our supervisors? Our customers?

> Usually, that sort of figure in a student's mind is sort of a stick figure. But if we were to add flesh and bones to that stick figure, and not interrogate that, that stick figure would turn into a White, cisgender heterosexual man who's middle-class and educated. Right? That means something. I try to invite students to think about other people and to think about the ways that emails and reports and policies and documentation they're composing also compose the environments and the context that other people live and work and play and consume within those contexts.

DENOUEMENT

A social justice-based approach to teaching writing situates the writing class as a site for inquiry and investigation. It seeks to interrogate how systems and structures privilege some and oppress others. Social, political, economic, and cultural norms ultimately help establish power and hierarchies. Teachers who embrace a social justice-based approach are committed to challenging and resisting these cultural norms that reproduce biases. Through this, the class becomes a space for critical reflection on how power is situated and constructed through and within systems and policies. No system is neutral. No structure or classroom practice is fully objective. Thus, social justice pedagogy reimagines the writing classroom and critiques exclusionary practices. Social justice pedagogies seek to establish more equitable practices and policies.

For example, a social justice approach resists departmental outcomes and classroom practices that uphold notions of standardized English, which are linked to whiteness. A social justice approach understands all language practices, dialects, and patterns are valuable meaning-making habits and activities for learning. Further, through the lens of writing program administration, a social justice approach confronts placement tests that disproportionately affect students of color. A social justice framework for teaching focuses on equity and uses classroom curriculum, readings, assignments, and assessments to value students' identities, languages, histories, cultures, and communities.

The following questions can be used to think more intentionally about this approach:

- Who are traditional writing classroom pedagogies and practices privileging? And what assumptions and biases are present in these constructions? What racial and linguistic identities are being disadvantaged within those assumptions and constructions?
- How can we invite and facilitate conversations on race, language, and power in first-year writing? Through what theories and practices (e.g., critical race theory)?
- How are we listening to students' lived experiences? How are we fostering student agency and dismantling hegemonic power?
- How are we paying attention to our local communities and the issues around us in order to better teach reading, writing, and other literacies?
- Whose voices and experiences are being amplified through readings and materials? Who's voices and experiences are absent and/or being silenced?
- In what ways can we rewrite departmental and classroom policies around social justice?

8

Disability Studies

> It is only by asking our students to think critically about the
> world around them, and to think creatively and productively
> about ways to change it, that we have any hope of transform-
> ing our future and working against assumptions that constrain
> the possibilities of what bodies and minds can and should ac-
> complish.
>
> —Ella R. Browning, "Disability Studies
> in the Composition Classroom"

> Many of us "pass" for able-bodied—we appear before you un-
> clearly marked, fuzzily apparent, our disabilities *not* hanging out
> all over the place. We are sitting next to you. No, we *are* you.
>
> —Brenda Jo Brueggemann, Linda Feldmeier White,
> Patricia A. Dunn, Barbara A. Heifferon, and Johnson
> Cheu, "Becoming Visible: Lessons in Disability"

One starting point for understanding how writing classes can focus
on disability studies and embrace inclusive and accessible pedagogies and practices in the 21st century is through universal design.
A universal design for learning (UDL) framework considers how
assignments, materials, assessments, and other classroom practices
can be constructed in ways that are most accessible for all students.
And while UDL doesn't solve all problems in academic spaces and
structures, it does offer ways for writing teachers to consider how
design affects learning and meaning-making. UDL provides opportunities for teachers to better understand how activities can be constructed to accommodate a range of students. This approach looks
like adding closed captions to videos, having transcripts for audio,
incorporating image descriptions, using alt texts, reconsidering

attendance and participation policies, rewriting writing program learning outcomes, reimagining font size and style choices on documents, and redesigning assignments and assessments.

A disability studies approach to teaching writing means problematizing how systems and structures advantage "temporarily able bodies" (Brueggemann et al., 2001, p. 369). It also means interrogating how traditional understandings of literacy privilege individuals based on their *bodies* and *abilities*. Disability studies is interdisciplinary and "disrupts the idea that disabled people should be defined primarily through their disabilities by others, retaining instead the right for disabled people to define their own relationships with disability" (Dolmage, 2017, p. 6). Most research in disability studies confronts ableism—or discrimination in favor of temporarily able-bodied individuals—and critiques how systems privilege movement and how society constructs and talks about disability. Societal constructions of disability are problematic because they often position disability as *abnormal, negative, wrong*, or something that needs *to be cured*. These "norms" and assumptions about disability are harmful and violent: "These norms have the discursive power to render people visible or invisible, privileging some by pushing Others out of categories of the human" (Cedillo, 2018, p. 11).

There's been great work over the last several years in rhetoric and composition on disability, including on autism (Yergeau, 2017), cripping time and neutrality (Ho et al., 2020; Wood, 2017), mental disabilities and mental health (Degner et al., 2015; Price, 2011), unbearable pain (Price, 2015), rhetorics of overcoming (Hitt, 2021), and disclosure (Kerschbaum et al., 2017). Taking a disability studies approach to teaching means addressing societal constructions and educational inequities and creating spaces and materials that are more inclusive. It means challenging "normate" assumptions about bodies and movement, and listening to the embodied experiences of disabled people writing about disability justice (Hubrig, 2020). Which for writing classes, this also means incorporating curriculum and conversation on disability. A disability studies approach to composition even disrupts notions of "composition" and what it means to read and write. The CCCC Position Statement on Disability Studies in Composition states that, "Disability enhances learning and teaching in college composition by helping us to think through and develop inclusive approaches rather than approaches based in deficit" (n.p).

In her 2017 article, Anne-Marie Womack poses strategies for universal design and constructing more accessible curriculum: "Accommodation is the most basic act and the art of teaching. It is not the exception we sometimes make in spite of learning, but rather the adaptations we continually make to promote learning" (p. 494). Teachers drawing on disability studies understand how classroom practices, like peer review and attendance and late work policies, can disadvantage students from participating in learning. Teachers need to reconsider definitions of time and labor. For example, students with processing disabilities are disadvantaged through traditional constructions of peer review that rely on sharing, reading, and responding to students immediately in class. And formatting text on a syllabi with serif font using single spacing with a white background and black text can disadvantage students with visual processing disabilities (e.g., dyslexia). Writing teachers committed to anti-ableism, then, advocate for inclusive practices (e.g., image descriptions, alt texts, captions). Accessible Syllabus is one pedagogical resource that encourages teachers to investigate their syllabi through the lens of accommodation, accessibility, and inclusivity.

A disability studies approach incorporates conversations on language, attitudes, knowledge, bodies, health, environments, power, and identity. This shifts the writing classroom and composition studies at large:

> Re-thinking composition from a disability studies perspective reminds us that we too often design writing instruction for individuals who type on a keyboard and too easily forget those who use blow tubes, that we have a habit of creating assignments for those who read text with their eyes and a related habit of forgetting those who read through their fingertips, that we too often privilege students who speak up in class and too often forget those who participate most thoughtfully via email. (Selfe & Howes, 2013)

Cynthia L. Selfe and Franny Howes remind teachers that classroom practices are never neutral. Simi Linton (1998) says this approach requires a complete reorientation of curriculum that "adds a critical dimension to thinking about issues such as autonomy, competence, wholeness, independence/dependence, health, physical appearance, aesthetics, community, and notions of progress and perfection—issues that pervade every aspect of the civic and pedagogic culture" (p. 118).

INTERVIEWS

In this chapter, I talk with Jay Dolmage, Tara Wood, Christina V. Cedillo, and Dev Bose about disability studies and teaching writing. The interviews focus on a range of ideas and concepts, like crip time and ableism, as well as accessible practices and future directions for disability studies and rhetoric and composition. One of the main themes in these conversations is how teachers can embrace anti-ableist frameworks by rethinking "norms" and implementing inclusive strategies. Dolmage starts by sharing myths about disability, which helps us see how disability is presented in society and what that means for writing teachers and classes. He talks about universal design and reconstructing classroom practices and assessment, like participation policies, in order to create a more inclusive space. Wood provides a definition for ableism and commonplace ableist assumptions about writing. She goes on to critique normative conceptions and constructions of time and offers "crip time" as an opportunity to resist ableism. Cedillo talks about critical embodiment pedagogy and invisible disabilities. Bose concludes by talking about challenges disabled students face in institutions and writing classrooms.

Shane to Jay Dolmage: What are some common myths about disability? [Episode 37: 01:57–05:02]

> I think that there's a lot. I think that disability is like highly mythological . . . for many people, their understanding of disability is shaped by these common cultural narratives we have about disability. Those narratives . . . the most important thing to say is those myths and narratives are not written by disabled people, in general. Disabled people's lives are not very well represented unless they conform in

a way to the myths that we already have. Those myths are generally about managing the affect, or the emotions or the relationship that temporarily abled-bodied people, or supposedly "able-bodied" people, have to disability.

That's a pretty problematic place to start because the myths have to conform to the fear that people have of being disabled. They manage those fears rather than reflecting on reality. I'll try to make this as relevant as I can to what's happening right now because I think we're seeing some really powerful myths about disability circulating, and one of the most harmful myths about disability is that it's a life not worth living. That temporarily able-bodied people or "normate" people assume that if they had a disability, they wouldn't want to be alive anymore.

That myth, that stereotype, that narrative means that we devalue disabled lives. Calling the myths or stories and tracing them through literature or film is one thing, but seeing how those things condition the actual lived experiences of hundreds of thousands of people is another. They really do come to be all about who lives and dies, who has access to privilege and who doesn't. The myths and stereotypes ensure the reification or the kind of solidification of social structures and choices, life choices for people. They shape people's lives. They reach into bodies in a rhetorical sense. The problem is that they come out of bodies that aren't disabled bodies. People who have no ability to imagine what a disabled life will be like, are the people who are making these dictates, right?

And on the flip side, the so called "positive" stories that we have around disability are all about overcoming, triumph over adversity, cure. Right? Miraculous cure. The ability to work hard or have a positive attitude and overcome the negatives of a disability. Again, you can see how those are really all about managing the emotions, the fears of temporarily able-bodied people, the idea that if I did have a disability, through hard work, I would be able to overcome it. I think those are the two biggest, unfortunately, forces, both positive and negative, shaping so many of the depictions that we have about disability. They're really difficult to escape and like I said, they reach into real bodies and they rearrange bodies in space, right? They determine access to so much.

Shane to Jay Dolmage: How can we make our pedagogies and practices more accessible in the writing classroom? [Episode 37: 17:04–22:43]

I mean, this is something . . . this is the major thing I think about. In terms of like any future work that I want to do, I think I'm more oriented around this idea of how we can make what we do more accessible to more people and extend that to the teaching that we do so that it reaches more people, and then more people have a genuine opportunity to learn and can contribute to the conversation and shape the future. Because it's not just about us portioning out this privilege. It's that we need more people involved in the conversation that shapes what higher education is going to look like. It sounds just like a magical solution, but universal design . . . it's a lot of work. We're talking about labor. Philosophically it is the idea that we should be planning for the most diverse group of students that we can. While the public paints higher education as this like radical place full of snowflakes and communists, it's a highly, highly conservative space. We keep doing the same things over and over and over, again. Universities claim to be evidence based, but all the good evidence around teaching we ignore for years and years.

People just keep doing . . . almost kind of like levels of hazing that they were put through as students, they put their own students through again. So even something like timed tests and exams. There's no data that shows students learn more. We just keep doing it. We structure entire universities, logistically, around timed tests and exams. They absolutely dominate the mental health of students for periods of time, and there's no good research. Then, for students to have accommodations, they have to jump through all these medical and legal hoops . . .

So universal design . . . there's three principles. One is that we should teach a variety of ways—the ways that we deliver information and structure conversations—we should just do it in a broad number of ways in terms of the cultural context we bring to the class, in terms of how we deliver it. You know, your podcast having a transcript and an audio version is positive redundancy, right? The more ways we do it, the more access there will be. The other thing is that we structure a variety of forms of assessment or ways for students to show what they know. Then, the final piece is just kind of dynamic ways to actively learn in the classroom.

I'll give you some tangible examples. For me, I will admit this, for like fifteen years, I assigned a participation grade in my classes, sometimes like 20–30%. I had no idea what I was assessing in a writing classroom in terms of participation. It was basically how much did you talk. Students would get good participation grades even if they were kind of like a negative force in the classroom because I was basically telling them, put your hand up all the time, interrupt people, like the more you talk, the better you'll do. That was really a problem. I was like assigning that grade like the day that I assign grades. It's just horrible. So I started thinking, what is the universal design approach to participation? I know there are a lot of valuable ways to participate in class without ever saying a word.

When we move classes online, we understand that some students are not going to have something to say in a 50-minute class. They may have a ton to say three hours later, or a day later, right? Universities are run like factories, like they're really on this kind of timeline as though we only can ever think or produce in these little chunks. Yet nobody comes to your office at like 9 a.m. and says, "I'll be back at 10:30 a.m. I need a publishable article."

Or in an engineering firm . . . people are working on their plans for a bridge and somebody comes in and says, "Okay, stop. Now whatever bridge you had, is a bridge we're going to build." But that's the way we structure classwork and things like participation. I developed this kind of means of saying to students, you tell me some of the valuable ways you're able to participate. I've been able to build this bigger repertoire of valuable ways to participate. Students taking pictures and doing visual descriptions of things that got written on the board. One student took minutes of every class . . . it was so valuable to me. Then, if a student missed, they could read the minutes, so it was valuable to other people than me as well. Right? Creating kind of this community of learning . . .

Opening that participation up to say to students, "You tell me some valuable ways to participate" has really exploded that for me and made it so much more valuable. I've landed on something that's much more equitable and valuable for everybody. That's a big one. It's almost like a philosophical explosion, right? Like you're changing the authority in the classroom, you're changing how you're assessing a big chunk of what it is you're doing, and you're giving over a lot of control . . . you can take little individual pieces of what we do, and if you think, "What's the way for me to engage every student in the broadest range of possibles?" . . . doing this, that's the philosophy behind universal design.

Shane to Jay Dolmage: What are some future directions for disability studies and rhetoric and composition? [Episode 37: 22:44–27:36]

I think there's some natural overlap with rhetoric and composition and disability in terms of their institutional history. You know, rhet/comp has been a sorting space. It's been a place to help students move ahead, but it's also been a place to intentionally hold students behind. So we need disability studies and we need an understanding of how disability is used and is attributed to groups to control access to privilege. There's that kind of disciplinary history that's backwards facing, but it's also never going to go away, right? That is going to continue to be writing studies relationship within the university. It is going to be used as a sorting gate.

I think the reason I got into teaching writing was because . . . like when I began, it was really deep in the process movement. The process movement gave us access to thinking about the labor that students put into the work they do. What does their writing situation look like? How do they think? What is the path from an idea, right? That is illuminating in ways that lots of other disciplines don't have. That much access to when you begin to try to understand the process of writing. It's inevitable that you understand it as a process that includes failure and difficulty, even though we romanticize it as something completely opposite . . . it requires stops and starts and failures.

When you look around, disability is everywhere. Not just in disabled students. It's that communication itself requires us to have some understanding of the incomplete nature of our bodies, and our need for other people, and our need for techniques and prosthetics . . . I mean, that's a pretty high-level philosophical argument to make. I think in a very tangible sense . . . my favorite class to teach, and I keep requesting it, is just first-year writing for students who don't want to take it in their first semester of university.

Because that's where we can begin to structure a relationship with university that is not about being the best all the time, but can be about asking for help, accessing and calling for more resources to support student life, student mental health, understand that we all need accommodations, and that some students are going to need to fight for their legal right to education . . . it connects us with the reality in our classrooms rather than the myth or fantasy that all students are going to find university life easy or even familiar, or welcoming . . .

So we have a responsibility to understand that 20% of those students are going to have disabilities that they're going to need to have accommodations for. And that everybody is going to experience the university as a disabling space that's putting up barriers that don't need to be there.

Shane to Tara Wood: How do you define *ableism*? [Episode 26: 02:04–03:02]

I think it has been useful for me in my own experience and in my own scholarship to think about it as sort of two pronged. It can either be social prejudice: attitudinal kind of prejudice aimed at people with various disabilities; and, it can also be a discriminatory act, something done in a discriminatory way toward people with various psychiatric, cognitive, mental, intellectual, physical disabilities. The flip side of that, or thinking about it in sort of inverted way, is that ableism is a sort of privileging of the able body or an attitude about the premises and ultimate "good" of the able-bodied for all.

Shane to Tara Wood: What are some commonplace ableist assumptions about writing? [Episode 26: 03:03–04:49]

I think the one that I've tackled the most in my own work is the idea that writing takes place in a normative time construct. The idea that people produce at certain intervals that are predictable and "normal." That has a tendency to enable or foster ableist approaches to teaching, writing or thinking about writing because you make assumptions about what the brain not only does, but should do and what's expected and normal in terms of producing text. Another ableist idea about writing is the labor involved, which of course is related to time, but it's the amount. Our assumptions about the amount of labor that goes into the production of a text, for example.

A really concrete example of this . . . is when a student swaps a paper with another student, which is a very common practice in writing classrooms. One student says,

"Oh, you must have just done this at the last minute. Me too," when they look at another student's paper because maybe it's not fully fleshed out. There's a lot of error that's visible to their partner. When in reality, it took that student hours and hours to produce that piece of content. These assumptions that we have about what people can produce and how much labor it takes to produce whatever is being asked of them.

Shane to Tara Wood: In "Cripping Time in the College Composition Classroom," you write about how when left unexamined these normative conceptions and assumptions privilege specific bodies. Do you mind talking more about the concept of crip time as an alternative pedagogical framework? [Episode 26: 08:05–11:16]

> Crip time is a concept that has emerged from disability communities and has since been leveraged by disability theorists to challenge certain ableist ideologies in a wide range of disciplines. I usually draw on Irving Zola's definition, which is a flexible approach to time. It seems really simple, but it's the idea that people will do things at different times and that people will approach a given task at different time intervals. It's just thinking about time in a nonlinear way. Yesterday when I was reading through your questions, I was like, "Oh, I'm going to come up with like a really good metaphor for crip time." Here's what I got. I even wrote this one down.

If normative time were like a *thing*, normative time would be like an uncooked spaghetti noodle. It's straight, it's firm, it goes from one end to the other. If crip time were a *thing*, it would be like a ball of yarn. Maybe we pull a little bit off, it's all loose, it's not never ending necessarily, but it's definitely not an uncooked spaghetti noodle. That's the metaphor. I think it gets to that idea of flexibility and even the rigidity of this idea of normative time, which most people can't deal with. Able or disabled.

There's an edited collection about bipolar disorder by Norton. There's a piece in there about labor and tenure clocks and the production, even now, that graduate students are expected to do. That everything has to happen on this completely unachievable and exhausting spaghetti noodle. It all has to happen like this and that if you can't meet it, what happens? It breaks. Something gets disrupted. You lose traction, whatever. Crip time for me is not only a concept, but it's also a sort of deliberate, theoretical acknowledgement that there are problems with normative constructions of time. If you think back to my comment about the two students swapping papers, one hour of time might mean something really, really different for one person than for another. So it gets a little bit complicated. How can you determine where that bar gets set if you're thinking about it in terms of minutes? Because one minute for one person is so different for another person, particularly for students with disabilities.

Shane to Christina V. Cedillo: In "What Does It Mean to Move?" you write, "Rhetoric privileges movement—emotional, ethical, physical. Hence, composition pedagogy aims to teach students to move others toward particular stances or courses of action. These goals often rely on normate standards of emotional engagement and activity, based in standards of White, Eurowestern ablebodiedness that associate certain kinds of movement with agency and expression . . . I argue that we must strive for critical embodiment pedagogies, or approaches that recognize and foreground bodily diversity so that students learn to compose for accessibility and inclusivity." Your teaching and research focus on affect and embodiment. Can you talk about what this looks like in terms of practices in your writing classroom? [Episode 29: 01:22–05:44]

Some of the things that I do have to do with pedagogy and then some of them have to do with more of the spatial practice. Of course it's all pedagogy in certain ways. So on the one hand, there's the more concrete hands on aspect of teaching writing. Some of the things that I do is that I deliberately center things like affect and embodiment when we're studying writing. One of the things that I'll have students do is, we'll do analysis of texts, but rather than talk about logical meaning, I'll have them go through and talk about their emotional reactions to specific aspects of the text and what that does for them to either agree or disagree, or pay closer attention or just check out. To get them to understand that that's what rhetoric really is, right?

Because I do agree wholeheartedly when Victor Villanueva talks a lot about how we've denigrated pathos so much in the teaching of writing assuming that it's wrong because it's being used wrong. That's one of the things that I really want to rescue. I always want to remind them that whether it's Cicero or Augustine or even today, that rhetoric always does the three things: to think, feel, and do. We usually do the *think*, but we never really stop to think about what we want people to *feel*. I also talk to them a lot about how the feel part of it is what usually gets people to *do*, right? That's where the teaching of ethics really has to stand out.

I have them do a lot of reflections also—a thing where it's like a shorthand version of speech act theory—where we talk about the different levels of meaning. I'll do some acting in the classroom. For example, even just the idea of saying "good morning," on the surface level, it's very much about just a greeting, but it's also a statement that enacts authority. Right? Socially it demands a response. Then, it has those psychological effects too, that if you don't respond when your professor says "good morning," it's like, "Oh no, what's she going to think?" These are a lot of the things that we talk about when students are writing. I'll have them actually write down what they would like people to experience and how well they thought that they did that. That goes a long way towards thinking a lot about who the audience is and being *actually inclusive* versus just thinking of them as generic fiction . . .

Shane to Christina V. Cedillo: You also write about your experiences as a Chicana living with several invisible disabilities. Do you think you could talk about how writing and rhetoric becomes oppressive or is oppressive for teacher-scholars and students with invisible disabilities? [Episode 29 08:34–11:33]

> That right there is the reason why I wrote this article in the first place. You hit the nail on the head. So one of the things that is a big discussion within disability rhetorics is the way in which nondisabled audiences tend to really think about disability in a specular way where people expect to see certain characteristics, or else you can't possibly be disabled. For example, when it comes to invisible disabilities, I recently had a conversation with somebody who's really close to me, who tends to be really thoughtful conversation, about "Well, you're not really disabled, why are you calling yourself disabled?" "Well, I have disabilities, they're mental disabilities I have to deal with. I have neurodivergence and it affects the way that I see the world. It's a very different experience from the normate."

> It became this thing about, "Well, you're only disabled because you say you are, if you didn't see yourself that way you could do all these other things." I'm like, "I never said disability was *wrong* or *bad*." I actually appreciate my disabilities because they give me very useful perspectives. They inform the way that you read yourself and others and I think in certain ways, they also make me more attuned to read people generously and from a relational standpoint, right? Like understanding, "Oh, well they might not understand things in this particular way."

> One of the things that I wanted to write about was the fact that if we really think about it, invisible disabilities aren't really that *invisible*. Because people tend to think that the material prosthesis looks a particular way, like there's a wheelchair or there's other technology that we need to use. But if we think about it, when I have to take my medication, that's a different kind of prosthesis, right? The thing about it is that the invisible isn't so invisible when you're sitting in class and people start thinking like, "Oh, that behavior is odd or why can't they understand this? Or why

are you writing like this?" Thinking about writing and rhetoric as normative proxies can be really oppressive.

Shane to Dev Bose: How do you define (in)visible disabilities, and do you mind talking about rhetorical conceptions to (in)visible disabilities? [Episode 45: 06:17–08:58]

(In)visible disabilities are those which are not immediately detectable, so to speak. My current research, I've actually been interested in caregivers and caregiving as a rhetorical construct. Now, I argue that disability does carry a sense of rhetorical presence . . . I'm relying on terms like agency, authority, delivery, identification, invention, and memory. I borrow just a bit from Kenneth Burke's *A Rhetoric of Motives* for making the case that disability can be identified internally and externally. You might even say, using Burkean terms, that a disability is "consubstantial" with shared interests between those who are disabled and those who are designing for the institution as a whole.

So . . . accommodations are an external factor for students to succeed in the classroom. More importantly, this is a motive for postsecondary institutions to improve upon themselves by delivering education that is universally accessible while keeping in mind the ways that marginalized groups operate within their boundary even to the extent of recognizing disability while erasing it. Stephanie Kerschbaum's recent article, "Signs of Disability," makes a case for how disability is shaped by a collective understanding of meanings which contribute to how we notice and erase it. I'm actually a big fan of Kerschbaum's writing. That particular argument speaks really well to what I want to think of in terms of (in)visible disability. In a nutshell, if one doesn't see a disability, it still exists but may not be likely to be reported. I'm particularly interested in scholars like Margaret Price. She's doing some writing on disabled faculty.

My own hypothesis is that (in)visibly disabled people might not be receiving as many accommodations due to the burden of proof being a challenge. You have to always kind of show something. I think going back to the rhetorical constructs that I was thinking about earlier, one can identify that a disability exists, and is therefore in need of accommodations if it's more visible, right? But if it's not seen, or if it's not immediately obvious I should say, some more challenges are there.

Shane to Dev Bose: Can you talk more about the challenges students face at the institutional level and in the writing classroom when it comes to accommodations? [Episode 45: 02:16–06:16]

Reasonable accommodations are essentially just adjustments made in the system after the individual has proven that their request is fair. However, accommodations often require expensive medical proof. Right? Which draws both a financial burden, but I also argue that that delineates privilege of sorts in terms. That's kind of the big answer for the university as a whole. Relatively easier, I think for a lot of students that ask for or think of the accommodations that one might need in a classroom that doesn't focus on writing or learning to compose it in written context, as it's like primary discourse or mode of assessment. However, I think for writing classrooms, students may not know necessarily what kind of accommodations to ask for, right? In my experience, for example, in working with writing instructors, this is a good thing, writing instructors oftentimes won't rely on quizzes or timed assessments. Timed assessments are often things that aren't really going to work very well for many people, right? Regardless of disability status. Having that clock on you as you're trying to complete your writing or finish your writing can be stressful. It can cause a lot of anxiety for someone who has anxiety or depression or OCD.

I kind of identify with all those things as well. Oftentimes timed writing assessments can just really be disastrous. Many writing instructors say that they don't use those things, but that's not to say though that there's not room for a crip time pedagogy. Tara Wood, of course, has that amazing article where she talks a lot about that. Essentially, the need for crip time, I argue, goes beyond just timed assessments because writing instructors will often say, "Well, I don't use timed assessment. I've already kind of passed that inaccessibility hurdle," but I think that there are still avenues for injustice to occur . . . I'm actually a big fan of portfolio assessment because I think that that's super helpful. If it's done right, that is, it's helpful for students to kind of identify their own path of success and provide evidence for that path of success through the various writing artifacts that they've put together in the classroom compiled in a portfolio.

When I was thinking about your question, I immediately thought of students coming in to self-advocate for themselves. First-year writing classrooms are often themed as being the threshold or the gateway for entering the college or the university. In fact, I tell this to a lot of grad students I work with, "Your class is more than likely going to be your students' first college class ever." So to me, I think that holds a lot of rhetorical agency for the instructor being able to be open to their students' needs. In addition to students hopefully being able to, if it's possible, advocate for themselves.

DENOUEMENT

A disability studies approach to teaching writing is activism—it demands us to resist inequitable systems. Disabled students have historically been and continue to be marginalized in academia (Dolmage, 2018). Accessible and inclusive pedagogies and practices help to deconstruct power and privilege. This work extends beyond the classroom, too. Stephanie Kerschbaum, Laura T. Eisenman, and James M. Jones (2017) argue that issues related to disability "have far-reaching consequences across higher education and beyond" (p. 2). Diversity, equity, accessibility, and inclusivity should be valued and centered in academic and public policies and structures. In the writing classroom, teachers can adopt frameworks, such as universal design for learning or crip time pedagogies, to help create more flexible learning environments and assignments. Teachers and students together can problematize how colleges uphold and maintain inaccessible spaces that privilege temporarily able-bodied people. And teachers and students can think intentionally about what it means to design and create curriculum that centers disability justice. In sum, a disability studies approach to teaching writing focuses on all student bodies and all possible paths for learning and engaging in the writing classroom.

I offer the following questions as an opportunity to think more about disability studies and teaching writing:

- What are some assumptions we make about students?
- How can writing teachers ensure classroom practices are accessible and inclusive? How can we make connections between language and disability studies?
- How are we designing curriculum with invisible disabilities in mind?
- What are some institutional constraints affecting students in your local context? How do students seek accommodations? What are some issues with that process?
- In what ways are cultural norms on knowledge, labor, time, and participation influencing writing assessment, and thus disadvantaging disabled students?
- How is the act of teaching writing connected to bodies, and what does it look like to facilitate conversations with students about the ways in which bodies move?
- How should undergraduate and graduate programs be reconfigured through disability studies? How can classes and institutions (and other infrastructures) build anti-ableist policies and practices? What outcomes and objectives need reconsidered and rewritten?

9

Community Literacies

> I like to believe that perhaps, even from our most privileged
> of positions, and perhaps, even in the smallest of ways, we can
> claim to have stood in alliance with those whose humanity is
> under assault, but who continue to try move forward. Perhaps,
> that is, we help create a world where birds can fly and young
> children are allowed to look at them in wonder.
>
> –Steve Parks, "I Hear Its Chirping Coming From My Throat"

All communities and cultures construct and disseminate knowledge. This chapter covers a range of pedagogical practices including community-engaged pedagogies and cultural rhetorics. Which
means this chapter invites us to consider politically and theoretically rich understandings of teaching writing within, beyond, between, and alongside communities. Community-engaged pedagogy is "grounded in the understanding of writing as a situated,
social act" (Julier et al., 2014, p. 56). This approach to teaching asks
us to investigate the nuances between language and power and to
examine who and what shapes our understandings of knowledge. It
challenges writing teachers to consider their own subject positions
and histories. In sum, a community and cultural framework for
teaching writing encourages us to reconsider our role as educators
and how we talk about literacies and to consider the relationships
we have with/in communities.

The rise of cultural studies in the late 1950s and early 1960s,
complemented with radical educational theories and philosophies
(Freire, 1968)[8] in the late 1960s and 1970s helped usher in the

---

8   In *Pedagogy of the Oppressed*, Paulo Freire proposes "problem-posing education," which resists the traditional "banking concept" that treats students as empty
vessels and teachers as givers of knowledge. The problem-posing method, accord-

"social turn" in composition studies in the 1980s (Berlin, 1988; Trimbur, 1994). In the late 1990s and early 2000s, the "public turn" (Mathieu, 2005) emerged through works like Thomas Deans's (2000) *Writing Partnerships: Service-Learning in Composition* and Beverly J. Moss's (2003) *A Community Text Arises: A Literate Text and a Literacy Tradition in African-American Churches* which focused on community-engaged practices and literacies. Through the 2000s and 2010s,[9] cultural rhetorics grew in response to the "unease with the facility of Western rhetorical theories and practices to account for the experiences of non-Western peoples *and* from the sense that the exigencies of Western culture itself have gone unexamined in that traditional canon" (Brata & Powell, 2016). These waves in composition theory and praxis have a throughline: writing teachers must pay attention to the social, economic, and political ideologies that affect systems, structures, and understandings about how knowledge gets produced and circulates.

Community-engaged approaches to teaching writing bring awareness to writing as socially situated and explore knowledges and meaning-making practices within communities. Thus, teachers and students investigate how writing has different purposes based on community needs, goals, and values. A community-engaged approach understands that curriculum must move beyond institutionally situated aims and English program outcomes. Some teachers, for example, might build curriculum that asks students to collaborate with community activists and organizations. Teachers might encourage students to partner with a community-based organization or initiative and complete a community-engaged project. Students, then, would work collaboratively with these partners to accomplish community-driven aims. The CCCC position statement on Community-Engaged Projects in Rhetoric and Composition states:

> We define community-engaged projects as scholarly, teaching, or community-development activities that involve

---

ing to Freire, makes education "the practice of freedom—as opposed to education as the practice of domination" (p. 81).

9   See Krista Ratcliffe's (2010) "The Twentieth and Twenty-First Centuries." See also Cobos et al. (2018) "Interfacing Cultural Rhetorics: A History and a Call" for a robust history of cultural rhetorics.

collaborations between one or more academic institutions and one or more local, regional, national, or international community group(s) and contribute to the public good. We use the word *project* to denote well-conceived activities pursued over time to provide reciprocal benefits to both academic and community participants.

University and classroom partnerships with community organizations should be carefully planned and should be designed with sustainability in mind. This approach to teaching also critically examines how colleges are positioned spatially within communities. Ellen Cushman (1996) writes that most universities sit in "isolated relation," socially and sometimes physically, to the communities around them. Cushman asks for a "deeper consideration of the civic purposes of our *positions* in the academy, of what we do with our knowledge, for whom, and by what means" (p. 12). Therefore, a community-engaged pedagogy concerns itself with issues of power and interrogates social and political realities. It encourages critical thinking and deconstructs borders between "academic" and "public" writing. There's good work in composition studies that has shown the value of community-engaged writing (Young & Morgan, 2020), public engagement (Flower, 2008), community publishing (Mathieu et al., 2011), and service learning as activities of empowerment (Deans, 2000; Gere & Sinor, 1997).

Another pedagogical approach that does deep investigation on community and meaning-making practices is cultural rhetorics. Cultural rhetorics decenters traditional systems that shape how knowledge is perceived, and thus valued. This approach means problematizing how teaching writing and histories of rhetoric and composition are often tied to Western orientations. It disrupts dominant narratives and "honors the cultural specificity of *all* rhetorical practices/productions" (Bratta & Powell, 2016). A cultural rhetorics pedagogy theorizes and makes visible non-Western meaning-making practices and knowledges. Jennifer Sano-Franchini (2015) defines cultural rhetorics like this:

> Cultural rhetorics theorizes how rhetoric and culture are interconnected through a focus on the processes by which

language, texts, and other discursive practices like performance, embodiment, and materiality create meaning . . . cultural rhetorics is an interdisciplinary field of study, a scholarly practice, and a category for interpreting the world around us. (p. 52)

Cultural rhetorics in the writing classroom might start by acknowledging the power of stories. Which also means identifying what community voices and traditions have been silenced. Maria Novotny (2020) says that *story as theory* "orients us to critically engage with whose stories are told, who is trusted to hear some stories, and why who listens matters" (para. 3). She writes that "stories wield power" and cultural rhetorics "reminds us that these stories matter" (para. 5). Through cultural rhetorics, writing teachers center the lived experiences of historically marginalized communities. In *Survivance, Sovereignty, and Story: Teaching American Indian Rhetorics,* Lisa King, Rose Gubele, and Joyce Rain Anderson (2015) write, "The stories we tell about ourselves and about our world frame our perceptions, our relationships, our actions, and our ethics. They change our reality" (p. 3). In the writing classroom, teachers and students can investigate what voices are present, what stories are shaping understandings of literacy, and how these narratives affect perceptions and realities. Sano-Franchini writes, "This may mean that, rather than building the rhetorical tradition around Aristotle or Kenneth Burke, we start with American Indian or Asian American or working-class intellectual traditions" (2015, p. 53–54).

Additionally, this might mean disengaging with traditional writing classroom practices, such as assigning letter grades on student writing, because of the colonial ideologies that are affirmed through these processes and practices. How can writing teachers disrupt the power imbalances attached with classroom writing assessment? Teachers might invite students to co-create and co-construct writing assessment instead. When different cultural experiences are shared, and when traditional systems and structures are examined based on their inherent biases, the classroom becomes more inclusive and engaging.

INTERVIEWS

I had the good fortune talking with Steve Parks, Paula Mathieu, Beverly J. Moss, Les Hutchinson Campos, Lisa King, and Candace Epps-Robertson about community literacies, community-engaged practices, and cultural rhetorics. Parks talks about how he became interested in community literacies and activism when he noticed the skills he was learning at the university as a first-generation college student "didn't do anything for the community" he came from. He also shares best practices for engaging in community work and building partnerships with local organizations. Mathieu talks about the challenges and constraints that hinder the "public turn" in composition studies and relationships between writing classes and community organizations. She urges teacher-scholars to "ask more questions, be humbler, and listen more." Moss talks about the importance of ethnographies as a methodology for listening and better understanding communities. Campos shares how writing classes can practice cultural rhetorics, and King connects cultural rhetorics with Indigenous rhetorics and offers applications for teaching writing. Epps-Robertson concludes by talking about the power of stories and silence: "The spoken word is powerful . . . but silence certainly is as well. And rhetorically silence always has a meaning. [Silence] has a function."

Shane to Steve Parks: How did you get interested in community literacies and using the classroom as a site for community-based activism? [Episode 4: 01:46–06:10]

> I was in Pittsburgh, and I went to high school during the period that Reagan was in office and all the steel mills shut down. So in my early memory are steel workers who became grocery baggers. There was this massive wreckage of working-class communities. I realized I had to get to college. I was the first person in my family to graduate college. I didn't do very well. It took me a long time to figure it all out, but one of the things that I had noticed throughout my whole education and through the master's degree is that all of the skills I was learning didn't do anything for the community that I had come from. It didn't do anything

for the people who were trying to figure out how to survive this wreckage of working-class communities.

I also thought that the way in which the communities were being described made them sound like there was nothing but deficits. That it was just wreckage. My memory is of people helping me figure things out, to stay in school, helping me with jobs. There was a whole communal feel to why I graduated that I didn't see represented in my master's program. When I went and stayed for the doctorate, I was even more confused on how our university sat within the midst of economic crisis. How it could go super elitist. I got into Pitt's program the year before [Gayatri] Spivak came. I got there, and I was stunned by how there was no relationship between what was going on in the community and the university. I was also very poor. I had two kids. No money. It was rough. I didn't think I would finish, so I picked a dissertation topic that would teach me the skills to survive outside the academy. I studied academic activist organizations to learn how to run an organization, so that when I left, I could get a job doing something.

I came to the writing classroom sort of depressed about its possibilities, and I came to the academy offended by its abandonment of the communities in which it sat. In my opening years of teaching, I didn't understand what the value of this classroom was. I was so poor and had kids, and I was working three other jobs. It took me a long time to figure out what the value could be. Until I began to think about, although the university was elitist, the students were still working class. I began to think, well, the skills I'm learning in my dissertation could be useful to these students. I began to think about the writing classroom as a place where you validated students' literacy and their identity, and you talked about writing not just as something that helps you get published in an article, but that those skills and the network of skills that support them can help the community in which you're coming from.

It was then that I began to think, "Okay, this could be a life for me. I understand the kids in these classrooms, I understand their communities, and I understand what it means to be taught skills that you see no purpose for," and to try to explain that. I kind of felt very at home in a basic writing classroom. I would say that the academy has always disappointed me, but I've always been intrigued by what it could do for people on the wrong side of privilege.

Shane to Steve Parks: Could you talk about your approach to building community partnerships? How do you suggest developing relationships with local communities and organizations? What are some best practices? [Episode 4: 18:18–22:15]

You shouldn't do partnership work where you don't have long-standing partnership beforehand. All the management stuff that you have to do is too hard if you're building the partnership and teaching at the same time. If you're interested in an issue, you should spend some time there. Spend time really knowing the people, understand the organization, what their needs actually are. Then, when you build your class, you can make sure it fits that actual need.

A lot of partnerships become burdensome because they're fulfilling fake needs that nobody cares about, so there's no commitment on either end. I think you should wait, have a longstanding partnership, really learn the need, and then align your class that way. I think programs should have two or three long term partnerships that their students return to throughout their career. You have a partner, you find the need, you develop your class.

The next thing that you have to do is have a meeting with your partner before your class begins, and each of you should give an honest account of your resources and your time. You should match what you're going to do to the resources you have. If you can only devote ten hours of your class to this project, and they can only give two or three meetings, then what you might do is a brochure, or it might be an event that people come and talk about an issue. But it'll actually happen. There's an urge to do some huge, massive thing that outstrips your resources. The students are disappointed, the community partner doesn't get what they need, and students get a sense that change can't happen.

Then, when you move into your classroom, very pragmatically, there is an elitism in the university that students are often quick to adopt because they don't want to fail. They want to succeed in college, so you have to begin your class with readings to disabuse them of the academy being the sole producer of knowledge. It disabuses them of what they think an intellectual is. That may be Gramsci, it may be Raymond Williams's "Culture is Ordinary." The next stage has to be teaching very pragmatic skills like: How do you run a meeting? How do you listen? How do you interview? Existing partnership resource meeting, disabuse them of academia is the only place, pragmatic skills that students bring into the classroom.

I would have students go off-campus and go to the place where the community lives, because it's arrogant to think they have to come to our shop. I would build in an assessment tool within the class. Like two students, maybe two committee members, meet every three weeks or something, and talk about what's going on and report back. At the end of the class, I would have the students do an assessment on how it went in dialogue with the community so that they can see that you have to be accountable, and that you can learn what you could've done better the next time.

The last thing I would say about this is when you work with a community partner, you should make at least a two-year commitment. Don't say you're going to come for a semester and leave. It teaches your students bad politics, it's unfair to the community, and it's not how change happens. I think you have to say, "I'm going to be here for two years. This is the type of work we're going to attempt." At the end of two years, you can leave ethically, or you can choose to stay.

Shane to Paula Mathieu: Do you mind providing a brief definition for community-engaged writing? [Episode 22: 11:33–12:49]

It's usually working with community groups, often who are lower income but not always. It's also taken the form of people doing community publishing . . . prison writing or writing between college students and prisoners. So it's not only student involved, it can be faculty involved. It can be also independent community groups who may have started in an institution but evolved to be their own non-profits. I think community writing is the extra curriculum where it's writing when people are doing it for some other reason. They're not doing it for a grade, they're not doing it for credentializing, but they're doing it for some other community purpose, whether it's to make change in their community or record something in their community or help address a problem in their community.

Shane to Paula Mathieu: I'm curious as to whether you think writing studies and writing classrooms have done a good job supporting the kind of public turn you talk about in *Tactics of Hope* (2005)? What challenges do you continue to see working against writing studies and classrooms when it comes to building relationships with community organizations? [Episode 22: 12:50–16:33]

I actually love this question . . . I just want to preface this by saying everything I'm saying is a generalization. I'm not trying to indict specific people or programs or ideas. I do think there's some amazing work going on in community-engaged writing. I think that the Coalition for Community Writing and the Conference for Community Writing is an amazing place for that to happen. The journal, *Community Literacy Journal*, is publishing a lot of that work. There's an incredibly vibrant aspect of our field that is just so exciting and so rich. But at the same time, I feel like the push for writing studies and that terminology, to me, threatens to be more about disciplinarity and what writing means only within the bounds of the university than the full life of a student or a community or the world. I worry about a push toward writing about writing, or threshold concepts and these kinds of very measurable outcomes-driven scholarship.

Empirical scholarship risks the conscience, and that Paulo Freire legacy of composition and the Lester Faigley legacy of composition: That we need to support the public sphere. That community-engaged writing, place-based writing, getting students to write about places, to think about the vibrancy of a place, to think about the engagement in the world. That can be quite different than, "What does it mean to be successful in your major." Those aren't opposite goals. I don't think it's wrong to teach students to care about success in the academy, but I don't think a writing class should be equivalent to success in the university. That's too small a vision for what writing should be, and certainly too small a vision for what writing studies should be. It's a generalization to say that's what people who support a disciplinary writing studies approach would support, but I think there is that tendency to want things to be measurable and to be scholarly and to be very intellectual, very thought based.

I feel like my commitments are to disrupting that a little bit, and to say sometimes *thinking* is the very problem. Sometimes our ideas about who we are as scholars is the problem. We need to ask more questions, be humbler, and listen more; be part of the community and do the antiracist work, and do some of this stuff that doesn't necessarily look like measurable outcomes-based writing, to be the best version of who we can be as a field.

Shane to Beverly J. Moss: You were a graduate student in the 1980s when rhetoric and composition was moving towards conversations on community literacies. You started examining African American community literacy practices and traditions in African American churches. What questions were you seeking about how literacy was happening in those locations? And how did ethnographies, as a methodology, allow you to investigate those rich practices? [Episode 9: 04:07–06:10]

I don't know that it's a deep question, but I think the question for me has always been, "What's going on here? What's happening? Let's go and look." I mean, and it seems like a simple question, but it's a question of invitation. Let's go see rather than make pronouncements about what people can do and not do. It also, for me, sets up community spaces . . . as spaces that are equally important to study as classroom spaces. What do people value in their community spaces? How can we have a conversation between what people value in the community spaces and what is valued in academic spaces? It was interesting because I think when I started graduate school ethnography wasn't a big thing in composition and rhetoric, but people had started to dabble in it and started to say, "Oh, this might be useful for getting to answer some of those questions about the what's going on here and what's going on there." We were beginning to move outside of the classroom because I think there was beginning to be a recognition that we need to know what literacy practices, what writing practices people are engaged in when they walk into a classroom.

Shane to Beverly J. Moss: How do you see community literacies as necessary to our understanding of teaching writing? [Episode 9: 06:11–08:01]

There's the impact that the research can have on what we do in classrooms. I also have been thinking about what it means to engage students in ethnographic work. Classrooms don't necessarily set up well to introduce students to doing an ethnography . . . but to use some of the methods and to think about it as a way of framing how we come to understand what's going on. I've engaged students in work that encourages them to think about themselves not only as students but as researchers, as people who are pursuing a line of inquiry. That allows them to think about and push against what the role of expert is, so they form a question that takes them out of the classroom. That expands the classroom beyond university walls to really start to see the complexity of literacy, the complexity of writing. When we talk about writing, it's not just what we do in those four walls in the classroom. It's not just what we do on a computer. We do it for different reasons. Let's look at the different reasons that people in these different community spaces write and how they use writing. Ethnography allows you to do that.

I'll introduce students to a different way of thinking about how knowledge is constructed: Who constructs knowledge? Who produces knowledge? What counts as knowledge? That's another way to think about ethnography. It's not just reading people's ethnographies, which I think is important, but it's also being in the middle of being an ethnographer.

Shane to Les Hutchinson Campos: Can you provide a brief definition of cultural rhetorics and explain how you incorporate a cultural rhetorics pedagogy? [Episode 32: 01:30–04:39]

So the way I was taught cultural rhetorics follows four sort of tenets of practice . . . those four tenets are *story, relationality, decolonization,* and *constellation*. There's no sort of ranking. All four of those things work together at all times. I'm going to go in reverse. *Constellation* means putting together different forms of knowledge—when you're constellating different kind of cultural approaches to rhetorics. At the heart of cultural rhetorics we believe that all rhetoric is culture and cultural, and all cultures are rhetorical. When you're constellating, you're constellating different rhetorical traditions. That decolonizes rhetoric by saying there's not just the Western rhetorical tradition. All of the other cultures throughout history have had rhetorical traditions. So really learning those and putting them together. That's a decolonial project in that it's removing the colonial imposition that the Western rhetorical tradition is the only, or most preferred rhetorical tradition. It's decolonizing our knowledge, returning to Indigenous epistemologies and respecting those, and the ways of being that those bring.

Relationality is really understanding that all of these knowledges and all of us all coexist together. When you put those things into a classroom practice, you're really sort of challenging the traditions that most of us were educated within which is a primarily Western rhetorical tradition and view of writing and all of that. One thing that I try to do is really encourage students to become more metacognitively aware of their own knowledge and their own rhetorical traditions that they come to the classroom with already.

So really prioritizing the fact that you all have so much knowledge already. You aren't necessarily here to have knowledge dumped into your brain, but we are sharing in a communal space of the classroom. A lot of my assignments, especially early on in the semester, are about students reflecting on those knowledges. I've had an assignment where it's very land-based. What were the traditional knowledges and Indigenous knowledges that you learned growing up in your homelands and how are those shaping the way that you've come to know where you are? At MSU (Michigan State University), most of my students came from, at the closest, different parts of Michigan, and, at the furthest, other countries. And then in sharing those knowledges in group settings and group conversations, students learn, "Oh, I see how these rhetorical traditions are all over the place." And then we start to practice respecting everyone else's knowledges.

Shane to Lisa King: Do you mind interconnecting cultural rhetorics and Indigenous rhetorics? [Episode 7: 01:53–04–51]

Indigenous rhetorics as a field of study is broad. It overlaps into Indigenous studies and cultural studies. In a sense, what we're looking at and what we're thinking about, and the places that we're writing from is the orientation towards Indigenous rhetorical traditions of these lands. The founding rhetorical tradition are Indigenous traditions. Of course, that means reorienting fundamentally the way we think about rhetoric as something that comes from the Greco-Roman tradition as it has been translated and enhanced and changed from the European tradition and imported here.

We have to rethink how we understand rhetoric as meaning-making with language. Indigenous rhetorics wants us to think about Indigenous peoples here, the traditions that already existed past and present. Contemporary work just as much as historical work—the ways in which Indigenous peoples have developed their own practices. Most of what we're interested in is ways in which Indigenous peoples have negotiated, especially with colonization, colonization in education, and what that represents now in terms of erasure of Indigenous peoples from the rhetorical tradition, from our campuses, from our understanding, from recognition in the United States. When we talk about Indigenous rhetorics, of course, that goes worldwide.

It's past but it's also very much present. It's imagining futures for us in terms of meaning-making practices. We talk about digital in terms of bits and bytes, but we can also talk about it in terms of fingers as Angela Haas talks about in her article, "Wampum as Hypertext." I love teaching that article because people don't think of digital in the older meaning, which is to say your digits, your fingers. I think those are the links that broaden Indigenous rhetorics application when we start thinking in broader terms of cultural rhetorics, right?

Of course, we work with language, we're working with English, we're working Indigenous languages, we're working with cross-cultural situations. We're working with the writing classroom. We're working with what goes on in Indigenous communities. We're also thinking about visual representations in terms of art, performance, mascots, stereotyping, how people think about Indigenous peoples. Where did those assumptions come from and what do we need to do to work through that and to change that? Or if invisibility is a problem altogether: How do we help cultivate a narrative of presence and encourage people to take that up rather than continuing to ignore Indigenous peoples?

Shane to Lisa King: How do writing teachers do this work in the classroom? [Episode 7: 04:52–08:36]

This kind of work is intimately tied to decolonial practices. I don't mean decolonial in terms of an academic buzzword. I mean it in terms of really thinking hard about the ways in which our classrooms, our institutions and programs, are structured along old colonial lines that are so taken for granted they're invisible to us. And about what it means to communicate well on paper in a particular language for this or that reason. What other possibilities are there? I think the field is moving into interesting and exciting directions in terms of opening up what rhetoric means.

When we think about Indigenous rhetorics in the classroom, it means thinking really hard about decolonizing our classrooms in terms of what kind of work or ideas we're promoting. I'm thinking perhaps about whose work matters and whose language matters and whose work is valuable and whose isn't, whether that's implicit or explicit . . .

It's almost something you feel in your bones and it's hard to articulate. It's a vision that hasn't quite materialized, but we're working on it. This is exactly the kind of work we need to do. It also means that if you're thinking about the rhetorical tradition . . . what other orientations can we take to rhetorical practice? What if we start thinking of it in terms of Indigenous terms that are fairly consistent across Indigenous communities, such as relationship, reciprocity, responsibility? What happens if we start teaching with those? What are the strategic alliances that can be made or strategic reorientation? What I think many Indigenous reorient us towards is *community* again . . . we're asking for a fundamental reorientation of the syllabus or that classroom practice. What does it mean to be in community for Indigenous peoples or for specific tribal community? What does it mean within your students' own community? This is how I structure my own classes.

Shane to Candace Epps-Robertson: Your book, *Resisting Brown* (2018), examines how African American community members in Virginia responded after Brown vs. Board of Education. You write about the Prince Edward County Free School. Can you talk about social justice-based work and the importance of listening while incorporating and amplifying marginalized community voices? [Episode 19: 04:28–07:54]

Really to be able to understand how social justice operates, you have to listen to the communities who are experiencing, who are fighting, who are working in these areas. That's become even more true for me as my research moves away from traditional archives to thinking about digital practices of citizenship and engagement in social justice and online spaces. My students certainly know what that looks like. I've learned a great deal from them just listening to their experiences both as participants and also as observers in some of these movements as well . . . so really to be able to learn from them is something that I'm indebted to and I really value. Listening plays a large role in terms of how I interact and even think about studying social justice, but also how I'm learning from my students.

I think also, in terms of thinking about my own research, listening is always where I begin. I can't think of another way really to start any of the work, especially a project that involves race, marginalized communities, or literacy because these are areas, Shane, that are so personal and so charged that it is my duty as a researcher to start with listening. My first project where I looked at the Prince Edward County Free School Association as a counter response to White supremacist ideologies really began long before I even went to graduate school because my grandmother was from Prince Edward County.

I grew up with these stories about what happened when the schools closed and how the Black community persevered through in spite of massive resistance. When I got to graduate school, I had identified this project. I knew that it would keep me connected to that community that actually helped me get to grad school in the first place. I knew there was an archive, but I also knew that there were going to be stories that just weren't represented in that archive. It was important that I found a way to have that community be able to speak and share their own stories. In many instances it just involved me doing a lot less talking and just a lot of listening.

Shane to Candace Epps-Robertson: In *Resisting Brown* (2018), you write, "My grandmother, like scholars of rhetoric and literacy studies, knew that stories were not just talk. For her stories were a tapestry of lessons and histories and often a catalyst for action . . . the experiences of my family members are with me through both the silences and the stories." Can you talk more about the power of silences and stories? [Episode 19: 10:04–14:28]

The spoken word is powerful. We'd all acknowledge that. But silence certainly is as well. Rhetorically, silence always has a meaning. It has a function. I can't say that I'll speak for all Black communities with my interpretation or with how I'm thinking about silence in this particular instance, but what I do know from my experience is that some stories, some experiences, are either so sacred or so precious or so painful that to make them public is a heavy decision. When I spoke with family members about my project on the Free School, sometimes they would say they had no problem talking with me and sharing their experiences in our own private home space, but they didn't want it to be made public for fear of it getting out into the world—into a space where it could be critiqued or misunderstood. I think this was especially the case for family members who were unable to relocate from Prince Edward. So who went the longest without having any access to public school.

There was often this sense of shame around not having access to literacy in that particular way through formal education.

The idea that people wouldn't understand or they would ask questions I think also comes from the fact that, oftentimes when researchers would come into Prince Edward, especially in those early days after the schools closed, and then once they reopened, researchers would sort of swarm into the community, do testing on the students, ask questions or whatever and they'd leave. Well, what happens once you have an interview with someone and you have no idea where that interview ends up, or you take a test and you have no idea what happens to the data that's being collected? I think the idea was that this is a way that we can exercise, or I can exercise some control. I can decide who actually gets to hear my story.

I think for many of us who are talking about race or writing about race, that certainly holds true. There's some instances where the material, the story can't be shared because the concern is about how it will be received. I think this is something that I'm thinking a lot about now with my second project, whether or not it'll be received at all. Just because you tell the story certainly does not mean that anyone has to listen to it or take time to pause and reflect and experience it with you. When I think about the Free School Project, and when I think about my current project now where I'm thinking about transnational citizenship and public pedagogy, I know that I often have a concern: Will people understand why I'm writing about this, or how will this get taken up in different spaces?

I have to believe in the work, and I do. But any time you share your story, you risk that people may not be as attentive or respectful as you want. It's something that I am very aware of any time I enter into a community as a researcher. And also it's just something that I'm attentive to as a person of color any time I'm sharing my own personal stories about race. Many of them are quite painful to reflect upon and to make those things public. It's a big risk.

DENOUEMENT

Teachers need to problematize traditional histories, standards, and power imbalances that exists within and beyond academia in order to center all rhetorical practices/productions in the writing classroom (see Bratta & Powell, 2016). I see community-engaged pedagogies and cultural rhetorics as practices that help make writing classes more inclusive and as approaches that break down the walls of the ivory tower (e.g., universities). Which is to say that these pedagogies address how power manifests in systems that ultimately oppress individuals and communities, and they help reimagine whose stories and histories are being told. These approaches resist the exclusionary status quo that reproduce biases, disenfranchise individuals, and privilege only some ways of knowing, being, meaning-making, communicating, and languaging.

For additional resources on community and cultural literacies, I suggest *Reflections: A Journal of Community-Engaged Writing and Rhetoric* (est. 2000), *Community Literacy Journal* (est. 2006), the Coalition for Community Writing, the Cultural Rhetorics Consortium, *constellations: a cultural rhetorics publishing space* (est. 2018–2019), *enculturation* (est. 1996), and the Working and Writing for Change series from Parlor Press. These spaces provide an abundance of research, support, and information for writing teachers. I also offer the following questions that might help teachers think about how to engage with/in communities and cultures in writing classes:

- How can we amplify and support the labor local community organizers and activists are producing and how can we build partnerships that are equitable and sustainable?
- How are we using writing curriculum as a means for community-based research and practice? And what does it look like to truly center diversity and inclusivity in writing programs and classrooms through course outcomes, goals, and assessments?
- In what ways are we promoting writing that takes place in and across various communities (e.g., prison writing, street newspapers) and actively listening and working toward social

change through pedagogies in the writing classroom?

- How are we emphasizing multiple modes and mediums for composing, including digital and oral practices, as opportunities for meaning-making and knowledge construction and circulation? How are we privileging other forms of communication beyond the alphabetic text?

- What identities and cultures are being silenced in rhetoric and composition and writing classrooms? In what ways are we listening to and amplifying histories and stories of marginalized communities?

- In what ways are we resisting dominant Western traditions, norms, and practices given the constraints they have on language and writing? And how are we embracing and making more visible non-Western histories and knowledges to students?

PART III. PROGRAMS

10

Writing Program Administration

Writing program administration (WPA) isn't defined by one kind of structure or role/position. It covers a lot of ground. It might mean directing a first-year writing program, basic writing program, second-language writing program, writing across the curriculum program, or writing center. These are distinct *writing programs* that carry their own tasks and responsibilities. This section, then, attempts to highlight conversations around different writing programs and administrative positions. Writing program administrators (WPAs) are often responsible for several things, including developing and mentoring faculty and students, establishing objectives and outcomes for their respective programs, building curriculum, conducting assessment and placement, staffing and scheduling, collaborating with university stakeholders, working with textbook publishers, and advocating for instructors and students. It's difficult to make a list of what writing program administration encompasses because these programs and roles/positions vary across institutional contexts (e.g., private universities, public institutions, two-year colleges, four-year universities).

That said, first-year writing program administrators often operate in precarious positions between upper administration (e.g., deans, provosts) and English departments. This has its advantages and challenges. Some WPAs have little to no department or institutional authority when it comes to making curricular or assessment decisions, while others have more autonomy to create change. Some WPAs have "authority but no power" (Ostman, 2013, p. 4). WPAs are always negotiating and shifting roles. Heather Ostman talks about writing program administration in the context of two-year colleges like this:

The WPA in the two-year institution holds a unique responsibility: to administer a writing program, or a core of writing courses, that meets the literacy needs of every student who walks through the college's doors; to simultaneously engage a faculty and an administration who may or may not have the time, energy, or background to support such a program fully; and to learn from and respond to the ever-changing environment of the community college. (2013, p. 4)

Each institution has its own set of expectations for WPAs. Some WPAs are more involved in conversations on staffing and cap sizes or enrollment, for example, whereas others are commissioned to do what they can with what they have. Some roles are focused on undergraduate students, whereas others are primarily connected to graduate students. All these different material realities and conditions shape what WPAs can/cannot do. Thus, the WPA position by nature is dependent on the context, environment, needs, opportunities, challenges, and demands of the program.

Nonetheless, there are a few institutionally overlapping tasks that WPAs are expected to perform. Most first-year writing program administrators are responsible for overseeing "first-year writing" or "first-year composition" courses. First-year writing courses are often connected to colleges and universities general education curriculum (GEC), and many students take first-year composition during their first year of college. WPAs are tasked with establishing program outcomes and goals that evolve from local aims and are tied to national organization statements for best practices of teaching writing (e.g., WPA Outcomes Statement for First-Year Composition). WPAs develop curriculum and mentor instructors teaching courses. One element to this is increasing awareness to composition pedagogies and theories, or different practices and approaches to teaching writing. First-year writing classes are dynamic, innovative spaces that engage in language and learning. WPAs have to think about how to best provide professional development and training for teachers, which also means WPAs need to know trends in research and scholarship.

Alongside curriculum development and serving as a mentor for writing instructors, WPAs are often expected to assess program outcomes and goals. WPAs coordinate program assessment which might take the form of randomly collecting student portfolios in first-year writing courses, collaborating with colleagues, conducting norming workshops centered on program standards and outcomes, and writing a report based on assessment results. This work can be used to help improve classroom teaching, or revise program policies and objectives. Program assessment helps administrators identify what is and is not working from a program perspective. And it ultimately provides insight into learning: "WPAs are usually called upon to provide data that show what and how the students and program are doing" (McLeod, 2007, p. 92). In addition to writing program assessment, WPAs are usually in charge of student placement into first-year writing classes. Of course placement takes different forms (e.g., indirect measures, direct measures) given institutional contexts and state mandates or policies. WPAs serve major leadership roles for programs and universities.

Writing program administration can be exhausting and energizing: "Administering a writing program can be equally exhilarating and tumultuous" (Costello & Babb, 2020, p. 5). For instance, being a WPA might mean producing a lot of labor with little to no recognition which can lead to burnout (Wooten, Babb, Costello, & Navickas, 2020). Conversely, being a WPA could mean having new opportunities and discovering personal and professional successes. Courtney Adams Wooten, Jacob Babb, and Brian Ray (2018) use "traveling" to describe WPA work:

> Traveling is never easy. Trips often involve sweat, tears, crying children, barking dogs and meowing cats, moving trucks, crowded airplanes, and cheap food. However, trips also open up new lives, lead to laughter and memories, and hold the promise of the unimagined and exciting. (p. 3)

The WPA role has come a long way since its beginnings due to the growth of first-year writing courses and writing-driven curriculum across colleges and universities. Susan H. McLeod (2007) reminds us of its history: "Although the work involved in writing program administration has existed for some time, it was not until the formation of the Council of Writing Program Administrators in the late 1970s that the work was dignified with a title that aligned it with other administrative positions in the university" (p. 3). Now, writing program administration is robust in theory, research, and praxis.

INTERVIEWS

In this chapter, I talk with Staci Perryman-Clark, Iris D. Ruiz, Melvin Beavers, Jacob Babb, and Elizabeth Wardle about recent approaches to writing program administration and different aspects of being an administrator. Perryman-Clark talks about what makes being a WPA rewarding and how programs can embrace more inclusive, equitable practices and policies. Ruiz intersects decolonial theory with WPA leadership and addresses future directions for antiracist writing program administration scholarship. Beavers describes how he mentors faculty and provides opportunities for professional development, and he talks about how he uses online writing instruction (OWI) principles in his program. Babb shares his advice to new WPAs: "You have to build trust among the people that you work with." He also discusses how WPA scholarship has influenced his administrative practices. Wardle concludes by reflecting on her work as a WPA in different institutional contexts and adds that "real change happens from the bottom up out of intellectual curiosity and interest."

Shane to Staci Perryman-Clark: What has been the most rewarding aspect for you as a WPA? [Episode 17: 01:26–05:22]

> This is going to sound cliché, but I'm going to unpack it a little bit. When we think about higher ed administration, one of the big trendy things to talk about right now is *student success*. Often they define that in terms of retention and graduation metrics. I'm going to start there . . . part of the reason for naming student success is because it directly impacts students. One of the things I loved when I was a WPA was the fact that I could take on a quasi-leadership role and it'd have more of a direct impact to students. I've been a dean, associate dean . . . but the one thing about WPA leadership is you get to work directly with students and with instructors teaching students. You get to actually design the curriculum that students will use to impact students.

When you're at a department chair and deans or associate deans level, the practices and policies you implement . . . sure they have impact on students, but it's not as direct. You're not necessarily designing pedagogy. You can't do it by yourself . . . when you're a WPA, you're doing the designing, you're doing the assessment, and yes, it requires some collaboration, but it's directed by you. You can implement specific pedagogy, specific assessment practices, and also retention initiatives.

When you can see the impact of that as far as students who would normally not come back to college coming back another semester, then eventually graduating, that's when you actually get to see the fruits of your labor. So yes, that is what student success looks like. Even though it does seem cliche, we do need to talk about our success in relation to retaining students in higher ed and graduation. Because if those things don't happen, then what are we doing? Why are we here? Why are we in higher ed? One of the things I think in terms of our discipline is that we need to be more active with the fact that higher education *needs us*. They need us for students. They need WPAs. They need first-year writing. They need writing across the curriculum programs. They need writing centers. All those things impact student success so students can be retained.

Shane to Staci Perryman-Clark: Your coedited collection *Black Perspectives in Writing Program Administration* includes experiences with issues of racism, institutional constraints, and challenges WPAs of color face. You talk about Blackness as a cultural epistemological framework that influences your work as an administrator. Can you talk more about this framework and how you encourage new teachers or instructors to embrace more equitable, inclusive, and accessible pedagogies and practices? [Episode 17: 11:40–18:00]

Recognize and empathize with what it feels for historically oppressed communities to have that discomfort by you feeling it yourself. This world could use some empathy, particularly right now. I recognize every instructor is not going to have the same expertise in Afrocentric language and pedagogy that I have. But you can design very broad assignments like personal narrative, learning outcomes that are really consistent, and pick a content that revolves around historically oppressed populations.

Afrocentric is one center, but we don't have to just have one center. We can have multiple centers, right? The other thing is the materials you include. Being very, very deliberate about what you include in a custom textbook and what you don't: Having the widest range of diversity content from the widest range of historically oppressed communities, even if that makes the volume look a little more massive. It's fine. The point is that students want to see themselves included. Those are a couple of things.

This is really where we need to start learning from HBCUs. The reason why I was so deliberate about putting them in the book is because, even in our field, the HBCU narrative is that they're way more traditional and more "skill and drill" than predominantly White institutions (PWIs). That they're a little stricter with language conventions. But that is not necessarily the case. For every HBCU that you find where you have "skill and drill," you can find a PWI that has a similarly backwards pedagogy. But often that was seen as the master narrative of HBCU experience, even in essays written in our field . . .

Now, as far as institutional policies, I haven't seen any, especially at Western Michigan. Part of the reason why is because institutions aren't ready to get real yet. They will say they have things, but they won't use those things to change systems. They will post an article in their magazines, or on their new sites about some sort of new initiative that's helping people of color. They'll have a few students of color the face of something, some success stories . . . you see these kind of surface, superficial things. They say, "Look, we celebrate diversity. We honor it." I know you don't honor it and celebrate it because the system hasn't changed.

When you still have lower graduation rates for African Americans; when you have zero African American deans or provost; when you have an institution that's got 20,000 students and you've got two Black department chairs, so hardly any in leadership, then the system is not changing. I can't lie and say I'm seeing policies that are embracing Blackness as a cultural epistemological framework.

Shane to Iris D. Ruiz: Your research focuses on decolonial theory and program administration. Can you talk more about how these intersect? [Episode 27: 11:06–14:05]

When we're thinking about administration, that's already a colonial construct in terms of all of the ideas and concepts that it invokes. The practices that administration invokes is to regulate. So we have to think about how that type of regulation or approach to regulation centers on a top-down approach than on a communal approach or collaborative approach. We have to think about the ways in which that program values the various voices of the educators that they're working alongside with. What do they value? What is their program's assessment built upon? What is the verbiage or the checks used within writing programs? Course learning outcomes or program learning outcomes? What kinds of skills are they valuing of their educators? What kinds of skills are they trying to impart and put value on that they're teaching students? How do those affect and apply to the student?

For me, that's decolonial practice. It's going to ask you to think about your own power position. It's going to ask you to think about how do you empathize with your potentially marginalized faculty, or your first-generation minoritized students as well? How are you going to be able to train your faculty and give them the ability to be able to value a diversity approach if you yourself don't value that? All of those questions and reflections are very decolonial. One of the actions I would say that really resonates with decolonial practice is self-reflection. Thinking about oneself in the world. Thinking about how others are a reflection of yourself. Thinking about the ways that you act upon the world and the way that the world then responds to you. This is a type of decolonial consciousness, I guess, state of mind.

If one does not have that experience or foresight or worldview, then they might have more of a top-down approach where we're not considering who our educators are; we're not considering who our students are; we're just considering we need to have these course-learning outcomes met and these learning outcomes met and that's all we need to worry about. That's a recipe for failure because, as we know, the demographics all over our country are changing. They're changing in a way that challenges that older structure that we could possibly call a symptom of settler, colonial structures within the university.

Shane to Iris D. Ruiz: In "Race, Silence and Writing Program Administration: A Qualitative Study of US College Writing Programs," you talk about the underrepresentation of teacher-scholars of color in writing studies and the silencing of teacher-scholars of color. What future direction can we take as teacher-scholars to amplify antiracist initiatives and aims and to intersect race and administration so that we can resist White supremacy? [Episode 27: 14:38–18:40]

I don't know if I could speak so much to scholarship as I would actually just speak to practice because . . . I really want it to be implemented and for people to be able to take action based upon our research. I was shocked, in some ways, with some of the responses that we had in our interviews. I understand that there are writing programs who are really struggling with how to implement antiracist measures in their programs. Locally, I would say for about the past two years, we've created what is called a diversity initiatives committee that is headed by a diversity initiatives chair. It's not necessarily only comprised of faculty of color because as a matter of fact, we have very few faculty of color in our writing program. It's comprised of who's ever interested in contributing to this particular conversation about diversity, about what it means, and about the mission of the program.

It does call for a commitment to creating structures, but also the commitment to being able to be open to revising current structures. To be able to understand the necessity of committing oneself in terms of your time and your labor to the practice of restructuring or revising a current program to value diversity. Bringing the value and meaning of diversity to the center and being able to have programmatic conversations about what does that mean to every individual. Why are some definitions proliferating more so than others? In which way is the department or program lacking in their understanding of diversity? So once you start getting those conversations taking place, then you start opening the doors for looking at deficiencies, possible deficiencies, or just possible places to grow within your program that are maybe your weak link right now as far as diversity awareness.

In our article, we mentioned that diversity is one of those standalone metatypical words that tries to bring up issues of race. But it doesn't necessarily go far enough. Some people are not ready to talk about *race*. They're not ready to talk about *antiracism* right off the bat. We get into those conversations in discussing *diversity*. Then, we can talk a little bit more about what race means and how we're valuing the race of our students, our own racial histories within the United States, our complicities and acts of bias. It kind of opens up the door to be able to talk about these things.

Then, it branches off into various areas. We branched off into bringing in a new mission statement for our writing program that values the students' diversity. Then we branched into discussions of course learning outcomes and how we could also revise those to reflect more of a commitment to diversity. Those are just a couple of suggestions of how you take what we studied and what we learned about some of the misgivings, or the misunderstandings about the role of race and diversity in writing programs. Take some of our findings and try to put those within practice in your own institutions.

Shane to Melvin Beavers: Your research focuses on preparing and professionalizing part-time contingent faculty, including providing pedagogical development for teaching writing online. Can you talk more about how you do this work as a WPA? [Episode 47: 06:00–08:57]

Part of why I focused a lot of my research on part-time faculty is because I was one for so long. I was trying to marry my experience and my research interests together. They came together within part-time faculty interests, concerns, issues with OWI training, and teacher preparation. Some of the approaches that are helpful and useful really come out of my dissertation research. Part of what I like to do or like to think of as training is the idea of being in the moment. When I say that, I think of things like . . . an open door policy. If someone comes in my office and they want to talk about their course syllabus, or they want to talk about an idea for an assignment, and it could connect to OWI, it may not, but if it does, that's an opportunity for me to talk them through their idea.

What do you want to do? What's the purpose of this? How are you going to present this information? What kind of language are you going to use to talk to your students and how is that different from how you might do something in the face-to-face setting? Or talk to them about accessibility issues, making sure that students have access to the materials or giving them materials in multiple ways, whether that's an audio recording, PDF file, or a recording of instructions, in addition to giving them a hard copy that they can read. Just being able to give somebody information or help them think through something. That's one way of approaching it.

Another way is providing all kinds of resources . . . you've got your OWI community. That information is readily accessible and I try to make sure that folks know about what's going on with the OWI community. If they want to participate in a workshop, or if they want to have access to a new book that's out, I make sure that they have those materials. If they have questions about it, then we can have a conversation. Ultimately what I try to do is make myself available if faculty want to have those conversations or share ideas.

Shane to Melvin Beavers: Is there a core principle that stands out to you, maybe more so than others, or one you emphasize more in your program as imperative to teaching writing online effectively? [Episode 48: 08:58–12:19]

Yeah, so you have the OWI principles of effective practices. That's an exhaustive laundry list of check marks. It's like, am I engaged in my course? Have I made it accessible? Am I doing things to be personal and interact with my students? This is really interesting that you asked me this question because I actually was thinking through the idea of engagement with students and increasing your presence and your interaction with your students.

. . . I don't really want to speak for the entire community, but I want to say that sometimes it seems that the push toward making sure that all these boxes are checked, I wonder if we're missing something in terms of just realizing that we're teaching something. I'm thinking about Marshall Gregory's article called "Curriculum, Pedagogy, and Teacherly Ethos." Part of that is thinking through what we are teaching and how we're conveying that information. Not necessarily thinking about what we're doing as the banking concept of pouring information into brains, but really thinking about how am I developing the course? How am I making sure that my students are learning and I'm actually teaching them something?

I think sometimes we get so involved in the design and in the ideas about engagement and presence and rapport and interaction. I think those are good. I think those are strong points to put on that checklist, but I guess I'm saying is to pay attention to those organic teacherly moments and that teacherly ethos you want to develop with your students. Remembering that our charge is to make sure that our students learn. To really coach our students through, whether it's writing or whatever the discipline may be. Sometimes I think maybe we need to take a step back and we just need to look at what we're doing inside the course . . . let's not forget that we are . . . especially in rhet/comp programs, teaching is our focus. That's one of the things I really try to emphasize with my graduate students. Think about who you are as a teacher. How do you see yourself in that role or within this online space?

Shane to Jacob Babb: Your coedited collection, *WPAs in Transition*, offers narratives and frameworks for teacher-scholars who are entering, navigating, or exiting WPA work. I was hoping we could talk about these transitions, specifically the person who is hired to be a WPA or inherits the role. Talk us through this transition and share how you would help someone navigate this new role. [Episode 50: 14:19–18:21]

> When someone is transitioning into the WPA role, it is impossible to be invisible. All of a sudden you are in a role that everyone else has seen someone else in. Everyone is looking to you a little nervous and a little anxious to see how you're going to operate. Inevitably, no matter how smoothly a transition goes, no matter how much time people have had to prepare for a transition, no single person is going to perform this role like any other person. There are always going to be differences in the way that we approach these positions. For somebody stepping into the role, a few things to bear in mind. First of all, you cannot solve every problem immediately. The best thing you can do is to sit back and listen for a little while and try to create a list of priorities. What are the demands that this job put on you and what are the kinds of things that you want to accomplish? What are the kinds of things that other people

in your department want you to accomplish? If you have interaction with other administrators, say for instance, deans, what are they looking for from you? Do your best to understand the landscape that you have stepped into. That's going to take time and patience.

One of the best pieces I've read in our scholarship . . . is by Laura J. Davies. She wrote a piece called "Grief and the New WPA." She published it in the *WPA* journal. It is a really effective examination of the emotional response of other people in a department when a new WPA steps in. It's a type of grief which is an understandable response to an absence. Those people need that time to make adjustments. In the beginning, while you are gathering your ideas of how to respond to the role, that same time that you are taking to do that is the time that others around you get to look at you and start accepting you in the role. So a bit of slowness in the beginning is really valuable for everybody involved.

Shane to Jacob Babb: You're the coeditor of *WPA: Writing Program Administration*. What scholarship has influenced your practices and the ways you've developed your program at Indiana University Southeast? [Episode 50: 01:47–06:00]

There are so many different avenues of scholarship to talk about here. For instance, I think about the types of scholarship that made me interested in doing this work to begin with: *GenAdmin*, a book that was published about 10 years ago now. *GenAdmin* helped me to think about my own scholarly identity and to think about how the work I had already been doing at that time in my PhD program and prior to coming into my PhD program shaped the kind of work that I wanted to do. Ever since I have been involved in studying writing, I had been involved in some form of writing program administration, whether it was helping to run a writing center or operating as an assistant director for different writing programs. I've always found that work to be extremely engaging and knew that that was a big part of who I wanted to be as a scholar and as a teacher. *GenAdmin* really captured the idea that WPA isn't just a job that we do. WPA is what gives shape to the work we want to do. It's what gives shape to the kinds of questions we ask in our scholarship. It gives shape to the types of communities we want to participate in.

I also think about pieces of advice I've gotten from WPAs over the years. One article in particular . . . Laura Micciche wrote about "slow agency." The idea that WPA work pushes us to feel like we have to solve problems quickly. We are always reacting. We're always responding to other things going on. But we need to think about how to slow down our work. We need to cultivate a philosophy of taking a slow approach to writing program administration. Because most of the types of problems that we wrestle with as WPAs can never be solved quickly. In fact, trying to solve problems quickly typically makes situations worse. When I was becoming a WPA here at IU Southeast, I participated in the WPA workshop that happens every year at the Council of Writing Program Administrators Conference. One of the people facilitating that workshop at the time was Linda Adler-Kassner. We had a meeting during this workshop to talk about the kinds of specific issues that I was trying to deal with as a new WPA, the kinds of curricular issues, whatever it was that I wanted to take on in this role.

I was brand new, not only to the role of WPA, but to the institution. I had only been here for a year and I wanted to solve everything. I wanted to do it now. One of the best pieces of advice I ever got was from Linda saying, "Be patient. You're not going to be able to do all of this at once. In fact, if you try to do all of this at once, you're probably going to burn many of the bridges that you need to try to wrestle with different issues." It's the advice that we have to pause and think what kinds of short and long-term plans do we want to make.

Shane to Jacob Babb: That's really good advice. What did you do, or how did you use that advice to come up with a plan or goal that you wanted to work on in your writing program? [Episode 50: 06:01–07:41]

> What it really involved was mapping out challenges and issues that I face at my institution. Heeding this call was valuable because it made me pause to look around and say, "Okay, what is it exactly that I think needs to be done most? Not necessarily what I, in particular, want to focus on, but what would be most beneficial to focus on?" That meant getting to know our part-time instructors. At IU Southeast, we don't have a graduate program. There are ten of us who teach writing full-time and the rest of the faculty are part-time instructors.

> I knew some of them reasonably okay in the beginning, but I didn't know them that well. In order to do anything else in a writing program, you have to build trust among the people that you work with. So for the next two years, it became a priority for me to get to know our part-time instructors, to observe their classes, to meet with them from time to time, to go into their shared office space and strike up conversations with them. Just to get to know who they were, get a sense of what they thought the challenges in their classrooms were like, and to get an idea of what they wanted from me as a WPA.

Shane to Elizabeth Wardle: You directed the writing programs at the University of Central Florida and the University of Dayton. I'm interested in what you learned about writing program administration from these earlier experiences and how those experiences helped you develop as a writing program administrator? [Episode 56: 01:29–06:01]

> At University of Dayton, I was just out of grad school. I had not gone there to be the writing program director. Then, halfway through my first semester, they were like, "Hey, would you like to be the writing program director next

semester?" I think most of us learned that job by just doing it. Very few of us are lucky enough to have extensive mentoring in it before we do it. In that particular job, I learned a lot of things about what it means to have authority or not have authority and how you help guide a program when you don't really have any institutional authority.

. . . I didn't hire people. I couldn't fire people. I didn't evaluate anyone. A lot of the people teaching in the program were literature faculty who really didn't have any interest in writing studies scholarship. Looking back now, I think, "Well, what actually was that job?" . . . the main lesson I learned from that is that if you can tap into people's intellectual curiosity, you can actually start working toward a really interesting and comprehensive program without any of the institutional authority. So that sort of ground up, "What are you interested in? Let's learn more about it together. What would you design out of your expertise if we were working from that together?" . . . I think that that was probably a really important lesson because even when I had more institutional authority, I still felt like that was a better way to do the work.

I think if you learn anything as a WPA, or just an administrator in general, it's that you can put things in writing and say that this is our policy about what you'll be doing in your classroom, but when people go into their classrooms, they're going to do what they want to do. Unless everybody has a collective interest and will in making a new curriculum, they're still going to be doing what they want to do. Mandating things from the top, even though it might feel satisfying, I actually think is not really how good writing program administration actually happens. I was really lucky to learn it that way at a place where I didn't have any authority, so I had to do it like that.

At UCF, I had more institutional authority, but I think that I still did it the same way. When I got there, I said, "Is anyone interested in piloting something new?" I didn't know anyone. It was a huge school. We had thirty-three adjuncts and a bunch of them just said, "I don't know you. I have no idea what you're talking about with writing about writing, but I'm really bored. I'd like to try something new." That's actually how we moved toward a writing about writing curriculum at UCF. It was not through me coming in and saying, "Now this is what you're all going to do." The entire project really came about because people were interested. We had reading groups, we shared teaching materials. Those people tried things. Then, they told their colleagues, "This was amazing, maybe you should try it." So about two or three years in, then we started saying, "Enough people are doing this. We have good assessment on it. We're going to start moving the program toward this." But it's because we already had like a tipping point of who said that this was working.

What's the principle here? I think that real change happens from the bottom up out of intellectual curiosity and interest, not really top-down mandate. So even if you have institutional authority, that's probably not the most effective way to run a writing program.

Shane to Elizabeth Wardle: Writing program administration is tied to local contexts and the affordances and resources, or perhaps constraints attached to those places. What have been some guiding principles or what tenets have helped shape your administrative philosophy? [Episode 56: 06:02–10:23]

> I'd like to go back to your comment about everything is tied to local contexts. I think that is true, but I also think as a field, sometimes we cop out on that or like, "Everything is different, so there's nothing that we can say is true across every context." But I actually think that there are real principles that could be at work across contexts. At least for me, there are things we know from the research to be true about writing and how writing works and those should inform whatever we do. I think that's true with anything, right? What's the point of expertise if we don't act from it,

right? I also think there are principles about how people do their best work: If they're acting from their own expertise and if they're able to have ownership and agency of something that they built together, then that's more effective than telling people what to do.

Regardless of the vagaries of the institutional context, I still think we can say, but some things are still just always true, right? Which is—we have research. We should see what it says. We should act from it. Otherwise, why do we have all that research? Then, there's just truths of our human nature. There's also quite a lot of stuff about leadership and change that, as a field we've not been as familiar with as we should be, that can really help us think about how to get things done. Really my principles have been act from the research and best practice, above all, but also empower people to act from their own expertise and have agency in terms of how curriculum operates so that everybody feels ownership over it.

. . . to be able to action those two principles empowers people to act from best practice, but also to have agency in terms of ownership over the curriculum . . . those two principles, I think gets you a long way toward having a program that is functional and also intellectual and where people also have a lot of goodwill toward each other and recognize each other's expertise.

DENOUEMENT

WPAs are committed to writing instruction and are always responding to local and national trends in higher education. WPAs fulfill the role of an administrator, leader, teacher, mentor, and colleague, and are primary sources of information on teaching writing for faculty, students, and other college administrators. Their roles are multifaceted and complex, and their work is inherently connected to institutional and program systems and needs. These interviews show how WPAs use research and theory to produce action for the betterment of teachers and students. Moreover, this conversation shows the joys and challenges of writing program administration, and the kind of dedication it takes to create sustainable systems and structures that empower teachers and students. For additional resources on writing program administration, I recommend reading the journal *WPA: Writing Program Administration*, Susan H. McLeod's (2007) reference guide titled *Writing Program Administration*, Staci Perryman-Clark and Collin Lamont Craig's (2019) coedited collection *Black Perspectives in Writing Program Administration: From the Margins to the Center*, *Landmark Essays on Writing Program Administration* coedited by Kelly Ritter and Melissa Ianetta (2019), and *Writing Program Architecture: Thirty Cases for Reference and Research* coedited by Bryna Siegel Finer and Jamie White-Farnham (2017). I also suggest reading *WPAs in Transition: Navigating Educational Leadership Positions* coedited by Courtney Adams Wooten, Jacob Babb, and Brian Ray (2018). I offer the following questions for you to consider on writing program administration, as well:

- What are the strengths and weaknesses of your writing program?
- What responsibilities do you want to prioritize as a writing program administrator?
- How are you shaping policies that complement your program's mission and aims?
- What resources are available to you, and how might you use those advantageously to support teachers and students?
- How are you considering the different needs of faculty and students, and in what ways are you drawing on their knowledges and skills?
- What theory and research inform your administrative philosophy and your program? What research can you do within your own program?
- What short-term and long-term goals do you have as an administrator?

11

Basic Writing

Basic writing programs have a tumultuous history in higher education. They were formed in response to inequitable systems and structures that failed to support diverse students and minoritized populations entering colleges and universities in the 1960s and 1970s. Ira Shor (1997) writes in his widely debated article, "Basic writing as a field was born in crisis" (p. 91). Basic writing is tied to the open admissions movement in the 1970s which altered the landscape of higher education. In 1970 at the City University of New York (CUNY), for example, first-year student enrollment increased from 20,000 to 35,000 (Otte & Mlynarczyk, 2010). Nearly every history of basic writing acknowledges Mina P. Shaughnessy at City College of New York, who was charged with creating a program for "'new' students who entered colleges under the open admissions revolution of the sixties" (Shaughnessy, 1976, p. 178). Shaughnessy, most notable for *Errors and Expectations* (1977), was important in helping establish basic writing as a field and site for research and rejecting assumptions and stereotypes used to describe students entering college through the open access movement.

In the 1970s, many administrators were responsible for developing programs and classes to support student writers who previously didn't have access to colleges and universities. Basic writing programs ultimately emerged from this. In the 1980s and 1990s, the term, definition, perception, and structure of "basic writing" became contentious in composition studies (Bartholomae & Petrosky, 1986; Bizzell, 1986; Greenberg, 1997; Lu, 1991; Shor, 1997). There were internal arguments about the name and even the nature of basic writing, as well as external pressures from policymakers that were affecting writing programs across the nation (Wiener, 1998). Basic writing programs were experiencing budget cuts and/or were being defunded because of public perception and hysteria on "error" in student writing and elitist language ideologies. In sum, there were national conversations on literacy that expressed discontentment about student preparation in college (see "Why Johnny Can't Write," Sheils, 1975; "Johnny Can't Write Because English Teachers Can't Either," Lambdin, 1980). Harvey S. Wiener (1998) felt that it wasn't the basic writing programs themselves that were at fault per se, but instead administrators' lack of response to these narratives on students and their writing: "Those with the responsibility for writing programs have not attended appropriately to public perceptions about the basic writing enterprise" (p. 97).

Basic writing programs have had to account for these national and institutional challenges while trying to support multicultural student populations. Further, basic writing has been marginalized in composition studies at large. As George Ott and Rebecca Williams Mlynarczyk (2010) write, "Research on basic writing is in short supply. Chronic marginalization of BW faculty is the chief cause of the dearth of scholarship . . . no branch of academia has been more adjunctified than composition, no subset of that more adjunctified than BW" (p. 122). Many program administrators have to contend with these ongoing issues and constraints, including a lack of institutional resources and support needed to develop sustainable programs. There are several basic writing program models, and in most of them, the larger mission seems to come from a desire to be inclusive, equitable, and supportive of students. Some programs offer credit for basic writing, while others don't. Some use directed self-placement measures, while others use standardized testing to place students. Some stretch and combine their basic writing class with first-year writing, whereas others have standalone basic writing courses. The goal is a good one—to promote and advocate for students, and to develop policies and practices that help foster success for diverse learners—but in reality, it's difficult given the internal and external challenges and pressures that surround basic writing programs and classes.

There are various basic writing pedagogical approaches, too. Some teacher-scholars have suggested a genre-based approach (Hall & Stephens, 2018), sociocultural and antiracist pedagogies

(Stanley, 2017), recommended multimodal assignments (Balzotti, 2016), and offered different ways to assess students' linguistic diversity (Athon, 2019). A recurring theme on teaching basic writing is the concept of "contact zones," which Mary Louise Pratt (1991) defines as the meeting and clashing of cultures: "Spaces where cultures meet, clash, and grapple with each other, often in contexts of highly asymmetrical relations of power, such as colonialism, slavery or their aftermaths as they are lived out in the world today" (p. 34). Basic writing classes are good sites for embracing pedagogies that center cultural knowledge and linguistic diversity. Teaching basic writing takes a willingness to listen and engage with students about their histories and communities. This contact zone framework, alongside critical pedagogies (see Paulo Freire) or feminist theories, could disrupt hierarchies between the teacher, who is traditionally positioned as the English language expert, and the basic writing student, who is traditionally positioned as deficient in English. There's great value in decentering and subverting power, and amplifying students' histories, languages, and cultures in and through basic writing.

INTERVIEWS

Through these interviews, you'll get a sense for how different teachers perceive basic writing and approach administration and teaching. I was fortunate to chat with Susan Naomi Bernstein, Darin Jensen, Bryna Siegel Finer, and Carolyn Calhoon-Dillahunt about basic writing programs and classes. Bernstein shares the history of basic writing programs in higher education and how they intersect "with social movements for reparations and restorative justice for ongoing and historical educational and social injustice." She talks about challenges facing programs and future directions for basic writing studies. Jensen talks about the label *basic writing* and Mina Shaughnessy's legacy, and he also describes how he approaches teaching basic writing. Finer mentions common assumptions about basic writing students and how she would go about training and developing graduate students to teach basic writing courses. And Calhoon-Dillahunt concludes by talking about her research on responding to students and what she enjoys the most about teaching basic writing.

Shane to Susan Naomi Bernstein: Do you mind providing a brief history of basic writing programs in higher education? [Episode 63: 01:18–05:39]

The history of basic writing programs or BW programs in higher education intersects with social movements for reparations and restorative justice for ongoing and historical educational and social injustice. In the 1960s, BW was part of a movement to create equitable access to higher education for BIPOC, poor and working class, queer and disabled, and other people who were historically closed out of postsecondary institutions by the material realities of White supremacists and elitist etiologies of higher education.

That said, I would suggest that there are many histories of basic writing, and that much depends on who is writing those histories and how basic writings historical contexts are evoked. For example, histories recounted by students and teachers of basic writing might be framed, and would be framed, quite differently from basic writing histories written by writing program administrators. Additionally, any history of BW in higher education needs to be grounded in a clear understanding of historic and ongoing inequities in K–12 public schooling in the United States.

By the second decade of the twenty-first century, many four-year colleges had eliminated basic writing and many two-year colleges no longer offer open admissions. For K–12 public school histories, I would recommend Bettina L. Love's book, *We Want to Do More Than Survive: Abolitionists Teaching and the Pursuit of Educational Freedom.* I'm reading that right now. It's amazing. I love it. I've been waiting for a book like this. It's just really pulls so much together. Valerie Kinloch's book *Harlem On Our Minds: Race, Place, and the Literacies of Urban Youth.* For a history of BW grounded in US social justice movements, I would recommend Conor Tomás Reed's article, "The Early Formations of Black Women's Studies in the Lives of Toni Cade Bambara, June Jordan, and Audre Lorde." What

Reed does is that he doesn't look at it from a writing studies perspective. He looks at the perspective of social movement at City University of New York. That's what it is. It's how basic writing grew out of social movements.

Really kind of look at what you're doing and why you're doing it. If you're saying that, as I've often heard people say about basic writing, "Oh, well it's too late. It was an experiment that failed." I'm like, "What are you talking about? What are you talking about?" It's about what Bettina Love focuses on—*potentiality*, right? It's not about numbers. It's not about enrollment management. It's not about kind of isolating, or they say, "Oops well, this doesn't look so good. So let's move a little money around." I've seen this in so many places. Let's get rid of things that could be looked at as remedial, rather than redefining it. Rather than making it more assets-based, it's instead, "Well, we don't want anything that looks like a deficit and anyway, it's not working. So we're just going to toss the whole thing." Rather than trying to think about, well, what do we need to do to make it better so that it is more inclusive, more equitable and more diverse in that it envelops, it works with, it is informed by more folks rather than fewer.

Moving from that I would generally recommend, and this has been informing everything I've done for the last four years, I would recommend James Baldwin's activist writing on bearing witness to Black lives and White supremacy, especially his *Collected Essays*, the [Library of America] edition that Toni Morrison edited, and his previously uncollected essays in *The Cross of Redemption*. I loved that book.

Shane to Susan Naomi Bernstein: What are some of the biggest challenges to basic writing programs? [Episode 63: 05:40–10:54]

The most significant challenge is that the burdens of administrators are borne by students and teachers of basic writing. This isn't new with me. Mina Shaughnessy wrote about this half a century ago and not in *Errors and*

Expectations, which of course is problematic, but her essays and her speeches and her writing outside of *Errors and Expectations*. It uses words like *democracy*, it identifies problems that we also now are facing. Half a century ago, Mina Shaughnessy identified the problems of basic writing or the challenges were being borne by students and teachers and unfunded mandates basically. One of those burdens is the misperception of basic writing as remediation.

Basic writing courses need to be fully funded and to be offered with full credit for graduation and transfer. No credit is a big, big problem. That made them easier to eliminate . . . something like directed self-placement, also not unproblematic, but nevertheless, creating a system as fair as possible with fully funded support services for tutoring, advising, counseling, and unimpeded access to healthcare, food, and housing. Sure, I'm leaving out other things as well. This would be for me the ideal model. Just the whole person, right? I mean the whole student and community concurrently. Basic writing courses and support services would be informed by a deep, deep awareness of racial and economic injustice, and the intersectional needs of queer and disabled people, and people from religious minorities.

Here I'm going to go a little autobiographical on you. It's always hard for me to know whether I should bring this up. It's not about me, but I have a much clearer understanding of the whys of why I got involved in this. I have ADHD and generalized anxiety that weren't diagnosed until I was fifteen years out of grad school. I had no accommodations, which is why I'm such a big believer in them. The other thing about that was that in kindergarten, in the 1960s, they were doing lots of experiments with us.

One of the things that I was able to be involved in back when I started school, they weren't teaching kindergartners how to read as a matter of course. That came later. Because of my hyper focus on things like books and magazines and things like that, they thought, "Oh, well, let's put Susan in this experimental class where we're teaching kids how to read." That saved me. That saved me because I learned how to read and learned how to write. Once I did that and we left that school district and moved to a much more conservative school district that wasn't doing anything like this, they were like, "Whoa, you're sort of ahead a grade level." That saved me when other things started tanking. It was literacy stuff that and I was like, "Whoa, that's like super important."

The other part is that back in '60s and '70s, there were some things that we're totally missing now. College needs to be free, as CUNY was for many folks until 1976. Or more fully subsidized. Free is better obviously, but more fully subsidized by state and federal funding. That's how it was for me. When I was an undergraduate in the late 1970s, one-third of my tuition was paid for by a needs-based state scholarship. While I still had loan debt, the indebtedness was much less onerous than student indebtedness in subsequent generations. Now especially, students' financial burdens and family responsibilities are an additional challenge for basic writing programs. Invisible, not invisible to many of us, but invisible to some folks who are making decisions. If my dad hadn't had access to low-cost education, a generation before me coming out of New Deal stuff, I wouldn't be here talking to you right now.

I mean, that stuff is intergenerational and significant. It breaks my heart isn't the right word. Enrages is a better word. It enrages me that that's gone. It just enrages me now that it's more necessary than ever. It's also more absent.

Shane to Susan Naomi Bernstein: What's the future of basic writing studies, or what future directions would you like to see scholarship and basic writing programs take? [Episode 63: 17:14–21:50]

It's got to be . . . action research and activist practice. This is what Bettina Love talks about, what Valerie Kinloch talks about. This is what it's got to be. It's got to be informed by our current and ever-evolving historical moment. It's got to be involved. It's got to be with an understanding of what happened and why it didn't work. Folks working on it have to be unafraid to challenge . . . I say "unafraid" and I totally, I'm like shaking all the time. I'm like, "Oh no, I didn't say it right." I'm going to use the word sacred because it involves potential, right? It involves something that's larger than us. That's larger than enrollment management. That's larger than universities. It involves the whole of the culture, all of our history and all of what is going to come.

As a teacher and as an administrator, it's got it involve your whole self and be informed by your life. That means that you have to look at your life in the way that Baldwin talks about to really, for White people especially, look at our own histories. Where are the gaps and absences? What are the stories we've been telling ourselves? What is missing from those stories? It's got to be informed by that. Most of all, I'm leaving out the most important part, it's got to be, it's got to be centered on students and what students need and where students are coming from and what they bring with them. It's got to not be a deficit thing. We have to stop looking at it as deficit model. It's got to be like Bettina Love says, it's got to be an assets-based model. That's what I see it as. All the places, all the points where it failed, were the, "Oh, well," or the idea of, "This is a failed experiment," or "It was too late for folks."

Some of the reading that I've been doing, I went back and I read about what CUNY was like before open admissions. I read some of the arguments in regular New York Times articles, that are not so different from now, in the early 1960s about what CUNY was like before. In reading James Baldwin's biographical history stuff that he, at one point, had thought about going to City College, but he couldn't get in because he didn't have an academic diploma. He worked when he was in high school and he went to an elite high school. Most of his classmates were Jewish.

Stan Lee graduated from the same high school a couple of years before him. He had to work. He had eight brothers and sisters. He had to help support them. He was growing up in Harlem and his family was working class, and there was a lot of suffering. City College had a requirement of, I believe, it was an A– average and what was called, at that time, an academic diploma, which would now probably become a Regents diploma if I remember right. He couldn't go. In a way that was good for him because he was able to leave us so much. In another way, he shouldn't have had to suffer and no one should have to suffer.

I'm not even sure if it would be called "basic writing" even. What it should be doing is alleviating suffering and not contributing to it. Everything needs to be offered for credit or the credit system needs to be imagined. I was the beneficiary of much work that was pass-fail. It meant it gave room to experiment and to find out more about what education could be. That's what the future has to be. It's got to be equity, inclusion, diversity. It can't just be performative. It's got to be active, it's got to be a real thing and viewed in everything.

Shane to Darin Jensen: The label "basic writing" was created, in many ways, to resist the dominant use of the word "remedial," specifically its attachment to "students" and/or "classes." In what ways do you feel like academia's understanding of basic writing has changed since Mina Shaughnessy's *Errors and Expectations* was published in 1977? [Episode 23: 07:47–11:56]

Hope Parisi wrote this magnificent essay in the *Journal of Basic Writing* about this and she has a retrospective of exactly the question that you're asking. Here's what I would say. I would say that I am sad that we even read Mina Shaughnessy's book anymore. I think that there's all sorts of problems with it even though she meant well, and that in most composition and pedagogy courses, when we read basic writing, we end up reading a chapter or maybe even the whole of *Errors and Expectations* and I feel like we should leave Mina as a wonderful important historical footnote, but that there's a lot of other work that's been done that is more interesting. I think Susan Naomi Bernstein would say that we shouldn't call anyone "basic writers." That there's no such thing as a basic writer. She's right. But I don't know what the hell to call people then.

I've been involved with NADE (which is now NOSS), National Association for Developmental Education, and they use this idea of "developmental education," which is somehow less damning to me than the notion of basic writing. But to answer one part of your question, our culture still thinks that we have "remedial" writers and our culture . . . I still spend time in the writing center getting students who come in and they just want to "fix" things, right? They have a notion of "correctness" that dominates their writing. So we do this still . . . every time I get a nursing student in the writing center who's buggered up about APA and it's just like, "You know, you're going to be fine and it doesn't need to be perfect." Except they have nursing instructors who want that to be perfect and it's an enormous part of their grade. So even outside of writing studies, the notion of correctness of the current tradition that's sort of grammatical is really, really important and it still dominates.

I think that one of the failures of writing studies, or maybe one work in progress of writing studies, is that we have not done a good job communicating how people really learn to write and how writing is a process and how writing is something that happens over multiple attempts. Not to be flippant, but I couldn't give the nursing faculty Anne Lamott's "Shitty First Drafts" and have them understand, "Oh!" because that's not what the nursing faculty want. They want students who can produce medical notes and case notes that are accurate and that have a shared grammar. I can't really blame them for that.

I don't know. There's lots of pieces to that question. I don't like the notion of "basic writer." However, if we get rid of the idea of basic writing or developmental writing, then we won't have a space. I'm really worried, especially the way developmental education has been under attack, that we won't have a space to give time to students who need the extra help, who need the extra instruction. I think that the other part of it is that we don't do a good job communicating to other publics what good writing instruction looks like.

Shane to Darin Jensen: You mentioned not wanting to lose the space and perhaps even the attention and resources attached to basic writing programs. Do you feel like there's a better conception of basic writing that moves away from that label but still very much gets to its identity or the work that happens in basic writing programs? [Episode 23: 11:57–14:03]

"Underprepared" or "underresourced." Christie Toth and Brett Griffiths write this chapter in a book on class and they use the term "poverty effects." I rarely have students who do not have the cognitive abilities to write at a college level. Whatever that is. Sometimes they're not motivated because of previous school experiences. Mike Rose writes about that kind of stuff. Sometimes they've had poor public schooling. This is not blaming high school teachers, but if you grow up working class, if you grow up poor and you don't have a lot of books in your house and nobody's really pushing you to read, there are a hundred things that happen by the time I get a student sitting in whatever we're calling it.

What I would say is that it's more about first-generation students. It's more about poverty effects. It's more about class. It's more about students not understanding the moves of "academic writing," or the moves of middle-class standards that we try to assimilate people to in post-secondary education. I want to resist that it has anything to do with their deficiency as a learner, as a thinker, as a human being. It has to do, in most part, with poverty effects, with class, with opportunities, with previous educational experiences that end up expressing themselves on a writing test or the Accuplacer or whatever measure people are using to sort students into classes.

Shane to Darin Jensen: How many years have you taught basic writing and how do you approach the basic writing classroom? [Episode 23: 04:19–07:46]

Eleven years. When I started at Metro (Metropolitan Community College in Omaha), the faculty there, Erin Joy and Susan E. Lee and some other folks, all had just revised their developmental writing sequence and they had this great course called "Read and Respond." It was very literacy focused and then building on writing skills. They had this kind of studio model that was called "Fundamentals of College Writing." . . . it really was an integrated reading and writing model. I say that because I think that, for me, forms the basis of why I do what I do. I saw the holistic model that Erin and Susan and others had developed as being the way to teach developmental writing. Obviously there's already been lots of critique of skill-based instruction, "skill and drill," building sentences.

The Metro program was really interested in having students write essays, write short essays, write responses, right? Lots and lots of writing and lots of reading. I think that my goal is to get students to engage in the process of writing and to understand writing as a process and reading as a recursive process. That they aren't deficient. And that is really important because I think one of the things that I took into my developmental writing courses is also a discussion of applied linguistics in the sense that many of my students, when you ask them what "good" English is, they'll say "proper," and they come with standard English ideology already embedded into them. They come with middle-class notions of language. The reason they've hated their English classes and they didn't want to go is because they had teachers who were still using current-traditional rhetoric methods.

So not only getting them to write, but also beginning to critically deconstruct the standard English ideology that has been foisted on them. When I taught at Omaha, I taught at a historically African American campus in an African American neighborhood. It was very clear the kinds of racism hidden in standard English. It was everywhere . . . it was immediately oppressive. We talk about that in my rural campus, too. We talk about rural English or working-class English compared to "standard" English.

Shane to Bryna Siegel Finer: What are some common assumptions about basic writing students and classrooms? [Episode 55: 00:57–04:02]

I've been teaching basic writing for a very, very long time. I've been doing a research project and collecting longitudinal data from nine basic writing instructors from across the country for the last two-and-a-half years. I've been spending the last couple of months analyzing that data. In terms of common assumptions, I think that there's a myth or there's an assumption that the students who are placed in basic writing are unmotivated or they don't want to be there. While I think sometimes that can be true, the reason for that has to really be explored. Right? By whoever's teaching the class, by the people who do the placement, by the WPA. The students aren't necessarily unmotivated just because that is their intrinsic nature . . . being placed in basic writing comes with a lot of emotional stuff. Students start to realize, "Oh wait, I was placed in this class, but my peers were placed in another class. Why didn't I get into this class?" Often, they're going to end up paying for an additional class that their peers aren't. So there's a lot of stuff that comes with being put into basic writing. It's not that students have a character trait of being unmotivated. So that is a really important thing that people should not assume about the students.

Also, there's an assumption that anybody can teach this class. A lot of the people who I talked to in the research study that I've been doing have talked about how they see this happening at their own universities where a lot of adjunct or graduate students or contingent faculty teach basic writing when they haven't had any training in it or any experience teaching it. And then, the students are kind of at a loss, right? They're not getting necessarily the best experience in the classroom. That's really a hard place for the students to be in. There are, of course, amazing instructors and adjuncts and graduate students who are great teachers, but I really think to teach this class—we talk about it at our own institution as a "specialized course"—you need some specialized training.

You need to have some experience working with students and working with students who need additional support and have some training on the sort of pedagogy that goes along with that, too. It's not like anybody can just sort of walk in and teach it.

Shane to Bryna Siegel Finer: I'm interested in knowing how you would suggest going about preparing someone to teach basic writing. What resources, texts, materials, or pedagogical strategies would you recommend? [Episode 55: 06:11–08:25]

What can best prepare somebody to teach basic writing is to be in the classroom with a teacher who's already doing it. With an experienced teacher. So either that they are assigned to be that person's graduate assistant or teaching assistant or something like that, or they ask if they can shadow that teacher so in some way they are in that classroom for once a week working as an in-class tutor. Spending time in an actual classroom. A lot of us get our PhDs from institutions that don't teach basic writing. So they don't offer basic writing to undergraduates. We get our PhDs in composition, rhetoric, or some related field, but we don't ever have the experience or the chance to teach basic writing. We teach something like English 101 and maybe some other kind of freshman writing course. We might learn about basic writing or we might read some books about it or some articles, but we don't get that hands-on experience.

I was really lucky because I taught as an adjunct in some places before I did my PhD I was kind of thrown into it and got a lot of practice doing it that way. But I think if you are a graduate student, if you can get some experience in the classroom, that's the best way. If you can't, I mean, there's a lot of great reading. Everybody will say read Mina Shaughnessy and Mike Rose. The Council of Basic Writing has a really great website/blog where people post tons of resources and articles and links to the journal. I mean, you really have to immerse yourself in that current scholarship to understand what's going on in that area if you're not able to get into the classroom itself.

Shane to Carolyn Calhoon-Dillahunt: In "Conversing in Marginal Spaces: Developmental Writers' Responses to Teacher Comments," you study basic writers' perception and attitudes on response. You research what basic writers do when they receive feedback from teachers. What did you learn from studying students' reactions to marginal comments? How has this research helped shape your teaching? [Episode 49: 12:26–18:01]

This was actually a three-year project Dodie and I did. The article only represents the first year . . . but it doesn't represent the third year, which was my favorite . . . the third project was actually case studies and that was awesome.

I interviewed, I think we had five or six students out of Dodie's class and we kind of went through that whole process that we did with the study, but just with those students and then follow-up interviews with them. It confirmed what we were seeing. It also provided a lot more support, for the most part, of the autonomous nature that these students are bringing in. Again, we still have these assumptions that developmental students—and they're not wrong, there's support for this—that developmental students want directive feedback and want to be told what to do. But they really do want to intellectualize . . . the majority of them, like most any other student, they're just students, they're just writers, they're just earlier more novice writers.

I think that was really helpful to try to get rid of that bias that I think I had and didn't intend to have because I love teaching developmental students. I was maybe being a little bit too nurturing, like, maybe this is my K–12 where I'm trying to show them the right way versus kind of treating them as they are adults with perfectly capable brains and plenty of ideas that just maybe need more practice at academic forms. It was great to work with another colleague and to kind of share these experiences back and forth. It was great to talk to students, even when it wasn't direct. We did interviews with the students, even in the first round, but you're getting to know them on the page pretty well and how forthright they are and how much they're willing to share about their experiences.

It was mostly very heartening to understand that our hunch that we felt like commentary was important. Both she and I devote far too much time to it. I haven't gotten any better. I get more efficient, but I'm slower. So it hasn't been a time-saver at all. It's still a hugely time-consuming process, but you're hoping that it makes a difference and our study suggested that it does. When you engage in it with this opportunity to discuss things with them on the page, that's what they're taking it as, that's what they want, that is how they are maturing . . . I think back to very early in my career teaching, I implemented portfolios, that's something I even did in grad school. I loved that idea of just having them revise and make some choices. What I remember is I would look at portfolios and all this stuff that I remembered had so much potential, and then I'd look at it and I'd be like so disappointed because it didn't live up to this potential that I had in my mind.

I think the study really brought home that 1) I'm taking ownership of their paper when I'm doing that, I'm imagining what it can be, and 2) I wasn't always being fair because I had imagined what their paper could be and it wasn't that they weren't passing, it was still satisfied, still credit . . . it was just like, it's not as good as I thought it could be. Like they were making changes. I'm just not seeing them because they weren't the changes that I was telling them to make necessarily, or they weren't changing in the way I thought they should change. So it's humbling and it's good. Then, to really think that the point is not to create a great paper. That'd be great if we both agreed and we're both really thrilled and proud of this work. The point is to learn how to change your writing and to learn how to make decisions about it; to make those decisions and to have a reason why you made those decisions.

Shane to Carolyn Calhoon-Dillahunt: What excites you the most about teaching basic writing, or what do you enjoy about teaching that class? And why? [Episode 49: 09:38–12:26]

I love the students, first and foremost. I love them because more than any other group, I think they are there to transform their lives, whatever that means to them. They feel very invested and they feel very grateful for their education. That's easy to work with. And they're with you, right? So they're very engaged in learning. They're less kind of "point oriented." . . . so they want to learn and we can all focus on learning and the course outcomes.

My commentary is better in those classes because it does feel less pressured without a particular grade that I have to assign at the end. One-hundred percent of them could be satisfactory, I would love that, that would be my goal. It's not really a gatekeeping sort of class, but it is, it still does prevent them sometimes from moving onto college level, even though there's not a test or whatever that they have to pass at the end, but they seem really focused on learning. When students are focused on learning, that's where I'm the happiest, because that's kind of what I'm there for. We don't have to do all the, I call it "point grubbing," where we're kind of distracted from what we're really doing here because we're so concerned about what the final grade will look like.

There's just a lot of freedom and flexibility, too, in developmental writing courses. Our campus has a lot of freedom. We don't have a standardized curriculum at all, we just have standard outcomes. I think that works really well for who we are, predominantly full-time, which is rare at a two-year college. We have developed collaboratively our course outcomes so we all have a clear sense of what we're looking for. We've done a lot of assessment. Everyone feels pretty comfortable doing what works well for you as a teacher, where your strengths are as a teacher, where your interests are as a teacher.

DENOUEMENT

To me, basic writing programs and classes start with an awareness of the sociocultural conditions and realities of students. The history of basic writing is one of *access*. It seems to me that investigating the question of access and understanding how power and privilege circulates and is reinforced in academia and public spaces is central to any work related to these programs and courses. Basic writing programs and classes, then, should be attentive to their students. They should be asset-based and should reject deficit models. Basic writing should be approached through potentiality and opportunity, not through limitations and needs. And ultimately, they should value linguistic diversity, social justice, and multiliteracies.

Most writing program administrators and teachers are aware of the larger cultural issues (e.g., racism, classism) that influence teaching basic writing. These biases have been reinforced through program practices, such as placement tests and standards that disproportionately affect students of color. As basic writing scholarship moves forward, administrators and teachers have to listen to students and reaffirm their literacies and languages. Some administrators might need to consider renaming their basic writing programs and classes given the negative perceptions and associations with the words *basic* and *developmental writing*. Tom Fox (1990) says that programs "have been limited by narrow definitions that misrepresent the languages and communities of their students" (p. 65). Composition studies and writing programs might need to further interrogate the labels used and assigned to classes and students.

For more research on basic writing theory and praxis, I recommend George Otte and Rebecca Williams Mlynarczyk's (2010) reference guide to basic writing titled *Basic Writing*, Susan Naomi Bernstein's (2013) *Teaching Developmental Writing* (4th ed.), Bruce Horner and Min-Zhan Lu's (1999) *Representing the "Other": Basic Writers and the Teaching of Basic Writing*, and the *Journal of Basic Writing* (JBW), as well as the *Basic Writing e-Journal* (BWe). I also offer the following questions to help guide more conversations on basic writing programs and classes:

- How are programs and classes supporting the needs of diverse student populations who have been and continue to be marginalized?
- What classroom strategies and practices are being used to value sociocultural, sociolinguistic, and socioeconomic diversity? Through what pedagogies, assignments, and assessments? And how are teachers providing feedback in ways that support students' language practices and differences?
- How are program administrators advocating for basic writing students through placement procedures, class sizes, and credit-bearing statuses?
- How are programs helping students transition into basic writing classes? And how are programs talking about and labelling these classes and what affects might that have?
- How are graduate programs preparing and developing instructors to teach basic writing? What basic writing studies research and theories are being amplified in graduate composition seminars and pedagogy courses?

12

Second-Language Writing

Second-language writers, often stylized as L2 writers, are a part of nearly every writing program across institutional contexts (e.g., two-year colleges, four-year universities) and "should be recognized as an integral part of writing courses and programs" (National Council of Teachers of English, 2020b, Part 1, para 4). Some colleges and universities have specific programs and classes informed by linguistic theories and second-language writing pedagogies dedicated to L2 writers. Second-language writing teachers, scholars, and administrators recognize and value students' cultural knowledge and histories, and develop practices that account for the diverse needs of students. One aim is to integrate L2 perspectives into writing programs and courses. Those who teach L2 students are committed to normalizing multilingualism and resisting monolingual assumptions and biases: "Classes based on monolingual pedagogies disable students in contexts of linguistic pluralism . . . valuing students' own languages—in this case, nonprestige varieties of English—helps in the acquisition of other dialects, including the socially valued dominant varieties" (Canagarajah, 2006, p. 592).

Second-language writing is connected to amplifying multilingualism and negotiating language differences. This requires an understanding of the language backgrounds of students within local contexts because L2 writers include "international visa students, refugees, and permanent residents as well as naturalized and native-born citizens of the United States and Canada" (National Council of Teachers of English, 2020b, Part 1, para. 3). Paul Kei Matsuda (2006) writes, "All composition teachers need to reimagine the composition classroom as the multilingual space that it is, where the presence of language difference is the default" (p. 649). This reorientation values multiliteracies. It is the responsibility of writing program administrators (WPAs) to support language diversity through program outcomes and classroom practices and assignments. This work is interdisciplinary and draws from sociolinguistics, applied linguistics, translingualism, and second-language writing theory and practice.

Establishing a writing program that brings awareness and attention to multilingualism and resists monolingualism, the assumed "norm" of many programs and classes (Horner, Lu, & Matsuda, 2010), requires curriculum that values language differences and problematizes monolingual English ideologies. And it requires creating policies and assignments that meet the needs of diverse students. This kind of shift in thinking and action has a complicated history in United States higher education. The influx of international students in US colleges in the nineteenth and twentieth centuries, for example, brought significant attention to issues around language preparation. In the late nineteenth century, most universities believed it was the responsibility of international students and sponsoring governments to prepare them for the linguistic differences: "US colleges and universities usually provided little or no institutional support for international students' cultural and linguistic adjustments" (Matsuda, 2006, p. 644).

Colleges and universities struggled to identify solutions and build sustainable structures that would help support L2 learners. Meanwhile, second-language programs doubled in size from 1953 to 1969 (Allen, 1973). Traditional approaches to teaching, assessing, and responding to language differences in writing were informed by a deficit model that assumed language differences were "bad" and that "error" in writing needed "to be fixed." Standard Edited American English (SEAE) was considered "right" and "correct." These traditional approaches and attitudes on language and writing are exclusionary. L2 writers were perceived as "outsiders" that needed to adapt to *standardized English*. This came across in classroom practices that focused on grammatical rules, which of course, reinforces privilege and reasserts power, further isolating L2 learners. Likewise, program assessment placement methods kept second-language writers from "mainstream" composition classes. These issues, alongside others like the English-only movement and the myth of linguistic homogeneity, or "the assumption that college students are by default native speakers of a privileged variety of English," continue to exist in twentieth century writing programs and classes (Matsuda, 2006, p. 641).

Here it should be noted that conversations concerning language differences are debated in second-language writing theory and practice, too. Most prominent now are conversations on the relationship between second-language writing and translingualism. In 2011, Bruce Horner, Min-Zhan Lu, Jacqueline Jones Royster, and John Trimbur suggest taking a translingual approach to language differences. A translingual approach honors all language users, recognizes language difference as a resource, views language differences as fluid, and confronts monolingual English assumptions and language practices more generally. Others have expanded on translingual approaches to writing instruction (Canagarajah, 2013). Meanwhile, some second-language teacher-scholars have urged writing studies not to conflate L2 writing and translingual approaches, and to recognize L2 writing as "its own field while acknowledging that it shares certain common foci with translingual writing" (Atkinson et al., 2015, p. 385). These teacher-scholars have stressed the distinctions between "translingualism and the field of second-language writing" and have noted how second-language writing has taken up the task to help L2 writers "develop and use their multiple language resources to serve their own purposes" (Atkinson et al., 2015, p. 384–385).

Not to be lost within these debates is a commitment to multilingual students. Second-language writing practice and theory is dedicated to helping writing programs and classes value multilingualism and to tap into the knowledge and experiences of L2 writers. Second-language writing theory and praxis has been influential in helping composition studies at large critically examine pedagogies and reconsider how to best serve students from varying sociocultural contexts and backgrounds.

INTERVIEWS

I had the opportunity to talk to some of the leading second-language writing scholars in the field: Paul Kei Matsuda, Suresh Canagarajah, Todd Ruecker, and Eunjeong Lee. The throughline in these interviews is their commitment to helping program administrators and instructors serve L2 writers. Matsuda provides a history of the emergence of second-language writing programs in the US, and he talks about mentoring writing teachers and preparing them for teaching L2 students. Canagarajah discusses current issues in second-language writing scholarship, and he shares how he creates a class where "multiple languages and cultures can thrive" and how he uses literacy autobiographies so that students can explore their histories with language and culture. Ruecker describes larger issues that writing programs face, such as budget allocations and placement methods, that often affect their ability to support L2 speakers and writers. He also reflects on meeting the diverse needs of students and negotiating language differences in the writing classroom. Lee concludes by offering her critical approach to language and literacy studies and how her pedagogy helps generate conversations on language differences.

Shane to Paul Kei Matsuda: You're the Director of Second-Language Writing at Arizona State University. How have second-language writing programs developed in the US, and what are some typical configurations and models of second-language writing programs? [Episode 61: 01:25–05:18]

> In the North American higher educational context, second-language writing programs, typically, are attached to or are parallel to first-year composition courses across the country. These days the goals and objectives tend to follow the WPA Outcome statement, which is the foundational document for our program. We have an adapted version of the outcomes statement, so there is an emphasis on writing skills, critical thinking, argument skills, and rhetorical awareness. Historically, L2 writing classes were created as a solution to a few international students who happened to be in first-year composition courses. The teachers of these courses didn't know what to do with this population so they segregated them. Sometimes they held students up to certain standards that were unreasonable.

> Sometimes they just let them pass. It was an administrative solution to the practical problem on the teacher's side.

Later these programs became a little more professional-ized. People who started teaching these students had some background in writing and some background in language teaching. The courses were reconceptualized to focus more on the students' needs and to provide the support that students need in order to cope with the challenges of academic writing, both in the first-year writing courses and beyond. There have been some unique proposals for different course designs and how to integrate or disintegrate "mainstream" writing students and second-language writing students.

The current trend is to mainstream students who want to be mainstreamed. But for students who feel uncomfortable being among native English speakers and who need additional language support to work with other students and instructors who are sympathetic to their unique needs and interests and experiences, separate sections of composition courses are being offered.

They are typically taught by experienced writing teachers who also have some background in language instruction and working with students from diverse backgrounds. A particular configuration where these programs are located is not so much a pedagogical or theoretical decision, but it's more of a logistic decision of where the expertise is. Sometimes, unfortunately, it's where the money is, so pragmatic and financial reasons. For institutions where there are separate and strong language programs outside of the English department or writing department, then you may find second-language writing programs that are located in a completely different department administered separately by a group of specialists. That degree of communication between writing programs and the "mainstream" writing programs and second-language programs also depends highly on . . . where they're located, how they are being administered by different people, and how they get along with each other or don't get along with each other.

Shane to Paul Kei Matsuda: What kinds of advice do you give or what assignments and assessments do you suggest instructors take up and implement in their second-language writing classes? [Episode 61: 06:53–10:53]

> Most of the teachers I work with come from different disciplinary backgrounds. Some of them are literature specialists. Some of them are creative writers. Some of them are applied linguists and TESOL specialists. Some of them are writing specialists. They all have their own biases and their own experience. I don't assume specialized knowledge of language teaching for first-year composition teachers who work with second-language writers, but I do expect them to have a broad understanding of the rhetorical situation, different genres, and also different contexts in which writing is being used and how it's perceived and how it's received.

> Awareness of the student population and a wider range of writing practices is essential. Sensitivity to language learning is also important. One of the things that I've observed over the years is that teachers, both first-language speakers and second-language speakers who tend to do really well in working with students, are not people who have certain types of expertise, but people who actually have experience as language learners. That really helps them put things into perspective as they try to work with second-language writers.

> In designing assignments, of course, being aware of cultural biases and some of the dominant assumptions, unspoken assumptions about literacy, about ways of arguing, about citation practices. These are also challenging for many teachers, so kind of breaking things down and explaining and raising the awareness of how little things like double spacing papers or using margins, not fully justified, but left justified, I mean, these little conventions. The idea that these little things that we take for granted are new to some students is an eye-opening experience for a lot of teachers. It's not one thing or a set of knowledge that teachers develop, but

it's repeated encounters with these little differences and new perspectives that are really important.

So expertise does play a role and people who have strong rhetorical backgrounds, they are good at articulating different aspects of rhetoric, persuasive appeals, and audience, and so forth, and people who are coming from language backgrounds are good at articulating and focusing on language issues. But people tend to overdo things and focus on what they're good at and what they're interested in and not have a balanced perspective in terms of what the students need overall. Even as we use the strengths that we bring to the table, I think it's important to take a step back and reassess what we don't know, and then start to feel comfortable addressing them. And also, remain uncomfortable. I think Chuck Schuster used to say this, in order to be a good teacher, you have to be comfortable not being fully comfortable. Paying attention to new things that we experience and trying to do our best in addressing them, knowing that there's always a better way to do the same thing. That kind of sensibility is really important for professional development.

Shane to Paul Kei Matsuda: How do you think writing programs can better prepare future faculty for teaching second-language writers? [Episode 61: 11:06–13:09]

Exposing more teachers to the world of multilingual writing and second-language writing is a good first step. At ASU, I try to do this systematically. So during the first year, everyone teaches the "mainstream" sections of English 101 and 102, the first-year composition sequence. Then after that, they can develop additional expertise in professional writing, second-language writing and other types of writing. I'm in charge of providing professional development and mentoring to people who are interested in developing second-language writing expertise. After they have taught L2 writing classes, they are exposed to a wider range of issues, assumptions, and challenges, as well as strengths that they may have not seen in "mainstream" writing courses. They are better prepared to work with a wider range of diversity.

Another thing that I've observed over the years of professional teacher education work is that people who have taught L2 writing tend to be much better teachers of "mainstream" writing classes as well. Because they are ready to identify issues and questions and possibilities for learning in ways that are not often visible in more conventionalized stagnated contexts. As a program, my goal is to expose more teachers to this new type of perspective, new experience, and then bring them back to the "mainstream" writing courses, as well as L2 writing courses, so that eventually everyone will be ready to recognize and address specific needs and to tap into the specific strengths that students from multiple linguistic cultural backgrounds bring to the program as a whole.

Shane to Suresh Canagarajah: What are some current issues being addressed in second-language writing scholarship, or what kinds of conversations are ongoing about teaching second-language writers? [Episode 53: 01:19–07:05]

I think all of us in second-language writing initially started with the assumption that second-language writers are "new" to English and therefore we have to focus a lot on grammar and language norms. So actually there are some scholars, we are good friends, Vai Ramanathan and Dwight Atkinson, they wrote a paper in the early '90s titled "Cultures of Writing: An Ethnographic Comparison." They said in L1 classes, teachers focus on voice and critical thinking and identity. All those nice things. But in L2 classes, they were looking at two departments in the same university, they said in the department that teaches L2 writing, they focus only on grammar. Those teachers don't talk about voice and critical thinking because they think students still need to learn the grammar before they can engage with that.

I think a lot of changes, now, relate to going beyond just grammar. One of the first shifts that I wanted to mention to you is treating writing as *rhetorical*, even second-language writing as rhetorical. One of my good friends, Jay Jordan, has been writing a lot about that recently, why don't we teach second-language writing as just rhetoric than just making a grammatically perfect text? That's one of the major shifts—treating second-language writing as rhetorical. This also comes into issues of the voice of a multilingual writer, identity, and even creativity. I guess earlier we were very "norm" driven. We were very concerned about getting the writers to learn the "academic" norms and "grammatical" norms. Second-language writing as rhetorical is kind of thinking more about where can students appropriate the grammar or use English for their own voices and identities in more creative ways.

The second shift, also moving away from language and grammar, is multimodality. We are saying writing involves a lot of other resources. Even in academic writing, we haven't really been sensitive to things like space, paragraph divisions, font. Writing as a practice involves technology, board processing systems, computers, but even more broadly academic writing draws from conversations we have. Students have social media posts. If I use multimodality in a broad sense to include all these practices—communicative practices that lead to the final text—a lot of us are now working on how all these other multimodal resources help writing. That's the second shift.

A third shift deriving from all of that is "translingualism." That is, how do students go beyond the grammar of one language in their writing? This gets people scared because they would say, "Well, English writing is English writing. You'll get punished if you bring a little bit of Chinese or a little bit of Arabic into your writing." That's true, but to begin with in the process of writing as people construct the text, we don't know what's going through their mind. They might be multitasking in multiple languages as they create the text. They might be writing a first draft in Arabic just to get the ideas going. They might try to outline in Arabic and then write the final draft. I think there's nothing to worry about . . . students are not going to suffer if we allow all the other languages to be part of the writing process.

My funny way of putting it to a lot of my students is to say, translanguaging might actually help your students write a more perfectly grammatical English essay. It's a paradox, but I think it's true in the sense that if somebody is just shuttling between different languages, they also develop a keen awareness of English grammar . . . I'm a secondary speaker, I use Tamil all the time. I'm always thinking to myself, "Why do we say this in English *this* way? When we say that in Tamil in *that* way?" I tell my students I'm always learning because I'm a multilingual. I'm always asking questions about languages and hopefully it's leading to a better appreciation of both grammars.

I think there's a fear from teachers that allowing multiple languages into the writing classroom or writing might affect the proficiency of English writing. I actually like to put it in a very paradoxical way: Students can actually improve the proficiency because moving between languages can create a better metalinguistic awareness to rise above both grammars.

Shane to Suresh Canagarajah: What are some resources that you would recommend teachers consider when teaching second-language writers? What advantages and affordances do they provide teachers and students? [Episode 53: 21:08–26:25]

Let me start with explanation because I guess the resources and affordances won't make sense without some justification. I'm coming from my background in social linguistics and migration studies and things like that. I feel that teaching has become more challenging for us because we are always confronted by new situations, new genres, and new interlocutors and audiences. Our texts travel to so many places. So teaching in a "product-oriented" way, that's a very familiar term for all of us, and also "teacher-fronted" way, that is, me taking the authority and telling the students these are the norms you need to learn, or this is the genre convention, and if you just learn the genre convention you are going to be fine, is not going to help. Students are always going to be confronted with new situations.

What I like to do in my classes is treat the classroom as a contact zone, like Mary Louise Pratt used in 1991. A class is a safe space where multiple cultures and multiple languages can collide. This is embodied by the students we have. Make all that diversity shine through. I'm kind of smiling to myself because a lot of people sometimes say, "How do you introduce diversity in your writing?" I say, "I just provide a space for it so that it comes out and I invite it rather than just teach it."

I create a classroom where, as a contact zone, multiple languages and cultures can thrive. Or another term that I've used in some places is the learning environment as "ecological." Ecological meaning all the resources in the classroom setting would become functional and influential and generative because every classroom has a lot of resources . . . I don't give texts that are only translingual. Sometimes I use my readings, but I also pair it with other second-language writers who would make a case for "norms" in writing. I want students to kind of work between these positions to see how would you formulate your own texts in the context of these persons? An ecological learning environment would be to draw from the affordances, try different kinds of texts, different kinds of technologies.

Shane to Suresh Canagarajah: Your pedagogy features the writing of literacy autobiographies. What value do you see in this genre for multilingual students? [Episode 53: 13:34–16:33]

So this comes from Vygotsky's idea that engaging with an activity by using certain tools helps you develop your identity, internalize your learning. Learning always is in the context of activity and tools. We think of writing a narrative as a tool, as an activity that mediates your development or identity in your learning of language . . . I've been teaching a class called "Teaching Second-Language Writing." It's for training future teachers who are becoming teachers of writing. It's a mix of undergraduates and early graduate students. I told them we are going to do a lot of the readings . . . and I use a lot of scholars from second-language writing like Dana Ferris who has a wonderful handbook for composition and for teaching composition. I use that. Also, Christine Pearson Casanave who is a second-language scholar. On top of the readings, I said, you will write your own literacy autobiography throughout the 15 weeks starting from a basic outline. You'll *negotiate*, that is, as you post your drafts, we will talk about it as a class to see how to improve it.

A lot of different things are happening. One is, they are engaging with their reading from the point of view of their own identities and their own backgrounds. Secondly, because it's kind of developed through the whole semester, they are also practicing what they should be teaching, which is draft several drafts and outlines and get feedback, including my feedback. I'm sure you could do it with any genre, all these things, even with expository writing, but with the literacy autobiography what I saw was that it's personal. It gives you a space to think about your own learning and your own background, all the languages that you speak, or the learning that you did. I tell my students, you are also assessing your own learning of writing so when you are future teachers, you can learn what didn't work and what did work. It's an important lesson for you also to kind of think critically about your own learning of writing. Maybe if I put it in one word, it's a very *performative* genre.

Shane to Todd Ruecker: What are some challenges that writing programs face in serving second-language writers, and what are some policies, practices, or procedures that can help overcome those challenges? [Episode 57: 01:14–04:40]

One of the first things that comes up is placing students and identifying students. There's been a fair amount of work on . . . the labels students use to identify themselves is pretty complex. I think back to Ortmeier-Hooper's piece in 2008 that's been pretty influential in the field. I've done some work on that. There's been some additional work in the *Journal of Second Language Writing*. Some students identify with the "ESL" label or the "non-native speaker" label, but then other students find that pretty problematic. Like we have a lot of students who grew up in the US speaking multiple languages and don't fit neatly in any one category but might be served well by a teacher who has training to better support their language needs along with their writing needs. So kind of figuring out how to get those students in the best classes for their needs. That kind of trickles into how we label the classes themselves, then what kind of placement mechanisms we use.

Another challenge that comes up is just finding qualified instructors and teachers to work with second-language writers. At the University of Nevada, Reno, it's been traditionally run and taught out of that intensive English program and they always haven't had the funding they've needed to support and pay full-time instructors. It's often taught by part-time, adjunct labor. By the nature of the exploitation of those positions, [teachers might be] distracted teaching other classes, they might not have the second-language writing expertise that we need to better serve these students.

Just in general, ideally, and various people have written about this, instructors of second-language writers should have experience and training in TESOL and applied linguistics and writing studies. Often we find that people have one or the other expertise.

So if they're just within TESOL, they don't necessarily know how to teach a writing class and provide students with that metaknowledge about writing and the writing process in order to transfer that knowledge into other classes that we find so common and prevalent in terms of writing instruction today. Or an understanding of genre theories as well, for instance. On the other hand, within "mainstream" composition programs, there's just not adequate training. I know there's been a lot of work on translingualism and everything, and there's a lot there about recognizing and valuing language diversity, but then sometimes it feels very theoretically focused and idealistic to some extent. So people aren't getting training and helping them progress in terms of their linguistic needs.

There's few programs who can prepare people within that. Like ASU is one, obviously with people like Paul and the established second-language writing program. They have dedicated second-language writing graduate seminars there. A lot of places don't have that. So people are kind of left to get that expertise through conferences, through reading and other means, or maybe the occasional faculty member they can work with on their thesis or dissertation.

Shane to Todd Ruecker: So you're talking about meeting the linguistic needs of students. I was hoping maybe you could talk more about what those linguistic needs are? [Episode 57: 04:41–07:27]

Our students end up being really diverse . . . you might have international students who've gotten a lot of formal training in the linguistic aspects of English so they can articulate grammar rules and things like that, while you have students growing up in the US who just kind of grew up in an underfunded school system and haven't had necessarily adequate support in any of the languages that they speak. They just kind of have an intuitive knowledge of the language and might be very fluent in spoken English, but then haven't had the training and support in written English, for instance. I think having people who understand the differences between the students and how to scaffold assignments to make sure people feel like they have the support and the time needed to succeed alongside all the other students.

Then, also providing language feedback. People like Dana Ferris have written a lot about how to provide feedback in a way that's useful and meaningful for students. Like I've seen instructors on different extremes. Some mark every error on a paper, and we know that that's not helpful or accurate for students. It just kind of overwhelms and demoralizes and they don't learn much from that. On the other hand, we have people who resist any kind of correction and teaching of this "standardized," privileged variety of English. I think that does students a disservice. They just don't have the knowledge to help the students see what's wrong with the sentence. They'll give advice like, "Oh, just read your paper out loud. You'll notice awkward spots." Some students don't necessarily have that intuitive knowledge where they can read their paper out loud and notice those spots.

Being able to identify things like . . . again, this is what Ferris has talked about, like those rule-governed errors and non-rule-governed. Like treatable and non-treatable, I think she called it, where some of it just take a long time. Like articles, they're going to take a long time. Don't spend a ton of time trying to focus a student learning articles unless they're really advanced. But things like verb tenses and the way sentences are structured, things like that can be pretty rule driven. If someone has the knowledge to explain that to students, then students can pick that up more easily.

Shane to Todd Ruecker: How do you negotiate language differences? What practices do you use as a teacher to help you negotiate linguistic varieties and differences in writing classrooms? [Episode 57: 18:46–24:02]

I'm proud to be trilingual, having learned different languages. I try to make that clear with my students and recognize that that's valuable. I also acknowledge that me being bilingual or trilingual has different connotations in the larger society than an immigrant, because for an immigrant it's often portrayed as a deficit. I think it's important that writing teachers take the time to learn other languages so they know . . . I guess teachers who have second-language writers, so they know kind of what their students are going through and how hard it is. Like even though I speak these other languages, I'm hard pressed to write in Spanish at a college level. Definitely not in Czech . . . I think it's important that we have that firsthand experience of learning other languages and especially writing in other languages so we can kind of understand what our students themselves go through.

I'm also conscious of positioning different languages and language diversity as an *asset* in the language I use in the classroom and assignment design. I'll use the term "second-language writer" in scholarship. I coedit the *Journal of Second Language Writing.* I use it in context like that, but in my classroom I talk about bilingual, multilingual and kind of lean towards that kind of labeling in classes. So any kind of student-facing language, making sure we're using as asset-based language as possible. When we're doing the research paper, I'll add a line in my assignment or say in class, "For those of you who are bilingual or trilingual, you're welcome to bring in texts in other languages. Like you have an asset. You have access to more information because of that." I'll work in language like that in my assignments as well.

One question that comes up then, like, if I invite students to analyze other texts, bring in other texts, "What do I do if I don't speak those languages?" The biggest thing, to some extent I try to just trust students and then also kind of draw on, where needed, maybe translation tools to help them. Like, even though it's not perfect, things like Google Translate have come a long way. Kind of alongside that, we talk about footnoting and the politics of footnoting. Like I always push for them to have the original language in the text rather than just give me a translation. And then, footnote the English translation. Like I do want the translation, for me and for the other students peer reviewing, but I always try to relegate that more to a footnote or at least below the original language in texts, if they want to do that. That's something I try to carry through in my scholarship as well . . .

I have some reservations about the fully translingual approach. I think a lot of students coming out of writing graduate programs, composition graduate programs don't necessarily have the expertise to work and serve second-language writers fully. So just reading translingual scholarship, which I think is important and I think it does a lot of good, isn't providing the level of expertise needed. I think you need to also draw on some of the scholarship by people like Dana Ferris and Paul Kei Matsuda, for instance. I co-authored a chapter with Shawna Shapiro on this recently, and it's in a collection edited by Tony Silva and Zhaozhe Wang. It brought in a number of second-language writing and translingual scholars to kind of explore the divides and try to look for some reconciliation.

. . . I'll always be positioning language diversity as an asset. I'm also still teaching and prioritizing to some extent the acquisition of this kind of privileged variety of English because I think that's what students are coming to us wanting. When they get beyond our classroom, they're going to be judged based on that in their math classes and their engineering classes, their science classes, and when they're applying for jobs as well. I do provide that . . . I don't fully subscribe to the approach that we can't teach some standards. Alongside that, I have discussions with students about how standards have come into play and how language variety of some are privileged over others.

Shane to Eunjeong Lee: Your teaching and research embraces a critical approach to language and literacy studies. Do you mind talking more about what this critical approach to language looks like and how this approach applies to teaching second-language writing? [Episode 42: 01:32–04:39]

I think for me, a critical approach to language and literacy studies is centering the issue of power and ideology and

how that's intersected and more specifically going to reproduce through structure. So these are also tied to the social
ecologies and inequalities and inequity, right? And kind of
the role that language specifically plays in them. The basic
idea to me is always to reveal that our language and literacy
use or practice or evaluation is not neutral and it reflects
and reproduces the power difference in differential social
categories, whatever that may be.

Particularly for teaching second-language writing, broadly
speaking, my understanding of second-language writing
and who is often discussed . . . it is many writers who have
different relationships or form different relationships with
English in different ways. I'm specifically talking about English because that's my focus in terms of second-language
writing. These writers often are positioned under different
oppressive systems that focus on monolingual ideology and
operates along other ideologies like standard language ideology, racial linguistic ideology, and . . . you know, Asao Inoue
most recently has termed this as "White language supremacy." This works in many different ways, including how we
think about what "good" writing is and who can be a "good"
writer and who is considered as a "legitimate" writer.

Taking this approach in teaching second-language writing
is thinking along with our students—to be more sensitive
to this aspect of language use and be more mindful in their
performance or in their positionality as a writer in writing.

Shane to Eunjeong Lee: So you emphasize how language is connected to social systems and structures. In short, how language is
linked to power. You talk about how ideologies inform how language is perceived, and you value linguistic justice and language
equality. How do you frame these conversations in class? What
practices do you use to invite students to think through inequalities and inequities attached or associated with language? [Episode
42: 04:40–10:05]

I think the key thing is opening up a space or creating a space with students to talk about this. How these

ideologies work in different ways in real life and what experience and practices are out there. We ourselves actually go through that . . . one thing that critical approach has taught me is over the years, along with different frameworks, I think taking this approach meant foremost what experience and practice I am able to provide or rebuild together as a class, rather than focusing on what kind of form or final "product" they will be producing . . . I prioritize more experience and practice. How do I produce that? How do I provide that? Or how do we create that together? As a result, what will that byproduct or particular form of writing be, right?

That kind of connection between experience and embodiment and product has been core to me. More specifically, this allowed me to kind of think about the core principle of language and literacy learning. Which is, any good language or literacy learning has to be contextualized and embodied, right? It's not just learning skills. You are experiencing it. You have your form of sincere and genuine embodied relationship with the thing that you're learning.

. . . I focus on multilingualism and navigating multilingual realities in a context here in Queens. My students talk about different language ideologies that shaped the way we think about writing and how we understand and value different language and literacy in certain ways. A lot of my students . . . are transnationals in different ways and immigrants in different ways. They bring a lot of firsthand experience of inequalities and inequities they experienced through school or outside school. I try to get them to reflect on their experiences and be able to kind of articulate what it is that influenced their experiences and why they had to experience those moments both individually, but also kind of tied to the structure that thrust into their whole life experience, both here and also other parts of the world that they have ties to because these ideologies are not just in the US. Right? These ideologies are not unique to English only.

They first begin this conversation by looking inward, kind of telling the moments where they noticed these ideologies, how they impacted them. The first assignment, often times, is a literacy narrative. Then they continue this conversation by extending this with other community members. They interview them and they collect literacy artifacts from them. They do this empirical inquiry borrowing from ethnography methods. They look at the firsthand primary data and analyze them in class and write a report. So if I talk in terms of the genre, they write this kind of research paper, right? Then that evolving reflection oftentimes culminates in the form of multimodal remix project, where they kind of frame it as a response to everything that they have learned and share it with the public.

I think that's the sequence that I have built over the last two or three years. To start from within and really engage in reflective practice throughout the semester, but kind of expanding out so that they kind of start this conversation not just with themselves, but with others and ultimately . . . share something that they would like to say about that in a context bigger than the classroom, engaging in different languages and modalities.

DENOUEMENT

Second-language writing theory is designed to help administrators and teachers support the needs of multilingual students. There are several approaches to teaching L2 students that are informed by applied linguistics and rhetoric and composition. Writing program administrators ought to provide instructors with training and resources for best serving second-language learners. Teachers need to be aware of the linguistic and cultural backgrounds of students in order to ethically and responsibly teach writing effectively. This also means teachers need to listen to students and their histories with languages and literacies. Multilingual students have resources that native English language (L1) writers don't have. Teachers and program administrators, therefore, should promote the multilingual resources of L2 students and encourage them to see their backgrounds as an asset to composing. This also means, at least to me, that teachers and administrators need to confront larger systemic issues, such as the history of admission as an exclusive gatekeeping practice in colleges and the harm caused by policies and initiatives like the English-only movement.

I suggest the following resources for teachers and program administrators to consider as they develop practices and policies around multilingualism and cultural diversity: *Second-Language Writing in the Composition Classroom: A Critical Sourcebook* (Matsuda et al., 2006), *Practicing Theory in Second Language Writing* (Silva & Matsuda, 2010), *Teaching L2 Composition* (3rd ed.) (Ferris & Hedgcock, 2013), *Literacy as Translingual Practice* (Canagarajah, 2013), *Composition Forum's* special issue "Promoting Social Justice for Multilingual Writers on College Campuses" (Vol. 44, 2020), and the *Journal of Second Language Writing*. Likewise, I offer the following questions for additional conversations on second-language writing theory and practice:

- How are writing programs and classes valuing linguistic differences? How are they utilizing the unique resources that second-language writers have?
- How are writing programs supporting teachers of L2 students? Through what kinds of professional development and resources (e.g., scholarship, conferences)?
- How are programs and classes drawing on students' rich cultural and linguistic identities? How are they positioning multilingualism as an asset to the writing classroom?
- In what ways are writing classes confronting monolingual biases through policies and practices? How are programs working towards more inclusive strategies that help support second-language writers?
- How are assignments and assessments equitable for second-language learners? How are teachers negotiating language differences? How are teachers responding to L2 writing?

13

Writing Across the Curriculum

Writing across the curriculum (WAC) programs engage in the intellectual and social contexts of writing and are designed to help administrators, teachers, and students learn more about how writing works across contexts and within disciplines. WAC seeks to answer questions about how writing activities are constructed and how knowledge is produced and circulated within disciplinary environments. WAC extends well beyond first-year writing programs and English departments. In fact, these programs emerged in the 1970s with the first faculty seminar being held by Barbara Walvoord at Central College in 1969–1970. The growing popularity of the writing process movement and new composition theories (e.g., expressive, cognitive) helped propel the expansion of WAC programs across the United States in the 1970s and 1980s. Since its early beginnings, there's been a relatively stable mission: to develop writing initiatives and workshops that increase attention on teaching and assessing writing, and to bring faculty together to talk about how and what writing can do within disciplinary homes to support students.

WAC is local, interdisciplinary work often led by an English or rhetoric and composition teacher who wants to offer strategies for curriculum development and help faculty and students see the power of writing. Walvoord (1996) reflects on its history: "WAC, like any movement, was influenced by societal factors. It may be seen in part as a move by writing faculty to extend their power and influence, helped by wide-spread perception that student writing was inadequate" (p. 61). WAC ultimately provides a space for faculty across disciplines to share their concerns about student writing, writing activities, and writing assessments (e.g., rubrics). Moreover, WAC is an opportunity to educate faculty about best practices, as well as a chance to collaborate with other faculty. Walvoord writes, "Workshops were the backbone of the WAC movement, and they tended to generate high energy and enthusiasm" (1996, p. 63). Chris Thaiss and Tara Porter (2010) find in their national study of WAC programs that faculty development workshops and seminars "remain the staple activities of WAC programs" (p. 555).

In the 1970s and 1980s, it was important for WAC programs to establish an identity that moved beyond national conversations on literacy which focused primarily on "errors" and notions of "good" writing. WAC didn't fixate on errors and grammatical rules; instead, programs were dedicated to developing ways for teachers and students to *use writing*. WAC programs provided a space for conversations around disciplinary objectives and writing curriculum: "WAC would never have spread had its advocates had nothing more to offer fellow teachers than correction symbols, syntax rules, and pious lectures about the need for 'good' writing" (Thaiss, 1988, p. 92). WAC programs are still concerned with helping faculty navigate the kinds of assignments and genres that will effectively demonstrate the skills and knowledge faculty/programs/disciplines want students to practice and transfer from class to class. And now, over the last decade, teacher-scholars have encouraged administrators to pay more attention to students' racial and linguistic identities when building faculty workshops and seminars (Anson, 2012; Hendrickson & García de Müeller, 2016; Poe, 2013). Mya Poe (2013) writes, "Integrating race in WAC practice has the potential to address very real teaching problems that are experienced by teachers across the curriculum. For this reason, I believe it is essential that we ground discussions of race in local contexts and in ways that have specific meaning for teaching writing" (p. 11).

WAC ultimately generates conversations around writing and helps faculty use writing to develop thinking and knowledge. The most common approaches to WAC are *writing to learn* and *writing in the discipline*. Writing to learn assumes "writing is not only a way of showing what one has learned but is itself a mode of learning—that writing can be used as a tool for, as well as a test of, learning" (McLeod, 2000, p. 3). Writing in the disciplines focuses on disciplinary knowledge and conventions and the rhetorical and social nature of an academic community (e.g., engineering, biology). WAC directors often use these approaches to help faculty better understand how incorporating writing into their curriculum can help meet teaching goals and departmental aims while reaching their student populations. WAC programs obviously offer extraordinary benefits to colleges and universities, especially in the sense that they bring greater attention to writing and help support faculty and students.

That said, there are some common issues that surround WAC, such as where and how programs are situated within institutional contexts. Some programs are connected to English departments, some standalone, some are tied to writing centers, and some are attached to centers for faculty development or centers for teaching excellence. The spatial location of WAC programs can be logistically complex. Further, some WAC programs have a full-time director and assistant director whereas others are led by a faculty member in the English department. These different orientations affect what these programs can do and can be. For example, given these precarious elements, sources for funding and financial allocations or budgets that WAC programs have vary. Some programs rely on external grants, whereas others have a university budget. And then, of course, programs have to think about how to get faculty invested in writing curriculum and initiatives. WAC program administrators have to consider how to reach faculty and encourage them to participate in seminars. Some directors have to incentivize workshops, for example. Despite these nuances, the goal is to create a campus-wide culture centered on writing. The structure of how to best accomplish this aim relies on administrators, faculty, and students.

INTERVIEWS

In this chapter, I talk with Chris Thaiss, Chuck Bazerman, Alisa Russell, and Linda Adler-Kassner about the development of WAC programs and the importance of WAC efforts in helping establish a university culture that values writing. Thaiss reflects on the early beginnings of WAC, identifies key moments in its history, and emphasizes how WAC is really about learning: "When you talk about writing across the curriculum, you are largely talking about *learning*. You are talking about writing as a tool of learning." Additionally,

Bazerman and Russell talk about the importance of WAC programs to colleges and universities in helping bring awareness to how writing builds and circulates knowledge within disciplines. Russell adds that WAC "inherently brings this interdisciplinary view to writing and to scholarship," and she shares how campuses benefit from the collaborative nature of WAC. Adler-Kassner concludes by talking about her decades of experience in different program leadership roles and how programs like WAC can use assessment to better understand "disciplinary interests."

Shane to Chris Thaiss: How did you get into writing across the curriculum (WAC)? [Episode 44: 01:51–05:04]

> Well, it's a good story. I remember it very vividly because it was back in 1978, which is not long after I started at George Mason, which was in '76. I was an assistant professor. In '78, I turned 30. It was that long ago. We had a situation at the school where we were being criticized in the English Department for not being able to teach our students how to write. We had this cross-curriculum committee from the faculty senate that was saying, "Well, what are you going to do about it?" It was coincidental at that time that we were setting up the Northern Virginia Writing Project, the site of the National Writing Project. We were doing a tremendous amount of reading and working with teachers in terms of the new research on which a lot of it was on writing across the curriculum (WAC).
>
> We decided to set up a program that we called the Faculty Writing Program, which was actually student-centered but it was also faculty-centered. We brought in Janet Emig, who had recently written her groundbreaking article on "Writing as a Means of Learning," and Donald Murray and a whole bunch of other people. The next year, we brought in Elaine Maimon and her folks from Beaver College who were doing great work on that. What we really decided to do was use a WAC approach to this question of preparing students to write. It was great because we got a lot of faculty from different disciplines involved in this.

They could see how they could contribute to helping students develop as writers rather than just pointing fingers at the English department.

That's really how we got started. We were working, as well, with writing groups for the faculty. They were working on their own writing. It was a great sort of combination of things at that time. One thing I want to really stress there is that a lot of WAC in the '70s came as a result of a collaborative effort between the National Writing Project and universities. Almost all the people that you could name who were really getting into WAC at that time in the US were also involved with K–12 schools.

I have to say, I would love to see that come again because it was a great collaboration. It was wonderful, actually, to see the kinds of cross-fertilization that would go on from environment to environment. That's really how I got started in WAC. Then, two years later, because we were working through the National Writing Project, which was already a national organization, I was able to start the WAC network for Conference on College Composition and Communication and NCTE.

Shane to Chris Thaiss: What would you identify as critical moments in WAC history, and what issues or questions were most significant to its development? [Episode 44: 05:05–09:46]

A lot of the questions that were significant then are still significant. When you're working with faculty and trying to develop policies and programs in schools, faculty . . . if they're interested in student writing and student learning through writing, they always have the questions about, "How do I find the time to do this? How can I add this to my curriculum?" Those are still questions that are make or break questions for whether WAC is going to work in a particular environment and whether there's going to be enough support for it as well. Those kinds of questions and those kinds of issues were really important then. They're really important now.

Of course, the difference between then and now is that virtually everybody, regardless of faculty, has heard of this thing called writing across the curriculum. A lot of people have had experience with it in graduate school or in universities that they might've been a part of. Then, it was brand new; it was a slightly different situation. Looking at landmarks and important things, I think the research that was going on in the '70s and then into the '80s was really important in providing a kind of a foundation or framework. A lot of different models for how you could do WAC at institutions. The British Schools Council Research from the '60s into the '70s with James Britton, Nancy Martin, a lot of other folks, was really important in creating a kind of theoretical framework. When you talk about writing across the curriculum, you are largely talking about *learning*. You are talking about writing as a tool of learning.

Sometimes we miss that in setting up WAC programs because, too often, what will happen is that a WAC program will develop as more or less sort of a continuation of a first-year writing course. That's not what it means. It means something very different from that. It is really focused in disciplines and focused in courses and teachers . . . some other landmarks that were really important at the time . . . the collaboration between the National Writing Project and the sort of nascent WAC movement in universities.

Also, writing and publication by certain people who were associated with both of those things are really important in creating that framework. I mentioned Janet Emig. I mentioned Elaine Maimon. Barbara Walvoord was an extremely important person early on and continues to be. Toby Fulwiler and Art Young, who at that time were both at Michigan Tech. Susan McLeod and Margot Soven and the kinds of works and edited publications that they've done over the years. Certainly the books by David Russell, the two volumes of the history of *Writing in the Academic Disciplines*. Those are very important things in creating a substance for the movement.

The WAC conferences that started in 1993 in South Carolina with Art Young and a number of other people in that region that then became this bi-yearly event that brought people together. Then in 2005, it became an International Writing Across the Curriculum (IWAC) Conference. I've got a couple others I want to mention . . . Mike Palmquist starting the WAC Clearinghouse. The WAC Clearinghouse has been extremely important. That's been over 20 years ago now. I'll also mention . . . in the past 15 years, there has been a lot of emergence of international and transnational and translingual research. That's going to become more and more important as time goes on. Then, the last thing I want to mention as sort of a landmark is the founding of the Association for Writing Across the Curriculum two years ago. That's going to be really important moving forward.

Shane to Chris Thaiss: What would you say to someone who might ask, "Why is writing across the curriculum important?" [Episode 44: 16:52–20:13]

This is a kind of question that actually I have been answering for more than 40 years. At George Mason, it was a question that arose all the time. At Davis, it's a question that arises. What happens is that sometimes one of the reasons why people will ask that question is because in some way, they've gotten the wrong idea of what writing across the curriculum is. There's sort of a natural assumption by academics who are not within writing studies or in English departments to think that writing across the curriculum— what we mean by that is, that a teacher in chemistry or a teacher in political science actually has to become a writing teacher or an English teacher. Well, that's never been what it means.

My attitude has been over the years to treat my role as not as a sort of a messianic person getting out there saying, "Oh, here are the wonders of writing," but actually . . . I learned this from Barbara Walvoord, one of my mentors. She said many years ago that when you do work in WAC, what you really are doing is research. When you have conversations with people and they ask you this question . . . I like to shift the burden . . . I want to learn from them. I want to ask them, "Well, as a teacher, what are the things that you do as a teacher that you think work? What are the things that you do that helps students to learn?"

. . . they'll say, "I can tell students are learning by the degree to which they're engaged in their learning" . . . then, I ask them to talk about engagement and what processes they have in their teaching that gets students engaged. They always involve some kind of dialogue; some kind of conversation; some type of opportunity for students to demonstrate their curiosity and interest in learning . . . so the question tends to answer itself.

Shane to Chuck Bazerman: How did you get into WAC? And what do you think WAC's mission is at colleges and universities? [Episode 13: 16:03–20:51]

I have never been a director of a WAC/WID program. In fact, none of the campuses I've been at has there been a successful WAC/WID program. I'm not the practice guy. I'm not the administrator. So it's kind of odd that I have become so engaged in it and in some ways I'm considered an expert in that area . . . it seemed to me that from the beginning that WAC needed to approach each of the disciplines with a great deal of respect and understanding. I think it took the field, as a whole, a while to get there because at first, they were very much taken with the practices they developed. Writing programs have been by and large the pedagogical innovators for the universities since the 1950s or '60s with things like writing centers, collaborative pedagogies, learning centers, importance of communication with students, even the question of writing as inquiry-based education.

Another thing I want to mention about writing across the curriculum . . . is the formation of knowledge and how people get knowledge. How does that enter into how they think and how they communicate and the bonds and commitments they make through writing? Where does that knowledge come from? As human beings, we're not computers on desks. We're not brains in a bottle. We have eyes and ears, and we walk around, and we touch things, and we get to know the world, and we try to make sense of it and bring it in.

Research methods is one of the main ways that knowledge of the world gets into texts and therefore enters into activity systems. There are related ways, like intertextuality is when knowledge from one system gets into another, but if texts are the place we communicate and we think through things, we analyze them and we make proposals out of them and we make plans and situations, it's important we get knowledge into them. And that the ways of getting our data about the word gets formulated into useful knowledge. That, to me, is of paramount importance.

. . . I think this is of paramount importance in the academic disciplines. Research communities have been one of the tremendous changes that have allowed us to think differently and gather knowledge and deal with our world in a more intelligent, sensitive, aware way. That's why writing across the curriculum is really important.

Shane to Alisa Russell: What excites you about the possibilities within WAC programs? [Episode 59: 01:20–05:18]

When I was a graduate research assistant for the WAC program at George Mason doing my master's, we did this huge assessment project of all the writing-intensive courses. That was a foundational project for me because what I got to do was interview a bunch of faculty across the disciplines. I think a lot of times, really all disciplines maybe, you get very siloed. It's very rare that you get to, especially as a grad student, talk to so many faculty all over the university. I got to talk to them about what challenges their student writers face and what challenges they face in integrating writing into their classrooms and teaching writing. I realized quickly, all faculty that I talk to value writing. They see how important it is. They see how much their student writers need it to be able to be part of the discipline and know in the discipline and do in the discipline. They want this. They want their student writers to succeed.

. . . I think one of the other things that's so important about WAC is that it inherently brings this interdisciplinary view to writing and to scholarship and an awareness of other disciplines. It lets you see how rhetoric and the work of the humanities is in all disciplines. I once taught a writing for engineers course. I had fourteen petroleum and chemical engineers in this course. They were forced to take it. They didn't really want to take it, but they were shocked when we started. I started piling them with all of these texts that engineers write all the time for lots of different audiences, for other engineers, for clients. They write standards. They write instructions. They have to make websites when there's a big public works project. They have to do all of these things and have all this rhetorical flexibility. You can know the engineering all day long, but unless you're able to then put it into a communicative form—write it up in a way that makes sense—it doesn't work.

WAC helps bridge that divide, I think, between the sciences and the humanities and shows that it's all implicated in one another. It's really fun to be in that position as a WAC administrator or as a WAC scholar where you get to see all those connections between disciplines and be in that interdisciplinary space.

Shane to Alisa Russell: How do you think WAC contributes to institutions and affects university campuses? [Episode 59: 05:19–08:06]

It's a culture of writing. Because WAC sees writing as, it's not just part of the English department, it's all the disciplines. This is how every discipline creates what they do and solidifies how they do their work. You end up with this wider understanding on a campus of how writing is situated, how it's a non-generalizable skill. It's an area of expertise. It takes time to study it and learn it and figure out how to teach it and how to develop. That's always a big plus when other disciplines see the validity of rhet/comp and of writing studies . . . you're helping foster this wider culture of writing on campus.

Because a lot of my other research focuses on the relationship between writing and access and how writing shapes access to different actions or settings or communities, I've been thinking a lot about social justice movements in writing studies and rhet/comp and what that looks like, you know, identity and difference in writing, alternative assessment practices, all these things. WAC, to me, is an inherently socially just practice. I'm not saying that it doesn't need renewed attention and critique and that there are a lot of things we could be doing to increase the way it contributes to social justice initiatives.

When we treat writing like it's a one-and-done skill, like you can just learn it in first-year comp and then . . . automatically you can do it in any discipline, what happens is those who already have some writing knowledge for different disciplines end up succeeding because of their experiences or backgrounds. While maybe those who don't, who are further away from those discourses in different disciplines, can end up not succeeding when you're not teaching it, or making it a part of the instruction, or making it explicit.

WAC increases students' access to their disciplines. It increases their ability to engage with course content and increases their ability to contribute by making writing part of the conversation. That's a really exciting place to be: To think of WAC work as a social justice initiative in itself.

Shane to Alisa Russell: What are some challenges WAC programs face? [Episode 59: 08:07–13:12]

All the things that I just said that make it so exciting and valuable are also the things that make it so challenging. It's a total double-edged sword. WAC work does happen at the administrative and student levels. I think it's a Mike Palmquist piece where he has this great WAC model, where it's not just working with faculty, but it's also working at these different levels. Most models still happen at the faculty level, like faculty development, faculty workshops, working with faculty on their assignment prompts, on their course design, things like that. That's part of what makes it so fun is working with all these different faculty. But it's also a challenge because faculty are strapped. Faculty are busy. Faculty have a million things on their plates and learning new pedagogies and redesigning your courses or assignments is hard. It's time consuming.

It also needs to be a collaborative conversation. Not just me, "I'm the writing expert and I'm telling you what to do." But actually, "I know a lot about writing, but you're the one who knows about writing in your discipline, so we have to collaborate and work together." But that takes a lot of time. It takes a lot of buy-in . . . I mean, we're touching on a bigger conversation of incentivizing and paying people for professional development.

You need incentives, or a stipend to do a seminar series. Or you need a developed program and a range of curricular options that different faculty can plug into based on the time or expertise they already have. You need ongoing support. A one-time seminar or workshop is wonderful, but we all have that high of coming out of a workshop, "Oh, we're going to make all these changes." Then we try one thing and it fails. And we're like, "Well, maybe not." You need that ongoing support.

All of those things require a budget. They require buy-in from upper administration. One challenge is . . . convincing everyone that the time is worth it, and that this is a valuable practice and that this is somewhere we should put our money because this is really important. That can be a challenge that varies from institutional context. Another challenge that's related is finding how WAC fits into an institution, especially if it's like a program. I just said that it's inherently interdisciplinary. So where does it go? Is it a standalone program, like in the provost office? Is it part of the English department? Is it connected to the writing center? Is it a branch of the Center for Teaching Excellence? A lot of that gets decided for a variety of factors, usually outside of the director or whoever's part of the WAC program's control.

Then, it's about how to stay sustainable in whatever institutional space you're in. If you are part of an English department, that presents you new sets of challenges to show that this isn't just an English thing, that this is an interdisciplinary thing. Or if you're connected to the writing center, that presents challenges in you're not just here for students, this is the faculty branch. Then budget lines get really complicated. It's all about wherever you are institutionally. Some of the things like partnering with other projects, layering your mission into other campus initiatives, setting up structures, they're going to outlive any one director or board or whatever your leadership is. A lot of those sustainability issues become an issue depending on where you are in the institution.

Finally, as maybe anyone who studies writing knows, the successful teaching of writing and writing improvement is famously difficult to measure and assess. Because WAC is usually having to answer to upper administration, we're always facing that challenge of how do we prove the efficacy of WAC? How do we prove that this is working? Chris Anson actually has a really great piece about different assessment data that can be effective when combined in different ways. I think this is a challenge that all of rhet/comp faces. How do we assess? How do we measure writing progress?

Shane to Linda Adler-Kassner: Through all your leadership roles and experiences, including being an associate dean, the Director for the Center for Innovative Teaching, Research, and Learning, and a writing program administrator, what have you discovered to be the most productive approach to facilitating workshops and generating conversations about writing across disciplines and contexts? [Episode 54: 13:08–18:03]

> Starting at people's points of need. So people like to engage with things when they find it meaningful for them. I'm lucky to be at a place, UC Santa Barbara, where, we're a relatively recent minority-serving institution. Within the last six or seven years, our student population is really changing here in California. People are very interested in how they can best work with the students in their classrooms. That creates lots of questions and lots of willingness to engage with different kinds of ideas. For them and for me, too. I have learned so much as I've worked with faculty from across the university.

> When people recognize that writing doesn't need to be like writing a five-page paper, but writing can do lots of things for them and that it's super important, that's another really great way to engage . . . so we talk about inclusive practice being about facilitating access and opportunity. Access means making the knowledge-making practices of your discipline explicit and providing opportunity to practice with them. Opportunity means creating ways for people to bring their identities, knowledges, and experiences to your discipline in order to push on those knowledge-making practices so that they are representative of and include the ideas of others . . .

> When we think about access and opportunity, we then engage in thinking about four domains of knowledge-making. Disciplinary knowledge, so what are the knowledge-making practices of your discipline? Representational knowledge, what does it look like or when you show what writing looks like. Empathetic knowledge, how can you form and confirm knowledge with others, mostly your students, and how can you even learn about their identities, experiences, and knowledges? That's especially important if you're teaching a class of 400 students, "How are

you going to do that?" There are ways to do that. Then, learning knowledge, what do we know about learning and learners that can help you do this?

Everything that we do operates through the idea of inclusive teaching and thinking about access and opportunity, and then those intersecting knowledge domains and how we can think about what those are and how teaching functions through them . . . the only way that leadership works is when you do it with other people. Basically what I try to do is take the knowledge of our discipline, build on that knowledge from other places, listen really, really, really, really, really hard to people, try to work with them to put some language around the things that they do, use that language and that thinking to develop new things that can help them advance their goals and their ideas within the contexts of our institution and its goals and our students, et cetera.

I'm certainly not the first person to say this, but leadership really is this sort of multi-dialogic process of listening . . . it's so not a solo activity. It's one that requires, at least for me, constant evaluation and sort of reflexive metacognitive practice.

Shane to Linda Adler-Kassner: Since you work closely with assessment, can you suggest ways directors can assess their WAC programs or what questions might be significant in helping programs better understand their impact across campus? [Episode 54: 18:04–21:15]

I think the kinds of questions people need to ask about WAC, first, need to be aligned with the disciplinary interests. It's probably easier to start with what not to do, which is something like a value-added model. If students take course X, does that improve their performance in course Y? Well, unless you can control, and I mean in the research sense, a whole lot of variables, like how has the writing handled in course X and course Y? How much of the grade does writing account? Are the values aligned? Is the grading consistent? I think that's not necessarily a successful model.

What we can do is understand writers' experiences and their writing knowledge as they move from course to course. That is an easier thing to follow. Then you can ask writers to submit artifacts that they think reflect different elements of their writing knowledge or the direct evidence for any kind of assessment. So I think we need to think about what are we assessing, writing and/or writers? What are the key attributes that we associate with growth and knowledge development? And what kinds of artifacts can be associated with that?

Asking writers to be involved in that process is really important. At UCSB, we're in the last year of a longitudinal assessment of general education that follows a cohort of students through the GE program every year. It's been really interesting to see what happens through that. So we're following students, but we're looking at the program and artifacts that students submit. We're seeing why students are taking things in general education. We're seeing the kinds of things that they tend to say that they're asked to do in GE courses. What kinds of knowledge do students say they're being asked to produce? How is that aligned with the overall goals? We're seeing some really interesting patterns . . . one of the things that emerged was classes where students write, that fulfill our writing requirement, students and faculty were consistently rating the artifacts more highly.

DENOUEMENT

These interviews indicate how WAC programs, when supported, can cause a shift in attitude and culture on writing at colleges and universities. WAC program administrators are in positions to work collaboratively with faculty across disciplines and to implement writing initiatives to help facilitate teaching and learning goals. What stands out to me is the kind of grassroots nature of WAC. WAC listens to the needs of faculty and students, and WAC responds appropriately. WAC ultimately supports faculty and students by connecting writing to learning. I also think it's important to see how WAC can come alongside larger university missions and goals and can complement those aims through their efforts. WAC is in one of the best positions to champion change. They can be sites that cultivate relationships, and they can be mediators and facilitators of teaching and learning.

For additional readings on writing across the curriculum, I recommend *Sustainable WAC* (Cox et al., 2018), *Writing Across Contexts: Transfer, Composition, and Sites of Writing* (Yancey et al., 2014), *Reference Guide to Writing Across the Curriculum* (Bazerman, Little et al., 2005), *Landmark Essays on Writing Across the Curriculum* (Bazerman & Russell, 1995), and *Writing Across the Curriculum: A Guide to Developing Programs* (McLeod & Soven, 2000). I also think these questions can further generate conversations about WAC programs:

- What would it look like to construct a first-year writing class that uses a WAC approach to teaching and learning? What WAC research might help teachers since many first-year writing classes are interdisciplinary?
- What kinds of university writing initiatives and writing curriculum developments are already happening in the institution?
- How does the spatial location of the WAC program affect what it can/cannot do? What are the limitations and constraints? What are the strengths of its alignment? What collaborations can happen with other programs?
- As an administrator, how are you listening to different perspectives and experiences with writing, both of faculty and students? How are you responding to those perspectives? How are you meeting the needs of faculty and students across disciplines and providing resources to assist them? How are you increasing the visibility of the WAC program on campus? What workshops or seminars would be most useful in your current environment?

14

Writing Centers

Writing centers grew substantially in the 1960s and 1970s during the open admissions movement when universities were experiencing a major shift in student enrollment and demographics. Moreover, there were national conversations about literacy and higher education that led to structures like writing centers which were designed to support student writers and to be a resource for teachers. Writing centers are a space (e.g., lab, clinic) where students can receive writing instruction beyond first-year writing classes and English departments; they are sites that provide a wider range of assistance and offer individualized feedback on writing. Writing centers take different forms, but for the most part, they offer one-on-one writing consultations or tutoring for students (e.g., face-to-face, asynchronous). Some writing centers are tied to a single space on campus, whereas some writing centers offer multiple locations. Writing centers are usually staffed by undergraduate and/or graduate students. Some are staffed by English majors and are closely connected with English departments, whereas others are more interdisciplinary. Whatever the case may be, writing center directors usually offer training and development workshops for staff. Directors offer strategies that might help tutors navigate sessions, and they provide additional resources from writing studies scholarship to help professionalize tutors.

Writing centers are sites for conversations on writing. They are collaborative spaces intended to meet students in their writing process (e.g., brainstorming, drafting, revising). Writing centers are truly student-centered. Tutors can help students build confidence in their writing and offer encouragement throughout their writing process; conversations are often guided by a particular writing assignment or draft a student is working on. This dialogic relationship between tutor and student is unlike any other writing instruction on campus because it is focused on feedback. Grades are never assigned. Students' papers are never marked with a score or with percentages. Therefore, writing centers are unique spaces that offer strategies for writing and revision and are ideal for building knowledge about what writing is and can do. They provide a low-stakes environment that can shift students' attitudes about writing.

Additionally, they are great sites for negotiation. Tutors and students can develop a plan and attempt to prioritize what is most important given where the student is in the writing process. Sometimes this means addressing larger revisions, such as developing a new idea that takes the piece in a different direction. Other times, it means reconsidering the structure or organization of the writing. Sometimes it might be revising the thesis or rewriting the conclusion. Negotiation is key. Tutors have to listen and set aside their own assumptions and biases in order to really promote student agency. As Nancy M. Grimm (2009) reminds us, "Effective tutors learn to shift perspective, to question their assumptions, to seek alternative viewpoints. These competencies are essential for ethical work, and they are practiced daily in a writing center" (p. 21). Some writing center scholars have advocated for incorporating mindfulness and meditation practices and centering embodiment in writing centers (Godbee et al., 2015; Johnson, 2018; Mack & Hupp, 2017). One of the main goals in each session is for tutors to foster writing engagement and to encourage students to dive deeper into the writing process after their thirty minute or hour-long consultation. Writing centers materialize writing as a social activity.

Writing centers also face adversity. For example, some writing centers face institutional marginalization. That is, writing centers often have to position themselves as theoretically rich sites for research and practice. They aren't subordinate to other departments and programs. This narrative is even more difficult to overcome when writing centers don't have their own space, or when centers are fully dependent on English departments, or when centers don't have a sufficient budget to build something sustainable. Likewise, most writing centers have to challenge assumptions about what it is they actually do. They aren't places to go to "fix error" in writing. Given those misconceptions, writing centers have to bring awareness to their mission. And hopefully, that mission includes actively resisting colonial assumptions (Bawarshi & Pelkowski, 1999) and racist views on language (Young, 2010).

INTERVIEWS

In this chapter, I talk with Harry Denny, Frankie Condon, Karen Keaton Jackson, Neal Lerner, and Rebecca Nowacek about writing center theory and practice. They reflect on their experiences in writing centers and share strategies for writing center practice, such as building centers focused on social justice and helping professionally develop tutors to navigate conversations about writing with students. Denny addresses identity politics in one-on-one consultations and talks about important characteristics of a writing center tutor: "What makes really good qualities of tutors is, to me, always empathy." Condon talks about writing centers as sites for antiracism, and she describes what it means to co-labor with others to advance social justice aims. Jackson reflects on the role of writing centers at Historically Black Colleges and Universities (HBCUs), and she addresses the absence of HBCU perspectives in writing center scholarship. Lerner talks about constraints and challenges to writing center work and describes how he mentors peer tutors. And Nowacek concludes by sharing how writing centers are a "great site for research."

Shane to Harry Denny: Your book, *Facing the Center: Toward an Identity Politics of One-to-One Mentoring*, takes up issues of power, agency, and language. Can you talk about identity politics in the writing center, and how social and cultural factors impact interactions between tutors and students? [Episode 51: 01:02–05:46]

> So what got me thinking about that idea way back when was the whole notion that a lot of our literature talks about writers, particularly in writing center scholarship at the time, as though writers occupy this uniform, unified, cogent identity. Those of us who have taken any postmodern, post-critical, feminist, critical race, you name it kind of theory, immediately think about identity positions as always complicated and fluid. When a writer comes to the writing lab, they're not just coming with that signifier,

they're coming with all sorts of identities and baggage and concerns, but it's not just the writer that we interact with at the table, we also have tutors or writing consultants or writing fellows who don't suspend who they are when they come to a session.

So over the years where that's become really tangible is when writers come in or tutors encounter issues and topics that can be really controversial. Whether it's a student writing about affirmative action and depending on what their position is being counter or pro and being in conflict with whoever they're working with, or someone writing about reproductive issues and having conflict there. Every once in a while, I haven't had it so much in Purdue, but at previous institutions, writing consultants really being frustrated that students aren't working hard enough, and sort of suspending an awareness of their own privilege when it comes to the ability to focus on education.

At many of our institutions, we have lots of first-gen students for whom college is one of many things occupying their time . . . we have lots of students here at Purdue that work, maybe two, three, four jobs, between 30 and 50 hours a week to pay for school. So that impacts people's connections to how you learn and how you experience teaching and how you do teaching. I also think about sexual minorities. We are in an environment where it's more or less okay to say offensive things or be the object of offensive things. Tutors and students alike are constantly struggling with that. I think a lot of times the impulse is to create bubbles of same mindsets rather than figure out how do we have dialogue about rhetorical situations, about genres, about expectations, and all those sorts of things.

So when someone meets another writer at a table, if only we could suspend the world—it would be a wonderful place, but the writing lab or writing center or writing studio, anywhere in the country, whether urban, rural, North, South is going to have everything that's percolating in that very space. We can't suspend and make the writing center a vacuum. So real life issues are going on. I think of my former tutor, who's now on her way to Oklahoma, who talks about tutoring while Black. That when she enters a session, her race isn't suspended, it's obviously always legible. Versus someone like me who may or may not pass as gay or straight. I can invoke that; I can play with that in sessions. But how our identities are legible and read or not legible and not read impacts interaction in so many ways.

I wish we could suspend all of society and all culture when we're talking about writers, but you and I know enough about comp theory to also be aware that you can never do that. Why would we want to pretend as if society and culture and politics and economics stop at the door? Writing centers, just like regular classrooms, are spaces where all it has to be hashed out and thought about. It becomes really, really interesting and really powerful and magical and tragic, you name it. It's a great environment.

Shane to Harry Denny: So let's take everything you just said—complex identities surrounding cultural and social systems, politics, and the exchanges between tutors and students in the writing center—and let me ask this question: What are some of the most important qualities and characteristics of a writing center tutor? [Episode 51: 05:47–10:26]

> I have a whole laundry list. I think at the top of my list is the whole notion of empathy that you need as a tutor, or a client needs. I think both sides of the equation are critical here. But thinking about what makes really good qualities of tutors is, to me, always empathy. That's an X factor that's hard to cultivate in a tutor training class or a tutor education class, how do you have empathy? How do you have some baseline regard in valuing of the human with whom you're working?

> I'd add another quality as being open, being inquisitive, ask open-ended questions, and understand that you aren't the

smartest person at the table all the time. We have enough people in our world and in our politics who think that they're the smartest people in the room.

I cultivate among my crew to ask questions and not necessarily baiting or rhetorical or leading questions, but, "Huh, tell me more." When I work with faculty across campus, I'm amazed at how many people I win over just because, "Hey, tell me more. I don't know anything about this." I think that's a good quality that really helps us be open. Don't always morph into, "Let me crack open your head and pour in what you need to know," but how do we have a really good critical dialogue? Another thing I always tell tutors that I think is really critical is having a mindset of always being willing to *learn with* rather than *learn from*. Embedded in that, to me, is this whole notion of valuing mutuality: "I respect you and I want to learn with you. I am not top-down, but we are horizontal with one another," if that makes any sense.

. . . they can teach me about their field. They can teach me about how their field thinks and how they do inquiry. Yeah, there might be things that I can teach them about writing, but it's not one way, it's not linear, but it's dialogic. Then, I would add to that is the willingness to be improvisational. I'm always trying to teach my folks, don't turn every session into a robot, like I've figured it out, here's the recipe, here's the template. How do you morph from session to session? How do you read the person that you're with and think about what their needs are?

I often joke, one session I'm the goofy gay uncle, the next session I'm very serious, the next session I'm reserved. I'm always trying to riff off of who I'm working with. I think that's another really good quality. Then, the last thing that I think is a really good quality and it's another X factor is approach teaching and learning moments with good cheer. If you approach teaching and learning like, "Aargh, I'd rather be off doing something else, but, oh, I've got to do this." That sets a vibe. Who wants to work with Debbie Downer or the Womp-Womp queen? I want to work with someone who's fun.

I have all these tutors who, I don't know how they keep the energy throughout their shifts, but they go from student to student, faculty to faculty, excited and energized . . . it's refreshing and it's encouraging particularly at big institutions for clients to meet someone who actually cares about them.

Shane to Harry Denny: How do you foster community in the writing center? What are some practical strategies? [Episode 51: 21:20–27:05]

I've done this at every institution at which I've worked. I start off with asking the staff, "What does community mean to us? What metaphor is going to govern how we understand who we are and what we're about?" I'm often very worried about a writing center becoming a clubhouse of exclusion, of elitism, of whatever. I always want us to be really thoughtful and mindful about what community means, who is included, who is excluded, who do we see in our staff? You know enough about me to know that I care deeply about, who's in, who's out, and how do we get there? But I also think that when we build community, we're actually in effect building communities.

At a very STEM school like Purdue, how do we make sure that our writing center has tutors from those fields? How do we make sure we have engineering students in the writing lab? How do we make sure that we have scientists and all the very interesting aeronautics and nuclear engineering, you name it, that happens at Purdue? But also commingle them with the interesting creative arts that's happening at a place like Purdue. How do we have theater students? How do we have English creative writing people from across the liberal arts?

As I talk to you about that, obviously, there is a bias towards the academic. What other communities might we build with? That's when we have to do really proactive outreach to other communities on campus. I think my staff does a really good job of reaching out to the LGBTQ Center and thinking about how might we be accomplices? But also how might we have representation among our staff of people from that community? All the while recognizing that there are people already on staff that are part of that community.

But similarly, any cultural center on campus, how do we build bridges to them? How do we make the writing lab or the writing center a space that's inclusive? I think about how do we imagine both the mainstream student, but also the marginalized student, the at-risk student and the not at-risk student? I think all those are really critical elements. I think that we also have to think about how do we create community in a way that's reciprocal? That we're not just poaching, but that we are fostering across communities, if that makes any sense. I think it also means showing up. Community means if you have tutors that are doing a reading or doing a performance or presenting research, that we support them, that we get out there and we make them feel valued. Community means not just doing our own thing, but community means being there for one another. I think that's really critical. I jotted down community means having fun with each other. It means eating with each other, it means doing things together.

. . . I suspect you know that in your heart, too, that if you want a community, it has to be material, it has to be tangible to people. You have to create a space where people want to be. You don't want a space where people are just punching the time clock. That they are invested in the space, that they get to put their imprint on that.

Shane to Frankie Condon: How did you get interested in social justice and antiracist practices, and how can writing centers construct a space committed to that kind of work? Perhaps some are asking, "Where do we start and how do we develop centers and programs in the most sustainable way?" [Episode 28: 03:10–10:31]

There's a personal aspect to that part of the story that I've written about in some depth in *I Hope I Join the Band*, so I'm not going to retell that part. So what I'll say about that is that when I was in graduate school, I already had this commitment to antiracist activism that was driven by my own family story, my personal history and my relationships. I was going to the University at Albany. I was working with a group called the Dismantling Racism Project, and really what we were doing is antiracism training predominantly in the medical and social services community in Albany, New York, particularly with those agencies and groups that were working with queer people of color who had HIV/AIDS, and making sure that they were culturally competent, culturally aware, and coming to that work from an antiracist perspective.

I was moving out of graduate school. I got a job directing the writing center at Siena College. I was writing my dissertation and it became increasingly clear to me that I could not proceed as an academic treating that activism work as if it was somehow unrelated to the work I was doing in the academy . . . so I just made a commitment to myself that I was never going to behave as if my work as a writer, as a researcher, as a teacher or as a writing center director and scholar was separate from my work as an antiracist activist.

That was 25 years ago or so, and I've just tried to live that way to the best of my ability . . . now with regard to the how do we start and how do we sustain, some of the things I think about, or maybe my first gut response is I really love the work that Myles Horton does. And Myles Horton has a phrase that I love and admire, which is he says, "We make the road by walking." So one response is well, how do you start? Well, you just do. You just start, right? But maybe that's too fast and maybe that's too simple. So maybe you start walking in order to make the road and maybe then you ask, "Who are my people," or, "Who are our people," right? Because I think one should never do this work *for* others. One should always do it *with* others.

So who are the people with whom I can conjoin the work that I'm doing in my writing center, or that we in our writing center can conjoin with? I look across an institution and I think, well the Multicultural Student Services Office is doing antiracism training. Perhaps I can work with them. So I go visiting people. The Faculty Development Center has somebody who's doing something. I go visiting people. Oh, I know this group of faculty are meeting and talking. I go visiting people, right? The job in some way is to start making connections with people, aligning with people and acting in solidarity with folks, building relationships with them.

I'd say another way to begin and to make the work sustainable in a writing center is to put it at the center. It can never be peripheral and be sustainable, right? It's not I'll add a unit to my tutor-training course, or I'll slap a reading in there. It really has to be at the center of the conversation and infused into all of the work that I'm doing and tutors are doing.

Then the last thing I'd say about sustainability . . . is you get tired, right? One of the biggest challenges to sustainability I think is the wear and tear of emotional labor and intellectual labor in doing the work. This is part of why I say you must always do it with people. First of all, doing it for people is that weird benevolence that actually does more harm than good, right? And that often has the effect of making people, White people in particular, feel better about themselves, feel like they're a better White person without actually having any effect on systemic racism or institutional racism.

But you get tired no matter what. So back in the day when Michele Eodice, and Meg Carroll, and Beth Boquet and Anne Ellen Geller and I were working on our book together, we talked a lot about the peloton, which if you are familiar with bike racing, you might know about the peloton, right? So there's a racing team and one person takes the front and they take the wind so that the people coming behind can ride with less wind resistance, and then when they get tired, somebody moves up to the front and takes the wind for the rest of the people. Canadian geese do this too, right? When you see geese flying in a V formation, there's one goose taking the lead and they're taking the wind and they take the wind for the other geese until they get tired, and then they fall back and another goose takes the lead. I think we need this in activist work and in particular, in antiracism work, right?

No one person is at the front of the peloton for too long. When people get tired, there's somebody who can move up to the front and take the wind. And of course, we need to be thinking about the degree to which so often people of color are put in the position of taking all the wind all the time. There are some White people doing antiracism work who need to be sensitive to when it's time to step up and take the wind without engaging in that illiberal benevolence, being with, not for.

Shane to Frankie Condon: I like how you talk about this as a communal effort. Knowing when to step up and take the wind and knowing when to come alongside and support. You mentioned walking the road with others. I'm interested in how you do this work with peer tutors at the writing center. [Episode 28: 10:45–14:23]

Engagement from the center with the center and also simultaneously looking outward. I think I was just talking with students this morning about this, right? There's that turn of phrase that people will say, "Change starts by being the change you want to be in the world." It starts with the individual, and I tend to think that that inward turn is always necessary and always insufficient. You never get to a point individually in your work on yourself where you could be like, "Dude, I'm done. I have the stamp of approval and I no longer need to work on this anymore. So now I'm ready to work on systems and institutions." That work is always mutually contingent and interdependent. Yeah? So we want, as individuals inside the writing center, to be thinking about who we are and what we're doing and the ways in which we are invested in racialized and racist ideologies with regard to language and teaching, and higher education or high school education, if those are the right centers that we're in. We want to be thinking about what our particular institutional site is and what its complicity is, or culpability is in broader institutional systems of racism, or marginalization and exclusion.

And then we want to be looking outward too with the institution as a whole. One of the things concretely that we could talk about is I want tutors to think carefully and critically about the languages for which they advocate as they're working with writers in a writing center. So when we say to a student writer, for example, "You really have to write things in this way because I'm not a racist and I like your home language and I think it's fabulous, but the teacher down the hall is a racist," then effectively we're acting as functionaries for the racist down the hall. I'm not sure how that makes us not complicit.

Or we say, "Well your employers will require it. That you do this, that or the other thing, because they're racist, not me." We're being functionaries for racism in the business world or the professional world or whatever. What people like Vershawn Young, and Asao Inoue, and Aja Martinez, and Elaine Richardson, Geneva Smitherman to name just a few, Victor Villanueva, are saying about the home discourses of peoples of color is those discourses are always being appropriated by predominantly White communities rhetors. But somehow, White folks get a pass on appropriating those discourses and all you have to do is have a Black sounding name or a Chicano sounding name and you don't get the pass. We need to think in more complex and critical ways about the languages for which we're advocating.

Shane to Karen Keaton Jackson: You directed the writing studio at North Carolina Central University. What role do you see writing centers playing in the context of HBCUs and what sort of differences are there compared to writing centers at PWIs? [Episode 34: 19:40–23:32]

> As I think about that, right as I was transitioning out into my current role, I really started to think about how I could articulate some of those differences with HBCU writing centers . . . I've talked about that at conferences and things. That affective component. I think that's always my bottom line, for me, that affective component. No matter where you set me, I'm always going to talk about the affective component of learning. Just one very basic level in our writing center at North Carolina Central University, we have an administrative assistant who makes all of our appointments so students can call or they can come in person.

> I know probably almost everyone else under the sun uses WC Online or something similar, and students can go in and make the appointments themselves. I think we tried that for all of two days. Part of it is probably my anal kind of temperament . . . I think our students turned our schedule upside down so much within two days, we were like, "Oh, we can't give them this much access to our schedule because we can't keep up with it." But again, thinking about our student population, a lot of our students really didn't know quite what they needed. Like they knew they needed help, but, you know, they thought they only needed fifteen minutes while they really needed an hour.

> Our administrative assistant, that's my frontline person. I was very intentional with who I hired for that position. Like to me, it's not just somebody answering phones. It's somebody who's calming a student who walks in and feels like, "Oh my gosh, I'm a horrible writer," or "My professor just tore up my paper," or "I hate my professor," or . . . I mean, there's a lot of emotion that comes when students walk in through the door. There's a lot of stigma attached with getting help. And that's not just in the Black community. I think that's across the board, but certainly for some

of our students, I think they felt some kind of way, you know, coming in for help. So for them to come through the door was like a big win already. I want to have someone there who was encouraging, again, that kind of other mothering mentor, right?

Like, "You can do this, we got you, I got just the right consultant for you." You know? So our administrative assistant is very intentional with who she would partner them with based on the different consultant strengths and weaknesses, and based on what they need that I don't think a computer system can do. We want us to keep our students coming back. We want to keep our enrollment up, our retention numbers, all of that is a big part of it. If you have a large number of your student population that's just totally unfamiliar with navigating this college thing, I'm a firm believer that that hands on piece makes a big difference in why we have so many repeat clients, why our numbers grew by leaps and bounds during the time I was director. And clearly it wasn't just me.

It was really the consultants and the frontline person. I was just kind of in the back. But they did an awesome job in being ambassadors for the writing studio. I don't think without that personal touch, that we would have drawn in as many students in that kind of way. So that's just kind of one thing that we do that I think is very different when I would talk to other writing center directors. That's something that I wouldn't bend on.

I mean, there was a time where they were trying to decrease our number of administrative assistants and that kind of thing. I was really advocating like, "No, I don't want a work-study student here just randomly scheduling students. Like I need a key person here."

Shane to Karen Keaton Jackson: Do you feel like there's an absence of HBCU writing center voices and experiences in writing center scholarship? How can that be addressed? [Episode 34: 23:33–26:34]

Yeah, so absolutely. I believe there's a gap for sure. I think a lot of similar approaches can be taken in terms of the collaborative pieces. I was a member of the SWCA board, the Southeastern Writing Center Association board. One thing I was really excited to do just before I transitioned off of that a few years ago was to help them establish a position for an HBCU representative. I'd been kind of talking about it for a couple of years . . . it wasn't really taken seriously for a while. Then, we had a really great SWCA conference at East Carolina University. You know I have to give a shout out, it was Will Banks and Nikki Caswell headed it up.

And it was dealing with issues of diversity and difference. It set the perfect tone of really digging into these honest conversations about diversity. Then, when we had our follow-up board meeting, it was almost like, how can we not say it now and do it now because the conference just set up the theme just so brilliantly. I think Vershawn Young was the keynote speaker that year. Again, I wasn't obviously the only person to do it, but, you know, that was kind of one of the things I was able to help usher in that position for the HBCU representative, having those intentional positions on the boards. And particularly, because of our region, most HBCUs are in the Southeast. So kind of like, how can we be so absent here, like regionally, and there are so many of us here.

I think having more representation on boards and actively reaching out to HBCUs. You know, we're smaller functions in general. A lot of us are wearing many hats, writing centers included. I think having to intentionally reach out makes a difference . . . being intentional, reaching out, and trying to mentor. Again, I think if people feel that their voices are valued, you know, then you're more apt to want to dig in and give a little bit of extra energy. I think that that part of being intentional is really, really, really key. You know, sharing the wealth a little bit more. I think we need to be everywhere, right? So maybe we can be at all different places. You just have a lot of different voices coming in at one time, which would be like our utopia.

Shane to Neal Lerner: You've seen writing center studies scholarship grow a lot over the past several decades. I imagine this development of scholarship has been exciting to see. But I also imagine you've seen reoccurring trends and threads in research that writing centers face, maybe at an institutional level, that has caused some sense of frustration? [Episode 35: 07:44–11:16]

> My frustration . . . and I'm not the only one to write about it, is that writing centers are in a funny place in terms of a constant need to justify their existence, a kind of perpetual funding and staffing crisis, partially because of their alignment, either with student services or student affairs or academic success centers. So there's this limit for many of them on what they could potentially be and do, that there's ways in which the role of writing center director is hamstrung by institutional realities.
>
> A writing center is a true research site. Or writing centers, themselves, as a kind of disciplinary enterprise, is never quite realized in ways that I wish it could. And that's not any individual's fault necessarily, but it's just a structural thing that just seems to be perpetuated. I mean, if you go back and you read stuff from the late '80s, early '90s, there's lots of same themes. The stuff that . . . even a little bit later, right? The things that Nancy Grimm wrote about in the late '90s and her taking the field to task in lots of ways, for certain kinds of practices and attitudes and beliefs, it's still true.
>
> I mean, Frankie Condon will talk about that too, right? You'll have plenty of people to say the field hasn't moved quite far enough for a whole variety of reasons. It's grown, but at the same time, it maybe hasn't grown as much as I think some of us would like. I've been frustrated in my own institution about grad students who haven't been as interested in studying the writing center as I would have been, right? Or as I was. That's for a whole variety of reasons.

Seeing writing center work as a career isn't as proliferated as I would like. I think I'm a bit frustrated by that.

At the same time, I've had many, many people work with me as grad students or in other roles who've gone on to direct writing centers. So that happens and that's a wonderful thing. But still generally, institutions . . . many have one writing center and then one writing center director and that's kind of the norm. One of the most fun pieces I've ever written was I drew on some studies from the 1930s of accounts of writing center directors in the 1930s. It's so many of the similar themes going on then as now. It seems endemic to institutions of higher education to have these kinds of limits on what the possibilities are.

Shane to Neal Lerner: In "Writing Center Pedagogy," you talk about how writing centers are social spaces and how centers inherently invite conversations on writing as process and are inherently collaborative. What are some of the constraints that affect social interactions in writing centers? [Episode 35: 14:12–16:39]

The thing I often think about is the role of interactants who aren't there, namely the classroom instructor, as well as a whole bunch of other people who aren't there who have an effect on the social scene for student writing. Whether it's their previous teachers, whether it's their perceived audience. How many things that students are writing in academia have actual audiences, right? Not very many. There are these hypothetical audiences. So they're trying to create and makeup and imagine these audiences that they might not have a cultural connection to, right? So some of the constraints are cultural, social, ideological, particularly around multilingual writers and the ways in which consultants have to play these multiple roles or have this kind of insider knowledge that they don't often have.

. . . I've spent 25 years thinking about the role of the instructor as a proxy within the session, right? The instructor's the third person making up that triad in a writing session, but the instructor is not there. The instructor might be there because of his or her comments on a draft or because of the assignment itself, but the person's generally not there. What kind of conversation is that when it's being driven by someone who's not there? I mean, outside of writing centers, we have those kind of conversations sometimes. You're talking to your sibling about something your parents said and trying to figure something out. But it seems so inexact and imprecise and constraining in a way that I think is worth understanding much more thoroughly than we understand it now. For me, the constraint of social actors who aren't present is maybe the most important one.

Shane to Neal Lerner: Do you mind talking about the ways you develop peer tutors and what it looks like to prepare them to give feedback to student writing? [Episode 35: 16:40–20:46]

Yeah, that's a great question. The kinds of things that we emphasized last year in the training . . . I had an assistant director, a PhD student. We designed the training together and did the training together. What that training consisted of just looks different in so many different places . . . I mean, in some ways there's a basic pedagogical function of it, which is, "How do you give people feedback on their writing to help them improve? What are the best practices around that?" And no surprise, it all has to be very kind of hands on. There's a lot of practice to it. I think the thing that I extend from any of my teaching is the ways in which these kinds of practices need to be out of what people want and where they're coming from and what their attitudes are.

So trying to explore what their experiences have been, what their attitudes are, what their beliefs are, because the way we practice teaching and tutoring is so shaped by beliefs that often we don't even realize, the implicit biases and sometimes simply fears, right?

I'll give you an example of that. One of the things I instituted more than it had been done up to that point was online consultation. And we do it synchronously. When

I started at Northeastern there was email consultation, nobody was ever very happy about it, and it was pretty low volume. There was essentially one person assigned to deal with it, so we eventually got rid of that. And we went to synchronous online using the WC Online platform. There's so many ways in which a lot of consultants really were uneasy with it because it was so different and the norms are so different than face-to-face consulting. Part of the issue around helping them be successful in that endeavor was facing those fears. What were they afraid of? Were their goals for the sessions not quite aligned with what the student's goals were and with what the medium might afford? So we just spent a lot of time talking about those issues and practicing those issues.

Training's always lots of scenarios and reflecting on problem solving in a way with different scenarios. We often have done a lot of that. It often involves reading and response to that reading pretty much every . . . last year we would have monthly staff meetings that were training sessions. We often had guest speakers with expertise. There's no way we can be experts of everything . . . 35% of the students who came in were multilingual writers, so we're always searching for expertise on helping us work most effectively with multilingual writers or with grad students or with disciplinary writers. Bringing in others to help gives us the benefit of their expertise and also pushes the writing center out into the consciousness of these other folks knowing that this is a place on campus that's doing a particular kind of work that's important and valuable. I think in general terms, that kind of covers it. I was lucky to have co-written a textbook with Paula Gillespie on training writing tutors. So I often draw from that, too.

Shane to Rebecca S. Nowacek: What has surprised you the most about being a director of a writing center? [Episode 43: 07:03–11:40]

This is particularly on my mind on the heels of all these exit interviews that I did with graduating seniors. I'm thinking about how much administrative work matters and constantly I feel like I have to . . . not reinvent my principles, I think my principles are pretty strong and constant, but the practice of it is constantly in progress. I've always believed that it's really important to have collaborative, transparent principles that guide our approach to writing program administration.

I've had such great role models in this. I was a graduate tutor at the University of Wisconsin, Madison, where I got to work with Brad Hughes, who was extraordinary in so many ways, including both how capacious his conversations about writing across campus could be, and also so profoundly humane in the way that he would listen to people and remember things that you said and the names of the people in your family that you care about and your dog. He was such a great model of both the scope of the ambition and how focused you need to be on the people you're working with in order to do that in a sustainable and humane way. Kris Ratcliffe was my senior colleague here at Marquette for many years and I learned so much from her about transparent, inclusive processes and how those are not just in what we say our values are, but how it plays out in committee work. And just seeing it on a daily basis was so powerful and I'm really so fortunate now I have a fantastic co-director in Jenn Fishman, my colleague, and we've moved into co-directing in the last year, year and a half. It has been such an extraordinary pleasure. It has always been the case ever since Jenn came to Marquette. I always say that all my synapses fire when I'm in conversation with Jenn. I think about more ambitious projects and better ways to achieve them.

. . . I've always had great models of how collaborative and transparent the work needs to be and yet I am surprised by all the things that I don't know about how to make that happen . . . the tutors will be fantastic partners if you invite them into the conversations and really mean it. If you just shut up long enough to listen to what they're telling you about, what they need and what writers might need, where the mismatch between your intention and how things played out was. I learned that through exit interviews . . . we have changed so many things about the way the writing center is organized and runs mentoring and various transitions. We have something called a "leadership team" and the structure of that adjusts depending on what we learned from people.

All of this is a really long-winded way of saying that in some sense I'm not surprised in the big picture, but I'm constantly surprised about how much, all of your little choices, all the administrative details matter for making our ideals of collaborative, transparent decision-making and administrative work. How much it matters for making that the lived experience for everybody who's in the writing center. Do they feel respected and included in the work?

Shane to Rebecca S. Nowacek: You've been a director for nine years. What do you find most fulfilling about your work? [Episode 43: 01:51–06:15]

There are so many things! I love, love, love writing center work. So we could spend all of our time talking about what's fulfilling in this work, most on my mind right now is the pleasure of working with the students who are our tutors. Some of them take the tutor education class in spring of their junior year so I get to work with them for that semester and two more, but many of them take it . . . their first semester of college. They take the class as a first-year student. I work with them for seven semesters, and it is a privilege. It is a pleasure to watch these students grow and blossom and try things out and fail with some things and knock other things out of the park.

Being a writing tutor isn't necessarily listed as one of the high impact practices that you know are batted about in university talk, but I stand by it. Being a peer writing tutor as an undergraduate is a profoundly transformative experience. I see it, we do exit interviews and many of our tutors talk about that.

I should say we're mostly an undergraduate-staffed writing center, but we also have a handful of truly fantastic graduate students who do extraordinary work in it. It's a great pleasure to work with and alongside of them and see them really growing as leaders and scholars, so that's one part of it. Another pleasure is I really like the work myself . . . I used to keep at least a shift or two on the schedule myself. As our writing center has grown over the past eight or so years, that's been increasingly difficult to do, but I do still work with writers coming into our writing center. It's a tremendous pleasure to learn about why people want to go to dental school or what they're working on in this capstone in their physician assistant's studies program or whatever. It's intellectually demanding and horizon expanding work just as somebody who gets to talk with writers from all different disciplines.

It's a great site for research. I'm interested in studying and learning more about transfer of learning. It's a brilliant site for research on that subject. So that's another pleasure and there are more . . . there is something deeply gratifying about being able to try to be a nimble program in our university, to try to build different kinds of programs that speak to the needs of our campus or the broader Milwaukee community. To be able to work with our office of admissions, to run workshops for area high school students who are writing college application essays and we hope that maybe they want to come to Marquette, but many of them end up in other places. But being in conversation with these young students on a Saturday morning, they show up at 8:30am or something extraordinary for high school students. And being able to build that with our undergraduate tutors . . .

Sure, there are lots of reports that need to generated and forms that need to be filled out. I don't mind doing that because the other part of the job is being able to build programming that seems to fill a real need. That's pleasurable in ways that I maybe didn't anticipate.

DENOUEMENT

The throughline in these conversations, to me, is the joy of collaborating with tutors and building a culture that advocates for student writing. Writing centers are unique spaces that can be a means for shifting attitudes and beliefs about writing across colleges and universities. They are sites for interdisciplinary interactions and research. And really, writing centers are places where student writers and tutors can be encouraged. There seems to be a constant need for centers to increase visibility within institutions and share their mission with administrators, faculty, and students.

Overall, writing centers offer an opportunity to educate a range of stakeholders about writing theory and practice. For example, centers can be a means for amplifying antiracist policies on language and can value cultural and linguistic diversity. They can be active participants of social justice initiatives and can advocate for equity and inclusion across campus. Centers can work collaboratively with other organizations and programs (e.g., office of diversity and inclusion, writing across the curriculum). They can provide workshops and seminars for faculty and students. Further, writing centers can be one of the best sites for researching response, and one-on-one consultations can serve as a great opportunity to observe how conversation helps writers think and engage in the writing process.

For additional resources on writing center theory and practice, I suggest reading *Writing Centers and the New Racism: A Call for Sustainable Dialogue and Change* (Greenfield & Rowan, 2011), *The Everyday Writing Center: A Community of Practice* (Geller et al., 2006), and *Theories and Methods of Writing Center Studies* (Mackiewicz & Babcock, 2019). Moreover, I recommend *The Writing Center Journal* and *Praxis: A Writing Center Journal*. I also offer the following questions to help generate more conversations about writing centers:

- How can teachers help support the mission of the writing center in first-year writing class? What can teachers learn from or about the writing center? How can teachers work with centers, and how can they encourage students to see writing centers as a resource for writing instruction?
- As a director, what administrative objectives and goals do you have? What kind of mission or culture do you want to help

cultivate in the writing center? What polices or practices need to adapt to current research and theory? As an administrator, how are you supporting tutors beyond providing resources to help with sessions?

- What kinds of writing center consultations (e.g., face-to-face, asynchronous, synchronous) are most beneficial to provide? What are the advantages and disadvantages?
- What does professional development look like in the writing center? What scholarship is being used (e.g., writing center studies, response, second-language theory)? What scenarios or workshops would be useful given the institution and student population?
- What cross-campus (and local community) collaborations can happen with the writing center?

References

Adler-Kassner, L., & O'Neill, P. (2010). *Reframing writing assessment to improve teaching and learning.* Utah State University Press.

Adler-Kassner, L., & Wardle, E. (Eds.). (2015). *Naming what we know.* Utah State University Press.

Alexander, J., & Rhodes, J. (2014). *On multimodality: New media in composition studies.* National Council of Teachers of English.

Allen, H. B. (1973). English as a second language. In T. A. Sebeok (Ed.), *Current Trends in linguistics: Linguistics in North America* (pp. 295–320) (Vol. 10). Mouton.

Alvarez, S. (2017). *Community literacies en confianza: Learning from bilingual after-school programs.* National Council of Teachers of English.

Andelora, J. (2005). The teacher/scholar: Reconstructing our professional identity in two-year colleges. *Teaching English in the Two-Year College, 32*(3), 307–322.

Anson, C. M. (2012). Black holes: Writing across the curriculum, assessment, and the gravitational invisibility of race. In A. B. Inoue & M. Poe (Eds.), *Race and writing assessment* (pp. 15–29). Peter Lang.

Arola, K. L., & Wysocki, A. F. (Eds.). (2012). *Composing (media) = Composing (embodiment): Bodies, technologies, writing, the teaching of writing.* Utah State University Press.

Athon, A. (2019). Designing rubrics to foster students' diverse language backgrounds. *Journal of Basic Writing, 38*(1), 78–104. https://doi.org/10.37514/jbw-j.2019.38.1.05

Atkinson, D., Crusan, D., Matsuda, P. K., Ortmeier-Hooper, C., Ruecker, T., Simpson, S., & Tardy, C. (2015). Clarifying the relationship between L2 writing and translingual writing: An open letter to writing studies editors and organization leaders. *College English, 77*(4), 383–386.

Baca, I., Hinojosa, Y. I., & Murphy, S. (Eds.). (2019). *Bordered writers: Latinx identities and literacy practices at Hispanic-serving institutions.* SUNY Press.

Baker-Bell, A. (2020). *Linguistic justice: Black language, literacy, identity, and pedagogy*. Routledge; National Council of Teachers of English.

Ball, C. E., & Charlton, C. (2015). All writing is multimodal. In L. Adler-Kassner & E. Wardle (Eds.), *Naming what we know: Threshold concepts of writing studies*. Utah State University Press

Balzotti, J. (2016). Storyboarding for invention: Layering modes for more effective transfer in a multimodal composition classroom. *Journal of Basic Writing*, 35(1), 63–84. https://doi.org/10.37514/JBW-J.2016.35.1.04

Banks, A. (2010). *Race, rhetoric, and technology: Searching for higher ground*. Routledge; National Council of Teachers of English.

Bartholomae, D., & Petrosky, A. (Eds.). (1986). *Facts, artifacts and counterfacts: Theory and method for a reading and writing course*. Boynton/Cook.

Bawarshi, A., & Pelkowski, S. (1999). Postcolonialism and the idea of a writing center. *The Writing Center Journal, 19*(2), 41–58.

Bazerman, C., Little, J., Bethel, L., Chavkin, T., Fouquette, D., & Garufis, J. (2005). *Reference guide to writing across the curriculum*. Parlor Press; The WAC Clearinghouse. https://wac.colostate.edu/books/referenceguides/bazerman-wac/

Bazerman, C., & Russell, D. R. (Eds). (1995). *Landmark essays on writing across the curriculum*. Routledge.

Berlin, J. (1988). Rhetoric and ideology in the writing class. *College English, 50*(5), 477–494.

Bernstein, S. N. (2013). *Teaching developmental writing* (4th ed.). Bedford/St. Martin's.

Bizzell, P. (1986). What happens when basic writers come to college?. *College Composition and Communication, 37*(3), 294–301.

Bleich, D. (1991). Introduction: Do we need sacred texts and great men? In G.A. Olson & I. Gale (Eds.), *(Inter)views: Cross-disciplinary perspectives on rhetoric and literacy* (pp. 1–26). Southern Illinois University Press.

Brata, P., & Powell, M. (2016). Introduction to the special issue: Entering the cultural rhetorics conversations. *enculturation: a journal of rhetoric, writing, and culture*. http://enculturation.net/entering-the-cultural-rhetorics-conversations

Broad, B. (2003). *What we really value: Beyond rubrics in teaching and assessing writing.* Utah State University Press.

Brown v. Board of Education of Topeka, 347 U.S. 483 (1954). https://supreme.justia.com/cases/federal/us/347/483/#tab-opinion-1940808

Browning, E. R. (2014). Disability studies in the composition classroom. *Composition Studies, 42*(2), 96–117.

Brueggemann, B. J., White, L. F., Dunn, P. A., Heifferon, B.A., & Cheu, J. (2001). Becoming visible: Lessons in disability. *College Composition and Communication, 52*(3), 368–398.

Calhoon-Dillahunt, C. (2011). Writing programs without administrators: Frameworks for successful writing programs in the two-year college. *WPA: Writing Program Administration, 35*(1), 118–134.

Canagarajah, A. S. (2006). The place of world Englishes in composition: Pluralization continued. *College Composition and Communication, 57*(4), 586–619.

Canagarajah, A. S. (Ed.). (2013). *Literacy as translingual practice: Between communities and classrooms.* Routledge.

Cedillo, C. V. (2018). What does it mean to move?: Race, disability, and critical embodiment pedagogy. *Composition Forum, 39.*

Ceraso, S. (2014). (Re)Educating the senses: Multimodal listening, bodily learning, and the composition of sonic experiences. *College English, 77*(2), 102–123.

Ceraso, S. (2018). *Sounding composition: Multimodal pedagogies and embodied listening.* University of Pittsburgh Press.

Civil Rights Act of 1964, Pub. L. 88–352, 78 Stat. 241 (1964). https://www.govinfo.gov/content/pkg/STATUTE-78/pdf/STATUTE-78-Pg241.pdf

Cobos, C., Ríos, G. R., Sackey, D. J., Sano-Franchini, J., & Haas, A. M. (2018). Interfacing cultural rhetorics: A history and a call. *Rhetoric Review, 37*(2), 139–154.

Composition Forum. (2020). Promoting social justice for multilingual writers on college campuses [Special issue]. *Composition Forum, 44.* https://compositionforum.com/issue/44/

Condon, F., & Young, V. A. (Eds). (2013). Introduction: Why anti-racist activism? Why now? [Special issue: Anti-racist activism: Teaching rhetoric and writing]. *Across the Discipline, 10*(3). https://doi.org/10.37514/ATD-J.2013.10.3.05

Condon, F., & Young, V. A. (Eds.). (2016). *Performing antiracist pedagogy in rhetoric, writing, and communication.* The WAC Clearinghouse; University Press of Colorado. https://doi.org/10.37514/ATD-B.2016.0933

Cooper, P. L. (1984). *The assessment of writing ability.* Educational Testing Service.

Costello, K. M., & Babb, J. (2020). Introduction: Emotional labor, writing studies, and writing program administration. In C. A. Wooten, J. Babb, K. M. Costello, & K. Navickas (Eds.), *The things we carry: Strategies for recognizing and negotiating emotional labor in writing program administration* (pp. 3–16). Utah State University Press.

Cox, M., Galin, J. R., & Melzer, D. (2018). *Sustainable WAC: A whole systems approach to launching and developing writing across the curriculum programs.* National Council of Teachers of English.

Cronbach, L. J. (1988). Five perspectives on validity argument. In H. Wainer (Ed.), *Test validity* (pp. 3–17). Erlbaum.

Cushman, E. (1996). The rhetorician as an agent of social change. *College Composition and Communication, 47*(1), 7–28.

Dangler, D., McCorkle, B., & Barrow, T. (2007). Expanding composition audiences with podcasting. *Computers and Composition Online.* http://cconlinejournal.org/podcasting/

Deans, T. (2000). *Writing partnerships: Service-learning in composition.* National Council of Teachers of English.

Degner, H., Wojciehowski, K., & Giroux, C. (2015). Opening closed doors: A rationale for creating a safe space for tutors struggling with mental health concerns or illnesses. *Praxis: A Writing Center Journal, 13*(1). http://www.praxisuwc.com/degner-et-al-131

Detweiler, E. (2021). The bandwidth of podcasting. In K. D. Stedman, C. S. Danforth, & M. J. Faris (Eds.), *Tuning in to soundwriting.* enculturation/Intermezzo. http://intermezzo.enculturation.net/14-stedman-et-al/detweiler-3.html

Dolmage, J. (2017). *Academic ableism: Disability and higher education.* University of Michigan Press.

Dolmage, J. (2018). *Disabled upon arrival: Eugenics, immigration, and the construction of race and disability.* The Ohio State University Press.

Elbow, P. (1994). Ranking, evaluating, liking: Sorting out three forms of judgment. *College English, 55*(2), 187–206.

Elbow, P. (1997). Grading student writing: Making it simpler, fairer, clearer. *New Directions for Teaching and Learning, 1997*(69), 127–140. Jossey-Bass Publishers.

Elbow, P. (2004). Writing first! *Educational Leadership, 62*(2), 9–13.

Elbow, P., & Belanoff, P. (1986). Portfolios as a substitute for proficiency examinations. *College Composition and Communication, 37*(3), 336–339.

Elliot, N., & Perelman, L. (Eds.). (2012). *Writing assessment in the 21st century: Essays in honor of Edward M. White.* Hampton Press.

Elliot, N. (2005). *On a scale: A social history of writing assessment in America.* Peter Lang.

Faigley, L. (1989). Judging writers, judging selves. *College Composition and Communication, 40*(4), 395–413.

Ferris, D., & Hedgcock, J. (2013). *Teaching L2 composition: Purpose, process, and practice* (3rd edition). Routledge.

Finer, B. S., & White-Farnham, J. (Eds.). (2017). *Writing program architecture: Thirty cases for reference and research.* Utah State University Press.

Flower, L. (2008). *Community literacy and the rhetoric of public engagement.* Southern Illinois University Press.

Flower, L., & Hayes, J. R. (1981). A cognitive process theory of writing. *College Composition and Communication, 32*(4), 365–387.

Fox, T. (1990). Basic writing as cultural conflict. *Journal of Education, 172*(1), 65–83.

Freire, P. (1998). *Pedagogy of freedom: Ethics, democracy, and civic courage.* Rowman & Littlefield Publishers.

García, R., & Baca, D. (Eds.). (2019). *Rhetorics elsewhere and otherwise: Contested modernities, decolonial visions.* National Council of Teachers of English.

García de Müeller, G., & Ruiz, I. D. (2017). Race, silence, and writing program administration: A qualitative study of U.S. college writing programs. *WPA: Writing Program Administration, 40*(2), 19–39.

Geller, A. E., Eodice, M., Condon, F., Caroll, M., & Boquet, E. (2006). *The everyday writing center: A community of practice.* Utah State University Press.

Gilyard, K. (1999). African American contributions to composition studies. *College Composition and Communication, 50*(4),

626–644. https://doi.org/10.2307/358484

Giordano, J. B. (Author), Hassel, H. (Author), Wegner, M. (Author), Sullivan, P. (Contributor). (2020). *TYCA working paper #2: Two-year college English faculty teaching adjustments related to workload.* Two-Year College English Association Workload Task Force. https://ncte.org/wp-content/uploads/2020/12/TYCA_Working_Paper_2.pdf

Godbee, B., Ozias, M., & Kar Tang, J. (2015). Body + power + justice: Movement-based workshops for critical tutor education. *The Writing Center Journal, 34*(2), 61–112.

Gonzales, L. (2018). *Sites of translation: What multilinguals can teach us about digital writing and rhetoric.* The University of Michigan Press.

Green, Jr., D. F. (2016). Expanding the dialogue on writing assessment at HBCUs: Foundational assessment concepts and legacies of historically Black colleges and universities. *College English, 79*(2), 152–173

Greenberg, K. L. (1997). A response to Ira Shor's "Our apartheid: Writing instruction and inequality." *Journal of Basic Writing, 16*(2), 90–94. https://doi.org/10.37514/JBW-J.1997.16.2.07

Greenfield, L., & Rowan, K. (2011). *Writing centers and the new racism: A call for sustainable dialogue and change.* Utah State University Press.

Grimm, N. M. (2009). New conceptual frameworks for writing center work. *The Writing Center Journal, 29*(2), 11–27.

Hall, A., & Stephens, K. (2018). Writing in context: Adopting a genre-based approach. *Basic Writing e-Journal, 15*(1). https://bwe.ccny.cuny.edu/Writing%20in%20Context%20Adopting%20%20Final.pdf

Hammond, Z. (2014). *Culturally responsive teaching and the brain: Promoting authentic engagement and rigor among culturally and linguistically diverse students.* Corwin.

Hassel, H., & Giordano, J. B. (2013). Occupy writing studies: Rethinking college composition for the needs of the teaching majority. *College Composition and Communication, 65*(1), 117–139.

Haswell, R., & Elliot, N. (2019). *Early holistic scoring of writing: A theory, a history, a reflection.* Utah State University Press.

Hendrickson, B., & García de Müeller, G. (2016). Inviting students to determine for themselves what it means to write across the disciplines. *The WAC Journal, 27,* 74–93. https://doi.org/10.37514/WAC-J.2016.27.1.05

Higher Education Act of 1965, 20 U.S.C. 1001 et seq. (1965). https://www.govinfo.gov/content/pkg/USCODE-2020-title20/html/USCODE-2020-title20-chap28-subchapI-partA-sec1001.htm

Hispanic Association of Colleges and Universities. Retrieved January 20, 2021. https://www.hacu.net/hacu/default.asp.

Hitt, A. H. (2021). *Rhetorics of overcoming: Rewriting narratives of disability and accessibility in writing studies.* National Council of Teachers of English.

Ho, A. B. T., Kerschbaum, S., Sanchez, R., & Yergeau, M. (2020). Cripping neutrality: Student resistance, pedagogical audiences, and teachers' accommodations. *Pedagogy, 20*(1), 127- 139.

Horner, B., & Lu, M. Z. (1999). *Representing the "other": Basic writers and the teaching of basic writing.* National Council of Teachers of English.

Horner, B., Lu, M. Z., & Matsuda, P. K. (Eds.). (2010). *Cross-language relations in composition.* Southern Illinois University Press.

Horner, B., Lu, M. Z., Royster, J. J., & Trimbur, J. (2011). Language difference in writing: Toward a translingual approach. *College English, 73*(3), 303–321.

Hubrig, A. (2020). "We move together:" Reckoning with disability justice in community literacy studies. *Community Literacy Journal, 14*(2), 144–153.

Huot, B. (2002). *(Re)Articulating writing assessment for teaching and learning.* Utah State University Press.

Inoue, A. B. (2015a). *Antiracist writing assessment ecologies: Teaching and assessing for a socially just future.* The WAC Clearinghouse; Parlor Press. https://doi.org/10.37514/PER-B.2015.0698

Inoue, A. B. (2015b). The living scholarship of composition studies: A case for students-as scholarship. *College Composition and Communication, 66*(4), 697–700.

Inoue, A. B. (2019). *Labor-based grading contracts: Building equity and inclusion in the compassionate writing classroom.* The WAC Clearinghouse; University Press of Colorado. https://doi.

org/10.37514/PER-B.2019.0216.0

Inoue, A. B., & Poe, M. (Eds.). (2012). *Race and writing assessment.* Peter Lang.

Jackson, K. K., Jackson, H., & Hicks Tafari, D. N. (2019). We belong in the discussion: Including HBCUs in conversations about race and writing. *College Composition and Communication, 71*(2), 184–214.

James, K. L. (2013). *First-year writing programs at Historically Black Colleges and Universities* [Doctoral dissertation, University of Alabama]. Institutional Repository https://ir.ua.edu/handle/123456789/1643

Johnson, S. (2018). Mindful tutors, embodied writers: Positioning mindfulness meditation as a writing strategy to optimize cognitive load and potentialize writing center tutors' supportive roles. *Praxis: A Writing Center Journal, 15*(2), 24–33.

Jones, L. (2010). Podcasting and performativity: Multimodal invention in an advanced writing class. *Composition Studies, 38*(2), 75–91.

Julier, L., Livingston, K., & Goldblatt, E. (2014). Community-engaged pedagogies. In G. Tate, A. R. Taggart, K. Schick, & H. B. Hessler (Eds.), *A guide to composition pedagogies* (pp. 55–76). Oxford University Press.

Kells, M. H., Balester, V. M., & Villanueva, V. (Eds.). (2004). *Latino/a discourses: On language, identity, and literacy education.* Heinemann.

Kells, M. H. (2007). Foreword. In C. Kirklighter, D. Cárdenas, & S. W. Murphy (Eds.), *Teaching writing with Latino/a students: Lessons learned at Hispanic-serving institutions* (pp. vii-xiv). SUNY Press.

Kerschbaum, S., Eisenman, L. T., & Jones, J. (Eds.). (2017). *Negotiating disability: Disclosure and higher education.* University of Michigan Press.

Khadka, S. & Lee, J. C. (Eds.). (2019). *Bridging the multimodal gap: From theory to practice.* Utah State University Press.

King, L., Gubele, R., & Anderson, J. R. (Eds.). (2015). *Survivance, sovereignty, and story: Teaching American Indian rhetorics.* Utah State University Press.

Kirklighter, C., Cardenas, D., & Murphy, S. W. (Eds.). (2007). *Teaching writing with Latino/a students: Lessons learned at His-*

panic-serving institutions. SUNY Press.

Krause, S. D. (2006). Broadcast composition: Using audio files and podcasts in an online writing course. *Computers and Composition Online.* http://cconlinejournal.org/krause1/index.html

Kynard, C. (2013). *Vernacular insurrections: Race, Black protest, and the new century in composition-literacies studies.* SUNY Press.

Ladson-Billings, G. (1994). *The dreamkeepers.* Jossey-Bass.

Lambdin, W. (1980, August 31). Johnny can't write because English teachers can't either. (1980). *The Washington Post.* https://www.washingtonpost.com/archive/opinions/1980/08/31/

Lee, V., & Selfe, C. (2008). Our capacious caper: Exposing print-culture bias in departmental tenure documents. *ADE Bulletin, 145,* 51–58.

Linton, S. (1998). *Claiming disability: Knowledge and identity.* New York University Press.

Lu, M. Z. (1991). Redefining the legacy of Mina Shaughnessy: A critique of the politics of linguistic innocence. *Journal of Basic Writing, 10*(1), 26–40. https://doi.org/10.37514/JBW-J.1991.10.1.04

Luther, J., Farmer, F., & Parks, S. (2017). The past, present, and future of self-publishing: Voices, genres, and publics. *Community Literacy Journal, 12*(1), 1–4. https://dx.doi.org/10.25148/CLJ.12.1.009113

Mack, E., & Hupp, K. (2017). Mindfulness in the writing center: A total encounter. *Praxis: A Writing Center Journal, 14*(2), 7–14.

Mackiewicz, J., & Babcock, R. D. (2019). *Theories and methods of writing center studies.* Routledge.

Mahon, W., & Schroeder, E. (2005). Cross-conversations on writing, interviewing, and editing: A meta-interview with Wade Mahon and Eric Schroeder. *Kairos, 10*(1), https://kairos.technorhetoric.net/10.1/interviews/rhetoric-and-composition.htm

Maraj, L. M. (2020). *Black or right: Anti/racist campus rhetorics.* Utah State University Press.

Martinez, A. Y. (2020). *Counterstory: The rhetoric and writing of critical race theory.* National Council of Teachers of English.

Mathieu, P. (2005). *Tactics of hope: The public turn in English composition.* Heinemann.

Mathieu, P., Parks, S., & Rousculp, T. (Eds.). (2011). *Circulating communities: The tactics and strategies of community publishing.*

Lexington Books.

Matsuda, P. K. (2006). The myth of linguistic homogeneity in U.S. college composition. *College English*, *68*(6), 637–651.

Matsuda, P. K., Cox, M., Jordan, J., & Ortmeier-Hooper, C. (2006). *Second-language writing in the composition classroom: A critical sourcebook*. Bedford/St. Martin's.

Mckoy, T. (2019). *Y'all call it technical and professional communication, we call it #ForTheCulture: The use of amplification rhetorics in Black communities and their implications for technical and professional communication studies* [Doctoral dissertation, East Carolina University]. The Scholarship http://hdl.handle.net/10342/7421

McLeod, S. H. (2007). *Writing program administration*. Parlor Press; The WAC Clearinghouse. https://wac.colostate.edu/books/referenceguides/mcleod-wpa/

McLeod, S. H., & Soven, M. (Eds.). (2000). *Writing across the curriculum: A guide to developing programs*. The WAC Clearinghouse. https://wac.colostate.edu/books/landmarks/mcleodsoven/. (Original work published in 1992)

Messick, S. (1989). Validity. In R. L. Linn (Ed.), *Educational measurement* (3rd ed., pp. 13–103). American Council on Education and National Council on Measurement in Education.

Miller, S. (Ed.). (2009). *The Norton book of composition studies*. W. W. Norton & Company.

Moll, L., Amanti, C., Neff, D., & Gonzalez, N. (2001). Funds of knowledge for teaching: Using a qualitative approach to connect homes and classrooms. *Theory into Practice*, *31*(2), 132–141.

Moss, B. J. (2003). *A community text arises: A literate text and a literacy tradition in African-American churches*. Hampton Press.

Moss, P. A. (1994). Can there be validity without reliability? *Educational Researcher*, *23*(4), 5-12.

Murray, D. (1972). Teach writing as process not product. *The Leaflet*, 11–14.

National Council of Teachers of English. (1974). *CCCC statement: Students' rights to their own language*. https://cccc.ncte.org/cccc/resources/positions/srtolsummary

National Council of Teachers of English. (2020a). *CCCC statement on disability studies in composition: Position statement on policy and best practices*. https://cccc.ncte.org/cccc/resources/positions/

disabilitypolicy

National Council of Teachers of English. (2009). *Writing assessment: A position statement.* https://cccc.ncte.org/cccc/resources/positions/writingassessment

National Council of Teachers of English. (2016). *CCCC statement on community-engaged projects in rhetoric and composition.* https://cccc.ncte.org/cccc/resources/positions/community-engaged

National Council of Teachers of English. (2020b). *CCCC statement on second language writing and multilingual writers.* https://cccc.ncte.org/cccc/resources/positions/secondlangwriting

National Council of Teachers of English. (2020c). *This ain't another statement! This is a DEMAND for Black linguistic justice!* https://cccc.ncte.org/cccc/demand-for-black-linguistic-justice

Newman, B. M. (2007). Teaching writing at Hispanic-serving institutions. In C. Kirklighter, D. Cárdenas, & Murphy, S. W. (Eds.). *Teaching writing with Latino/a students: Lessons learned at Hispanic-serving institutions* (pp. 17–36). SUNY Press.

Novotny, M. (2020, July 22). Cultural rhetorics in precarious times. *Writing & Rhetoric MKE.* https://www.writingandrhetoricmke.com/blog/cultural-rhetorics-in-precarious-times

Ostman, H. (2013). *Writing program administration and the community college.* Parlor Press.

Otte, G., & Mlynarczyk, R. W. (2010). *Basic writing.* Parlor Press; The WAC Clearinghouse. https://wac.colostate.edu/books/referenceguides/basicwriting/

Palmeri, J. (2012). *Remixing composition: A history of multimodal writing pedagogy.* Southern Illinois University Press.

Paris, D., & Alim, H.S. (Eds.). (2017). *Culturally sustaining pedagogies: Teaching and learning for justice in a changing world.* Teachers College Press.

Parks, S. (2017). "I hear its chirping coming from my throat": Activism, archives, and the long road ahead. *LiCS, 5*(1), 85–91.

Perryman-Clark, S. M. (2016). Who we are(n't) assessing: Racializing language and writing assessment in writing program administration. *College English, 79*(2), 206–211.

Perryman-Clark, S. M., & Craig, C. L. (Eds.). (2019). *Black perspectives in writing program administration: From the margins to the center.* National Council of Teachers of English.

Pimentel, O., Pimentel, C., & Dean, J. (2016). The myth of the colorblind writing classroom: White instructors confront white privilege in their classrooms. In F. Condon & V. A. Young (Eds.), *Performing antiracist pedagogy in rhetoric, writing, and communication* (pp. 109–122). The WAC Clearinghouse; University Press of Colorado. https://doi.org/10.37514/ATD-B.2016.0933.2.05

Poe, M. (2013). Re-framing race in teaching writing across the curriculum. *Across the Disciplines, 10*(3), https://doi.org/10.37514/ATD-J.2013.10.3.06

Poe, M., Inoue, A. B., & Elliot, N. (Eds.). (2018). *Writing assessment, social justice, and the advancement of opportunity.* The WAC Clearinghouse; University Press of Colorado. https://doi.org/10.37514/PER-B.2018.0155

Pratt, M. L. (1991). Arts of the contact zone. *Profession, 33*–40.

Price, M. (2011). *Mad at school: Rhetorics of mental disability and academic life.* University of Michigan Press.

Price, M. (2015). The bodymind problem and the possibilities of pain. *Hypatia, 30,* 268–284.

Purdy, J. P., & Walker, J. R. (2010). Valuing digital scholarship: Exploring the changing realities of intellectual work. *Profession,* 177–195.

Ratcliffe, K. (2010). The twentieth and twenty-first centuries. In L. L. Gaillet & W. B. Horner (Eds.), *The present state of scholarship in the history of rhetoric: A twenty-first century guide* (pp. 185–236). University of Missouri Press.

Redd, T. M. (2014). "Talkin bout fire don't boil the pot": Putting theory into practice in a first- year writing course at an HBCU. In D. Coxwell-Teague & R. F. Lunsford (Eds.), *First- year composition: From theory to practice* (pp. 146–183). Parlor Press.

Relerford, J. (2012). Looking back in composition studies: What a narrative history of composition at HBCUs can contribute to the field today. *CLA Journal, 56*(2), 116–128.

Ritter, K., & Matsuda, P. K. (Eds.). (2016). *Exploring composition studies: Sites, issues, perspectives.* Utah State University Press.

Ritter, K., & Ianetta, M. (Eds.). (2019). *Landmark essays on writing program administration.* Routledge.

Rodriguez, G. M. (2013). Power and agency in education: Exploring the pedagogical dimensions of funds of knowledge. *Review of Research in Education, 37*, 87–120.

Roen, D., Yena, L., Pantoja, V., Waggoner, E., & Miller, S. K. (Eds.). (2002). *Strategies for teaching first-year composition.* National Council of Teachers of English.

Rose, M. (1989). *Lives on the boundary: A moving account of the struggles and achievements of America's educationally underprepared.* Penguin.

Royster, J. J., & Williams, J. C. (1999). History in the spaces left: African American presence and narratives of composition studies. *College Composition and Communication, 50*(4), 563–584. https://doi.org/10.2307/358481

Ruiz, I. D. (2016). *Reclaiming composition for Chicano/as and other ethnic minorities: A critical history and pedagogy.* Palgrave Macmillan.

Sano-Franchini, J. (2015). Cultural rhetorics and the digital humanities: Toward cultural reflexivity in digital making. In J. Ridolfo & W. Hart-Davidson (Eds.), *Rhetoric and the digital humanities* (pp. 49–64). University of Chicago Press.

Second Morrill Act, 7 U.S.C. 321 et. seq. (1890). https://www.govinfo.gov/content/pkg/USCODE-2020-title7/pdf/USCODE-2020-title7-chap13-subchapII-sec321.pdf

Selfe, C. L. (1999). Technology and literacy: A story about the perils of not paying attention. *College Composition and Communication, 50*(3), 411–436.

Selfe, C. L. (Ed.). (2007). *Multimodal composition.* Hampton.

Selfe, C. L. (2009). The movement of air, the breath of meaning: Aurality and multimodal composing. *College Composition and Communication, 60*(4), 616–663.

Selfe, C. L., & Howes, F. (2013). Over there: Disability studies and composition. *Kairos, 18*(1).

Selfe, R. J., & Selfe, C. L. (2008). "Convince me!" Valuing multimodal literacies and composing public service announcements. *Theory Into Practice, 47*(2), 83–92.

Shaughnessy, M. (1977). *Errors and expectations: A guide for the teacher of basic writing.* Oxford University Press.

Shaughnessy, M. P. (1976). Basic writing. In G. Tate (Ed.), *Teaching composition: Twelve bibliographic essays* (pp. 177–206). Texas Christian University Press.

Sheils, M. (1975, December 8). Why Johnny can't write. *Newsweek,* 58–65. http://engl4190fall2011.pbworks.com/w/file/

fetch/46866774/sheils_johnnycantwrite.pdf

Shipka, J. (2011). *Toward a composition made whole*. University of Pittsburgh Press.

Shor, I. (1997). Our apartheid: Writing instruction and inequality. *Journal of Basic Writing, 16*(1), 91–104. https://doi.org/10.37514/JBW-J.1997.16.1.08

Silva, T., & Matsuda, P. K. (Eds.). (2010). *Practicing theory in second language writing*. Parlor Press.

Sinor, J., & Gere, A. R. (1997). Composing service learning. *The Writing Instructor, 16*(2), 51- 63.

Smitherman, G. (1977). *Talkin and testifyin: The language of Black America*. Houghton-Mifflin.

Spencer-Maor, F., & Randolph Jr., R. E. (2016). Shifting the talk: Writing studies, rhetoric, and feminism at HBCUs. *Composition Studies, 44*(2), 179–182.

Stanley, S. (2017). From a whisper to a voice: Sociocultural style and anti-racist pedagogy. *Journal of Basic Writing, 36*(2), 5–25. https://doi.org/10.37514/JBW-J.2017.36.2.02

Stone, B. J., & Stewart, S. (2016). HBCUs and writing programs: Critical hip hop language pedagogy and first-year student success. *Composition Studies, 44*(2), 183–186.

Sullivan, P. (2020). *Sixteen teachers teaching: Two-year college perspectives*. Utah State University Press.

Sullivan, P., & Toth, C. (2016). *Teaching composition at the two-year college*. Bedford St. Martin's.

Tate, G., Taggart, A. R., Schick, K., & Hessler, H. B. (Eds.). (2014). *A guide to composition pedagogies*. Oxford University Press.

Thaiss, C. (1988). The future of writing across the curriculum. In S. H. McLeod (Ed.), *New Directions for Teaching and Learning, 36* (pp. 91–102). Jossey-Bass.

Thaiss, C., & Porter, T. (2010). The state of WAC/WID in 2010: Methods and results of the U.S. survey of the international WAC/WID mapping project. *College Composition and Communication, 61*(3), 534–570.

Tinberg, H. (1997). *Border talk: Writing and knowing in the two-year college*. National Council of Teachers of English.

Toth, C., Griffiths, B., & Thirolf, K. (2013). "Distinct and significant": Professional identities of two-year college English faculty.

College Composition and Communication, 65(1), 90–116.

Trimbur, J. (1994). Taking the social turn: Teaching writing post-process. *College Composition and Communication, 45*(1), 108–118.

University of California, Davis. (2019). Special issue on two-year college writing placement. *The Journal of Writing Assessment, 12*(1). https://escholarship.org/uc/jwa/12/1

University of California, Davis. (2020). Special issue on contract grading. (2020). *The Journal of Writing Assessment, 13*(2). https://escholarship.org/uc/jwa/13/2

US Department of Education. Hispanic-serving institutions. Retrieved January 20, 2021. https://sites.ed.gov/hispanic-initiative/hispanic-serving-institutions-hsis/.

Vaughan, G. B. (1982). *The community college in America: A pocket history.* American Association of Community and Junior Colleges.

Vélez-Ibáñez, C. G., & Greenberg, J. B. (1992). Formation and transformation of funds of knowledge among U.S.-Mexican households. *Anthropology & Education Quarterly, 24*(4), 313–335.

Villanueva, V. (1993). *Bootstraps: From an American academic of color.* National Council of Teachers of English.

Villanueva, V., & Arola, K. (Eds.). (2011). *Cross-talk in comp theory.* National Council of Teachers of English.

Walvoord, B. (1996). The future of WAC. *College English, 58*(1), 58–79.

White, E. M. (1993). Holistic scoring: Past triumphs and future challenges. In M. M. Williamson & B. A. Huot (Eds.), *Validating holistic scoring for writing assessment: Theoretical and empirical foundations* (pp. 79–108). Hampton Press.

White, E. M. (1985). *Teaching and assessing writing.* Jossey-Bass.

White, E. M. (2004). The changing face of writing assessment. *Composition Studies, 32*(1), 109- 118.

Wiener, H. S. (1998). The attack on basic writing—and after. *Journal of Basic Writing, 17*(1), 96–103. https://doi.org/10.37514/JBW-J.1998.17.1.07

Womack, A. M. (2017). Teaching is accommodation: Universally designing composition classrooms and syllabi. *College Composition and Communication, 68*(3), 494–523.

Wood, S. A. (2020). Engaging in resistant genres as antiracist teacher response. *The Journal of Writing Assessment, 13*(2), http://

journalofwritingassessment.org/article.php?article=157

Wood, S. A. (2018). Multimodal pedagogy and multimodal assessment: Toward a reconceptualization of traditional frameworks. In S. Khadka & J.C. Lee (Eds.), *Bridging the multimodal gap: From theory to practice* (pp. 244–262). Utah State University Press.

Wood, T. (2017). Cripping time in the composition classroom. *College Composition and Communication, 69*(2), 260–286.

Wooten, C. A., Babb, J., Costello, K. M., & Navickas, K. (Eds.). (2020). *The things we carry: Strategies for recognizing and negotiating emotional labor in writing program administration.* Utah State University Press.

Wooten, C. A., Babb, J., & Ray, B. (Eds.). (2018). *WPAs in transition: Navigating educational leadership positions.* Utah State University Press.

Wysocki, R., Udelson, J., E. Ray, C.E., Newman, J.S.B., Matravers, L.S., Kumari, A., Gordon, L.M.P., Scott, K.L., Day, M., Baumann, M., Alvarez, S.P., & DeVoss, D.N. (2018). On multimodality: A manifesto. In S. Khadka & J.C. Lee (Eds.), *Bridging the multimodal gap: From theory to practice* (pp. 17–29). Utah State University Press.

Yancey, K. B. (2004). Made not only in words: Composition in a new key. *College Composition and Communication, 56*(2), 297–328

Yancey, K. B., Robertson, L., & Taczak, K. (2014). *Writing across contexts: Transfer, composition, and sites of writing.* Utah State University Press.

Yergeau, M. (2017). *Authoring autism: On rhetoric and neurological queerness.* Duke University Press.

Yergeau, M., Brewer, E., Kerschbaum, S., Oswal, S., Price, M., Salvo, M., Selfe, C. L., & Howes, F. (2013). Multimodality in motion: Disability and kairotic Space. *Kairos, 18*(1).

Young, D. D., & Morgan, R. (2020). The impact of critical community-engaged writing on student understanding of audience. *Composition Studies, 48*(3), 35–52.

Young, V. A. (2010). Should writers use they own English? *Iowa Journal of Cultural Studies, 12*(1), 110–118.

Author

Shane A. Wood is an assistant professor of English and director of composition at the University of Southern Mississippi. He teaches first-year writing, digital literacies, technical writing, and a graduate practicum in composition theory. He received his BA in English from Western Kentucky University, MA in composition theory from Fres-  no State, and PhD in rhetoric and composition from the University of Kansas. His research interests include writing assessment, teacher response, and multimodal pedagogy. His work has appeared in journals such as the *Journal of Writing Assessment*, *WPA: Writing Program Administration*, *Composition Forum*, and *Reflections*.

Contributors

LINDA ADLER-KASSNER

I started teaching writing in classes labeled "basic writing" more than 30 years ago. I was lucky, though, to be hired by a mentor and in a program that challenged that definition and the very ideas that underscored it—a challenge that resonated with me because I had my own experiences of learning failure and exclusion. From the mentor, my students, and colleagues, as well as my graduate studies, I realized that teaching writing was about learning, listening, and advocating with others. Since that time, I've worked with students, faculty, administrators, and people in communities on two sides of a common coin associated with these practices: understanding how people (students, faculty, others) define and act on ideas about "good" learning and literacy and how those are connected to values and ideologies; and creating more explicit ways for faculty to teach/students to learn about and expand on those ideas of "good" so that they are more inclusive and equitable. I've taught undergraduate courses from first-year writing to writing and civic engagement, grad classes, and faculty seminars; I also work on pedagogical innovations to support learning and teaching. I've studied and written about all of this in recent research like *Naming What We Know: Threshold Concepts of Writing Studies* and *(Re)Considering What We Know*, both coedited with Elizabeth Wardle, and in articles like "Designing for More: Writing's Knowledge and Epistemologically Inclusive Teaching."

CHRIS M. ANSON

My parents were British, but I was born in the US (on Thanksgiving) when my father was transferred to the New York office of his firm. Lore has it that my very pregnant mother, not used to a huge meal, declared that there wasn't enough room in her for two turkeys, and was taken to the hospital to give birth. A couple of years later, my father was reassigned again to his firm's Paris office, and I spent the next six years in a small town nearby and attended a local French public school. My father had grown up in a working-class family in Birmingham, but his parents sacrificed so he could attend excellent schools, as did my mother. As a result, I was steeped in literature and the world of ideas as a kid—a "born English major," as my high school guidance counselor would call me, and an avid writer. Initially I wanted to be a novelist, and I ended up earning an MA in creative writing at Syracuse University. But faculty there exposed me to early work in writing studies. Fascinated, I pursued another MA and a PhD at Indiana University, focusing on language and linguistics with a concentration in composition. That preparation landed me a tenure-track position at the University of Minnesota, where I spent 15 years working in the Program in Composition, nine of them as its director. At Minnesota, many departments asked me to help them with writing instruction, which drew me into research on writing in the disciplines and to speaking or leading workshops for faculty at universities across the US and in many other countries. In 1999 I left Minnesota to direct a newly established WAC program for faculty at North Carolina State University, where I continue to enjoy teaching and research in writing studies and WAC. You can find a rather dry but comprehensive summary of my work at www.ansonica.net.

CHUCK BAZERMAN

Working with inner-city children in the 1960s, I saw how poorly they had been served by their schools, their societies, their governments. I had previously been caught up in finding my own way, using the literacy tools my fortunate public middle-class suburban education and private elite university education had provided me, but now I saw how inequitably these tools were made available and the consequences of that inequity. At that moment I understood the necessity of "spilling the beans," sharing the class secrets of dominance. After initially teaching what I had already learned, I had two further realizations. First, people had different experiences, motives, perceptions, and needs, so I shouldn't try to lead students down the same path as myself. In fact, that could not even succeed as students needed to follow their own paths. Second, I didn't know as much about writing as I thought I did. So I needed to do some research to find out what writing was, how it worked in the world, and how people developed as writers, whether in school or out. Since that time those three realizations have guided me.

MELVIN BEAVERS

For as long as I can remember, I have loved to read and write. In fact, my first-year writing teacher taught me to think of myself as a "good" writer. I was the student she often called upon to read my work and help others in the class. Although I still have difficulty thinking of myself as a writer or even a good one, I certainly enjoy helping others engage with the writing process. I have taught writing for 15 years, as a full-time instructor at the University of Central Arkansas, and as an assistant professor and First-Year Writing Director at the University of Arkansas, Little Rock. My research has focused on access to professional development opportunities and workplace equity for part-time faculty. I have an article titled "Administrative Rhetorical Mindfulness: A Professional Development Framework for Administrators in Higher Education" in a special issue of *Academic Labor: Research and Artistry* on "Prioritizing Ourselves and Our Values: Intersectionality, Positionality, and Dismantling the Neoliberal University System."

SUSAN NAOMI BERNSTEIN

My parents grew up in Chicago, and my father, who died at 90 from COVID-19, was a first-generation American and a first-generation college student. I was raised and attended public schools in predominantly White, redlined Chicago suburbs. My work focuses on writing for educational justice, and draws on Bettina L. Love's and Valerie Kinloch's research for Beloved Community and educational justice, and on James Baldwin's lifelong work in bearing witness to Black lives and White supremacy. I live and work in Queens, NY, and I write a blog for Bedford Bits. My book for Bedford is *Teaching Developmental Writing 4e*.

DEV BOSE

I am from Los Angeles and grew up as a first-generation Indian American in the 1990s hardcore metal and punk scene. As a neurodivergent person, disability and writing studies intersected in a revelatory diagnosis during my late 20s as a grad student; that moment defined my research trajectory. As a college writing instructor since 2001, first as a graduate student then later as a professor, my teaching philosophy accentuates accessibility from a universal design perspective while considering multiple writerly identities (with the past six years emphasizing graduate teacher training and writing program administration). I have written about these topics in forthcoming work (*Disability Studies Quarterly*, *Intermezzo*, and Parlor Press), as well as previously in *Chronicle of Higher Education*, *Technoculture*, and *Computers and Composition Digital Press*.

CAROLYN CALHOON-DILLAHUNT

I was born and raised in the agricultural Yakima Valley—Spanish and sprinklers the soundtrack of my youth. Following my dad's footsteps, I became a teacher, teaching Spanish and language arts at the middle and high school level. In graduate school, in Washington State University's nascent composition and rhetoric program, I found my disciplinary home, and a few years later, I found my professional home, teaching English at the two-year college. I began teaching at "home," at Yakima Valley College, more than twenty years ago, first on its rural Grandview campus, where I directed the campus writing center, and now on the larger Yakima campus, where I am involved with placement, accelerated learning, programmatic and institutional assessment, and equity work in addition to teaching. I have been active in professional organization leadership (former TYCA and CCCC Chair). My scholarly work centers on writing pedagogy and assessment.

LES HUTCHINSON CAMPOS

I am Xicanx with Yaqui descendency, and I was born and raised in the territories of the Serrano, Southern Paiute, and Mojave peoples. My ancestors travelled to these lands from England, Germany, Italy, and were also displaced due to Native removals across what is currently referred to as Texas and Guaymas. I have learned and done community organizing in Kumayey land for my master's degree, and in Nkwejong, where the rivers meet, land of the Anishinaabeg, for my doctoral work at Michigan State University. I currently teach in occupied Nuwe territory at Boise State University in the English department. My teaching and research focuses on social media content strategy, cultural rhetorics, and indigenous studies. I also serve as the Executive Director of the Indigenous Idaho Alliance.

SURESH CANAGARAJAH

I had my foundational education and early teaching career in Sri Lanka. My schooling was in the vernacular (Tamil) medium, with English as a second language. Sri Lanka is a former British colony, and we speak a local variety of Sri Lankan English for our purposes. The country is multi-religious (Buddhists, Hindus, Christians, and Muslims) and multilingual. After my doctoral work in sociolinguistics at the University of Texas at Austin, I returned home to teach in the University of Jaffna in 1990. However, the civil war between the majority Sinhala-speaking Buddhists and minority Tamil-speaking Hindus became more aggressive, and I was evacuated with my family out of the besieged Tamil-speaking territory by the Red Cross. I was fortunate to gain a teaching position at the City University of New York (Baruch College) on my return to the US as a refugee in 1994. After teaching in a rural university in Sri Lanka, I was suddenly thrust into a megalopolis with students from different countries and races. Though these social experiences can be unsettling, they have blessed me with a critical orientation to language and pedagogy, and a fierce commitment for justice and inclusivity. I am currently the Edwin Erle Sparks Professor of Applied Linguistics, English, and Asian Studies at Penn State University.

CHRISTINA V. CEDILLO

Born and raised in Laredo, Texas, on the Mexico-US border, I grew up familiar with a variety of cultures, languages, and practices—as well as the limits imposed on those of us from marginalized communities. After getting a master's degree, I taught middle school in Los Angeles, California, and then in Laredo, Texas. I also adjuncted at Laredo Community College and Texas A&M International University. After graduate school, I taught at Northeastern State University in Oklahoma before arriving at the University of Houston-Clear Lake. If rhetoric is all about movement, I think my itinerant experiences reflect that. My research and teaching go hand in hand, both dedicated to promoting decolonial, antiracist, and anti-ableist futures. My most recent publications are "Disabled and Undocumented: In/

Visibility at the Borders of Presence, Disclosure, and Nation" in *RSQ* and a book review titled "(Inter-)Cultural Literacies: Towards Inclusive Writing Pedagogies and Practices" in *Composition Studies.*

FRANKIE CONDON

I was raised among the rolling hills of western Pennsylvania in a poor rural county. As a White member of a multiracial family in an overwhelmingly White community, I grew up with an acute awareness of the venality of racism and White supremacy in the life of one whom I love most dearly. Over time, as I have studied, taught, written, and been generously mentored, I have acquired a powerful sense of responsibility to stand up and speak out and a more tender as well as unremitting conviction about the need to practice those forms of stillness that enable deep listening and through which humility may be learned, embodied, and learned anew. The project I am currently most excited about is a new book I'm writing in which, through a composite counterstory called "The Annals of Bean," I talk about the why's, how's, and wherefore's of critically reflexive antiracist pedagogy.

STEVEN J. CORBETT

I've been teaching and tutoring writing since 1997. I started as a peer tutor at the Edmonds Community College (near Seattle, WA) writing center, and the way I feel about teaching and learning are underscored by my experiences in teaching one-to-one and in small groups. Like many writing teachers and tutors, I believe that writing is certainly social, but also a very personal issue. This is evident in just how personally we take comments about our writing, how elated we feel when someone praises our writing and writing performances, how deflated we might feel if someone comments carelessly on our writing. With students and teachers of all levels, I try to cultivate relationships that combine scholarship and friendship with collaborative intellectual rigor and reasonable expectations. Then I write, and rewrite, about those relationships.

GINNY CRISCO

As a literacy specialist, I honor my father for sending me on that path: he struggled with reading and writing because of his disability, so Elspeth Stuckey "violence of literacy" was a concept I saw in action based on my father's experiences of the world. Additionally, after high school, I was an au-pair Mädchen for a family in Wiesbaden, (West) Germany. I had learned German for six years, but I was not prepared for the challenge—and the prejudice—that language learners face, and this experience would later inform my thesis research on teaching second-language learners at the college level in California. These experiences and many others have led me to where I am now: a professor at California State University, Fresno, working on a large federal grant in collaboration with teachers at the secondary and college levels across California and Washington, to implement curriculum that includes culturally sustaining language pedagogy and universal design for learning for the first-year college and secondary English language arts classrooms.

HARRY DENNY

I grew up in Davenport, Iowa, one of the Quad Cities along the Mississippi River. My family was and remains working class, and I was the first to complete an undergraduate degree as well as to attend graduate school and receive advanced degrees. All of that makes me a proud first-generation academic. I've helped lead writing centers for twenty-eight years, from LIU/Brooklyn and SUNY Stony Brook to St. John's and now Purdue. In West Lafayette, I am the faculty director of the Writing lab and its widely-used website, the Purdue OWL. My teaching, research, and leadership seeks to focus on the role and dynamics of identity politics on access and success around writing and rhetoric and literacy practices. Apart from a recent book with Robert Mundy (*Gender, Sexuality, and the Cultural Politics of Men's Identity in the New Millennium: Literacies of Masculinity*) and an edited collection (*Out in the Center: Public Controversies and Private Struggles*), I have a current project that explores activist rhetoric in amici briefs around civil rights and the Supreme Court under review.

JAY DOLMAGE

I have a lovely partner named Heather, a dog named Bingo, and three hilarious children named Vern, Francine, and Murphy. I am committed to disability rights in my scholarship, service, and teaching. My work brings together rhetoric, writing, disability studies, and critical pedagogy. My first book, entitled *Disability Rhetoric*, was published with Syracuse University Press in 2014. *Academic Ableism: Disability and Higher Education* was published with Michigan University Press in 2017 and is available in an open-access version online. *Disabled Upon Arrival: Eugenics, Immigration, and the Construction of Race and Disability* was published in 2018 with Ohio State University Press. I am the Founding Editor of the *Canadian Journal of Disability Studies*.

JOHN DUFFY

I am a professor of English at the University of Notre Dame, where I teach classes in writing and literature. I arrived at Notre Dame after a peripatetic journey that included a PhD from the University of Wisconsin, and MA degrees in applied linguistics from Teachers College and in Irish studies from University College, Dublin. These were punctuated by four years working in refugee camps in Southeast Asia. Although I have lived in the Midwest for some thirty years, I still think of myself as a New Yorker.

CANDACE EPPS-ROBERTSON

I was born and raised in Richmond, VA. My mother was a social worker, and my father, a correctional officer. I grew up acutely aware that words had power. As an undergrad, I wanted to be an orthopedic surgeon because it felt impossible, and I could see how they helped people. My career ambition changed when I began to take classes in philosophy and literature because I could also see how working with language felt impossible and could help people. My research is driven by a desire to understand how people learn to be present in the world. How do we use language to build communities, resist oppression, and seek joy? My first book, *Resisting Brown: Race, Literacy, and Citizenship in the Heart of Virginia* (2018), examines the literacy curriculum of a free school established during the American civil rights movement. My second book project examines pedagogies for global citizenship through music and fandom.

BRYNA SIEGEL FINER

When I was a kid, I spent lots of my free time writing stories and poems in blank books, and if I wasn't writing, I was usually reading.

My teachers always told me I was a good writer, so the idea that people struggle with writing was new to me when I started college and met friends who hated to write. I supported a lot of these friends, and this was partly what made me realize that I wanted to be a teacher and work with students who had the most challenges with their writing. Thus, I've been teaching basic writing for over twenty years now, first as an adjunct in New York City and its suburbs, then in Rhode Island, Vermont, and now as a professor and Director of Writing Across the Curriculum at Indiana University of Pennsylvania. In my classes, students write about their communities and social issues that are important to them; they write in real genres for real audiences. Like them, I also write about communities and social issues through my research in the rhetoric of health and medicine, and in my two coedited collections, *Writing Program Architecture: Thirty Cases for Reference and Research*, and *Women's Health Advocacy: Rhetorical Ingenuity for the 21st Century*.

LAURA GONZALES

I was born in Santa Cruz, Bolivia. I immigrated to Orlando, Florida with my family when I was 9 years old. My early learning experiences in the US were shaped by the English as a Second Language (ESOL) program I attended, the stigma I faced as a multilingual learner, and the work my mom and grandpa did to teach me English in community. Stemming from these experiences, I decided at an early age that I would be an "English teacher," specifically so that I could tell students like myself that not speaking English as a first language is not a bad thing. Now, I write about the power of language diversity in professional, academic, and community contexts, and I have the privilege of working with multilingual communities who continue to show me how language is a dynamic, powerful technology. My first monograph, *Sites of Translation: What Multilinguals Can Teach Us about Digital Writing and Rhetoric*, provides insights into how multilingual Latinx communities translate and localize information by leveraging various cultural and rhetorical practices.

DAVID F. GREEN JR.

Raised by two teachers in the heart of central Newark, NJ, I was provided an eclectic introduction to urban life and Black culture at an early age, which continues to shape the way I engage the world. My father was a natural philosopher, gymnastics coach, and jazz enthusiast and my mom was a well-known English teacher in the Newark public schools system, and a passionate consumer of film and drama. Following in their footsteps, I taught junior high school written communications for a year in Norfolk, VA, and after being advised by past professors to apply to a graduate program, and against the wishes of many of my students, I applied to several graduate programs. Soon after my acceptance to Penn State University, I was formally introduced to rhetoric and composition by Keith Gilyard and Elaine Richardson. I was trained and specialized in African American literature, language, and rhetoric during my time at Penn State, and would go one to receive a master's in English and a PhD in rhetoric and composition from the Pennsylvania State University. I have been teaching at the college level for about 15 years beginning at Penn State University, then Hampton University, and then Howard University. Currently an associate professor of English at Howard University, I teach courses in rhetoric, African American literature, and writing in addition to serving as director of Howard University's writing program. I rely on a hip-hop influenced understanding of African American rhetoric and culture to shape much of my teaching and research, particularly in regard to social justice approaches to teaching and critical pedagogy. My current research interrogates hip-hop discourse and its various cultural and composing practices as an analytical approach to conversations about rhetoric, writing, race, and language.

JENNIFER GROULING

I grew up as the only child of two academics. My early memories of the university are of my mother driving between locations as an adjunct faculty member in multiple departments at multiple schools. I'd sit in the back of her classroom or office and write. The first negative feedback I received on an essay was my overly specific description of her office chair. It's not a surprise, then, that I ended up as an associate professor and Director of the Writing Program at Ball State University. I care deeply about labor issues, response, and teacher development. My work is driven by a fascination with the tension between choice and constraint, whether that tension is in how much freedom to give new TAs in teaching writing, how national rubrics for writing are modified for local context, or in how game masters control role-playing narratives. When not working, I love playing board games and hanging out with my wife and cats. http://www.jgrouling.com/

CODY HOOVER

I'm an English instructor at Clovis Community College in Fresno, California. I grew up in a working class, Mexican American family, and I was the first member of my family to graduate from college. I completed my BA and MA in English literature at Fresno State, where I worked in the writing center and as a TA. My first job at a community college was in a writing center at Long Beach City College, and I started adjunct teaching at Moreno Valley College, on top of teaching as a TA at University of California, Riverside. I moved back to my hometown of Fresno and have adjuncted at Clovis Community College, Fresno City College, and West Hills College Lemoore. I'm proud to have returned to work in Fresno at a variety of community colleges (urban, suburban, and rural colleges), where I hope to both promote open-access schools and challenge the institutions that have systemically oppressed and made learning difficult for people like my family and others in my community.

ASAO B. INOUE

I was born in Englewood, California, to a White-identified mother born in Oregon and Japanese father born in Hawai'i. I was raised in various poor and working-class parts of Las Vegas, where I attended public schools and where most of that time I was a remedial English student. I am also a product of a single-parent home. My mother worked three jobs so we could be poor, and I love her for it. Today, I am a teacher of color who does antiracist language work, often published by academic presses. Sometimes my language work is in classrooms, but more often these days it is with colleagues in academic settings, as a good part of my life is as the Associate Dean of Academic Affairs, Equity, and Inclusion at ASU in the College of Integrative Sciences and Arts. I consider myself first and foremost a languageling of color who works daily at confronting and dismantling the White language supremacy in the world and in me.

KAREN KEATON JACKSON

I was born in Detroit, Michigan, and I've wanted to be a teacher for as long as I can remember. I am a proud graduate of Hampton University, an HBCU that alum lovingly call "Our Home by the Sea." There I majored in English secondary education; however, when I did my student teaching, I realized the high school setting wasn't quite the space for me. So, I went back home to attend graduate school at Wayne State University. Like many people, I thought English only consisted of literature, so I was beyond excited when I fell in love with composition studies after one class. I realized I could combine my passion for teaching with my love for writing. It was the perfect match. I've since worked my way through the assistant, associate, and full professor ranks at North Carolina Central University, the first public liberal arts HBCU in the country. I directed our writing studio and writing program and also served time on the Southeastern Writing Center Association and Council of Writing Program Administrators executive boards. I've been a facilitator for the International Writing Center Association Summer Institute and I'm currently a Trustee on the NCTE Research Foundation Board.

DARIN JENSEN

I am the son of a printer and a bookkeeper and a first-generation college student. I have spent most of my career teaching in community colleges and shouting about their importance to anyone who would listen. I teach writing, work on professional issues, edit, and write. I still believe in the democratic potential of literacy and education and that we can make a more just, fair, and equitable world, although I should probably know better by now. My students and I are trying to figure out what good writing is and we'll be sure to tell you as soon as we find out. Currently, I'm editing *Teaching English in the Two-Year College* and am raising a puppy. I have no idea which of the two is more difficult.

LISA KING

I was born and raised in rural Kansas, close to the Oklahoma border. My dad farmed some, worked as a journeyman lineman for the regional power company, and worked as a head building engineer/

head janitor until his recent retirement; my mom sold Tupperware part-time and substitute-taught for years in local schools until she decided to go back to college to complete her special-ed teaching degree at the same time I completed my own BA (and we were simultaneously in graduate school together, too). I'm a first-gen PhD, and I've taught writing for 20 years, from the University of Kansas as a grad student, to John A. Logan Community College as an adjunct, to the University of Hawai'i-Mānoa and now the University of Tennessee-Knoxville. I was raised to honor all the parts of my heritage, though as I grew up it became apparent that some (whiter) parts got more honor than others, and the history of colonialism is writ deep in my family history. My writing and teaching, then, have been dedicated to help make visible the settler-colonial narratives we take for granted as "true" no matter what land we live on, and to help support Native American and Indigenous voices and self-representation inside and outside the writing classroom. I've had the honor to coedit *Survivance, Sovereignty, and Story: Teaching American Indian Rhetorics* with Joyce Rain Anderson and Rose Gubele to talk about the work we can do in our classrooms, and written my own monograph *Legible Sovereignties: Rhetoric, Representations, and Native American Museums* to draw attention to other powerful educational sites and how Indigenous peoples self-represent.

EUNJEONG LEE

My scholarly work has a lot to do with who I am—an immigrant-generation, multilingual scholar of color who has constantly moved across language and various geographical settings. Born and raised in South Korea, I learned to pick up the Busan dialect to avoid getting called "sassy" or "snobby" for speaking the Seoul dialect (which is considered as the standard Korean). Following my immigrant mother, I moved to the US and taught in different places—first in West Texas, next in Central Pennsylvania, where I completed my doctoral degree at Pennsylvania State University, then in northern California. I began my first Assistant Professor position at Queens College, City University New York, and now currently work at University of Houston. I learned, and continue to learn, how complex and rich language histories and practices multilingual students bring to my class, which shapes my teaching and research on how literacy classrooms and research can better sustain and amplify multilingual students' language practices. My recent work on this thinking has been published in *World Englishes* and *Composition Forum*.

NEAL LERNER

Having grown up in suburban New Jersey, I was eager to leave home and start college. Unfortunately, the University of Pennsylvania and I did not see eye to eye, nor did my choice to be a math major quite work out. By the time I graduated from SUNY Purchase with a BA in English, I vowed never to set foot in a classroom again and went to work in Silicon Valley as a production manager for a four-person company making plug-in boards for the then brand-new personal computer. After several years of life in the matrix, I took a year off to write a novel, ran out of money and realized that if I pursued an MA, I could live off of student loans and spend more time writing. Over 30 years later, I find myself as the chair of the English Department at Northeastern University after time spent as a writing teacher, writing center, writing program, and WAC director. Writing continues to sustain me though it's primarily been academic writing since putting aside that last novel to pursue my doctorate in education. I do plan on returning to fiction writing in a few years, as well as riding my bicycle from Portland, OR, to Portland, ME.

ALEXANDRIA LOCKETT

I was raised by a working-class family in Fort Campbell, Kentucky; Fort Eustis, Virginia; and Texarkana, Texas. For over twenty years, my dad served in the military while my mother was a dedicated housewife and certified childcare provider. They divorced shortly after his retirement, which led my mother to rejoin the workforce. She retired from Christus St. Michael Hospital where she served over twenty years as a dispatcher. I'm a first-generation student. I've been in the workforce since I was 15. My pursuit of higher education would not have been possible without computer literacy. With the generous assistance of my mother, I purchased my first computer at 16 and took high school courses in business computer applications and telecommunications. This access combined with a Bill Gates Millennium scholarship played a major role in my ability to attend a four-year college. I went to grad school after learning about and being accepted into the Robert E. McNair postbaccalaureate program, which enabled me to do undergraduate research. I went to the University of Oklahoma where I was introduced to composition, rhetoric, and literacy courses and began teaching and administering first-year writing. I've taught writing for fifteen years: as a grad student at the University of Oklahoma State and the Pennsylvania State University. I am currently an assistant professor at Spelman College where I teach professional writing and technical communication that center Black women's epistemologies, narratives, and Herstory.

PAULA MATHIEU

I am the youngest of nine children and was born and raised in the south suburbs of Chicago where I attended Catholic school. I spent my undergraduate years at the University of Illinois, Urbana-Champaign, and then moved to Chicago where I lived for more than a decade and completed my MA and PhD at the University of Illinois-Chicago and worked with the nonprofit, StreetWise, offering work and writing opportunities for individuals experiencing homelessness or poverty. I have taught writing in some form or another since 1995 and at Boston College since 2001. The question that defines my array of writing and research interest is both simple and maddeningly complex: when, how, and for whom is language powerful and performative, and when, how and for whom is language insufficient or destructive? In other words, to paraphrase Rebecca Solnit: when is language the bars of our cage and when is it the crowbar that pries open those bars? I love writing and it humbles me. I live with my husband, daughter, and two dogs in Lexington, Massachusetts.

PAUL KEI MATSUDA

I was born and raised in Japan as a monolingual speaker of Japanese. I started taking required English classes in junior high school, but I did not enjoy them because of the emphasis on memorization and translation, and I developed no proficiency. Four years later, I became interested in becoming proficient in English, and devised my own curriculum based primarily on reading and writing news articles, which led to an undergraduate major in communication and journalism. Seeing the limited support for second-language writers at the time in both language and writing programs at all levels, I decided to become an expert in both language studies and writing studies, and to help bring various disciplinary perspectives together. I continue to advocate for second-language writers by helping build the disciplinary infrastructure and by working with teachers, researchers and administrators from around the world.

TEMPTAOUS MCKOY

Straight out of Harnett County, NC, I am ya country girl with a love for all things Black, writing, and smiling—a lot. Child of two military veterans, including one that went on to be an educator, I am out here making my way through this rhet comp and technical communication world. I am also a member of Sigma Gamma Rho Sorority, Incorporated. For undergrad, I went to the illustrious Elizabeth City State University, an HBCU in eastern North Carolina, Armstrong State University in Savannah for my master's, and came back home for my PhD in writing, rhetoric, and professional communication at East Carolina University. There is where I wrote my two-time award-winning dissertation, "Y'all Call It Technical and Professional Communication, We Call It #ForTheCulture." Upon graduation in 2019, I took my talents back to an HBCU where I am an assistant professor of English and Coordinator of Graduate Studies for the Department of Language, Literature, and Cultural Studies at Bowie State University. I've chaired the CCCC Black Technical and Professional Communication Task Force in addition to currently serving as the Associate Editor of the *Peitho* journal. From my teaching, writing, and general day-to-day practices, I'm out here making sure I center the lived experiences of Black and other historically marginalized communities.

CRUZ MEDINA

I'm the son of two first-generation college students turned educators. My father earned his master's degree and taught English at the community college level and my mother earned her master's degree in TESOL and taught at the elementary school level. After graduating undergrad, I taught third grade in Costa Rica. I tutored writing at Chapman University while earning my master's degrees and taught writing at the University of Arizona, where I earned my PhD. The courses I teach at Santa Clara University and for the Bread Loaf School of English incorporate digital writing as it relates to cultural rhetoric and decolonial approaches. My article in *Rhetoric Review* "'Publishing is Mystical': The Latinx Caucus Bibliography, Top-Tier Journals, and Minority Scholarship" provides data and perspectives on publishing from members of the NCTE/CCCC Latinx Caucus that I've co-chaired since 2017.

SHARON MITCHLER

I grew up in rural Iowa, and after high school attended Iowa State University. After switching to four different majors, I found my way to an English major and a minor in secondary education. After teaching at high schools in Iowa, North Carolina, and El Salvador, Central America, I dipped a toe in remote graduate work while I was living in Panama and served as the "branch campus" for Panama Canal Community College at Fort Davis. Two master's degrees later, I made the switch to full-time community college teaching, first at Fayetteville Technical Community College in North Carolina, and for the last 23 years, at Centralia College, in rural Washington State. I teach multiple courses in the English and Humanities Department, with freshman composition a continuous part of my schedule. Helped by the generous support of Centralia College, I recently completed my PhD in English in my 50s, while teaching full time. My teaching focuses on meeting students where they are and helping them reach their next goals. Teaching for transfer and critical rural pedagogy are my current research interests. I have published primarily in *Teaching English in the Two-Year College.*

BEVERLY J. MOSS

I was born in York County, South Carolina, and grew up in Charlotte, North Carolina, during the time that Charlotte-Mecklenburg schools were going through court-ordered busing for desegregation. What that mean for me was a dramatic shift from an all-Black elementary school to an integrated junior high and high school. For the most part, I was the only Black student (or one of two) in many of my junior high and high school classes. When I graduated from high school, I attended Spelman College, an HBCU for Black women. Choosing an HBCU was the best decision of my life. Attending a school dedicated to educating and celebrating Black women was important for me as an 18-year-old introvert who needed the grounding in Black women's history and accomplishments. I was fortunate to have Jacqueline Royster as my first-year writing and advanced composition professor at Spelman. She introduced me to the field of Rhetoric and Composition and to the idea of attending graduate school. My desire to do research on literacy practices in African American community contexts is very much connected to the African American communities I grew up in and to which I belong now.

JESSICA NASTAL

I am one of a long line of union members on both sides of my Irish Lebanese American family. Born on the south side of Chicago, I became the first woman on either side to earn a bachelor degree. After many jobs in many different arenas—including as a janitor and as a technical writer—I found rhetoric and composition/writing studies. When I decided to pursue a PhD, it was to work at a two-year college, primarily to connect with working-class students like I was, from communities that have long been excluded from higher education. I teach exclusively composition classes, where my focus is to help students understand the cognitive, interpersonal, and intrapersonal domains of writing (White et al., 2015). I strive to encourage students to gain confidence in and awareness of their writing; one way we do this is by using the guidelines of *Queen City Writers* for our research projects, and submitting essays for publication consideration. I want to make the cultural expectations of academia transparent, especially for New Majority college students. My research focuses on equity in writing assessment, placement, and pedagogy, and has recently been published in *ETS Research Reports* and the *Journal of Response to Writing*.

BEATRICE MENDEZ NEWMAN

I spoke only Spanish probably the first four years of my life. When it was time to start kindergarten, my immigrant parents started teaching me English so I wouldn't be behind my peers, and gradually, English became my dominant language. Sadly, I do not speak Spanish easily now, but the structure, cadences, and mindset of Spanish are indelibly in my linguistic make up. That has been an advantage in working with translingual students because I see and hear what they are doing as they merge structures and ways of thinking across languages. As a professor at one of the largest Hispanic-Serving Institutions in the country, I write a lot about translingualism. However, these days, I am also exploring pedagogies that support writing growth in online settings. My latest publication, a piece in the November 2020 *English Journal*, shows how I guided my dual enrollment students in preserving their translingual creativity even in the sometimes leveling environment of online writing.

REBECCA S. NOWACEK

When I was a sophomore in college, my sociology professor handed back a paper to me saying, with a smile and a shake of his head, "You write like an English major." I was both confused and intrigued by that backhanded compliment, and much of my subsequent research has been devoted to understanding how students learn to distinguish and write for various disciplines and what teachers can do to facilitate that learning. I've grown especially interested in the question of "transfer"—how writers connect what they know and who they are in one context with what they know and who they are in another context. I completed a book (*Agents of Integration*) on this subject and have also explored the powerful role that peer writing tutors can play in helping writers to integrate their knowledge across contexts (in *Writing Center Journal, Composition Forum, Naming What We Know*, and elsewhere). Much of this more recent research has been conducted in collaboration with the marvelous undergraduate and graduate peer tutors at Marquette University's Ott Memorial Writing Center, where I serve as co-director.

STEVE PARKS

I have spent my career attempting to repay the labor of all those who enabled me to attend college, survive graduate school while raising small children, and enjoy a comfortable life. Through experience and research, I have come to understand the university as an institution writ large designed, inherently, to exclude those on the wrong side of privilege. My own work as a teacher has been to create classrooms which enable students to navigate such environments while still maintaining a deep connection to the values and communities which enabled them to succeed. Some of this work has appeared in *CCC*, *College English, Literacy in Composition Studies,* and *Reflections*, as well as in *Class Politics: A Students Right to Their Own Language, Gravyland: Writing Beyond the Curriculum in the City of Brotherly Love,* and numerous edited collections. This work has also enabled me to create and sustain *New City Community Press.*

STACI PERRYMAN-CLARK

I grew up in Toledo, Ohio, and attended an all-girls Catholic college prep school offering AP English literature. Though I did poorly on the AP exam, I thought my college prep high school would prepare me well for higher education. It did; my first two years of undergraduate education at the University of Michigan seemed much less challenging than my prep high school. This education laid the foundation for a career and love for the study of writing. After taking a first semester narration course in college, I knew I wanted to major in writing, with creative writing being the only option for a course of study. At the time, I thought I would pursue an MFA in fiction and become the next best author. Instead, I was only accepted into a graduate program that focused on teaching writing, where I fell in love with writing studies and would later pursue a PhD in rhetoric and writing at Michigan State University. I currently serve as the Director of the Institute for Intercultural and Anthropological Studies at Western Michigan University, housed within the College of Arts and Sciences. I am professor of English and African American Studies at Western Michigan University, and served as program chair for the annual 2022 CCCC Convention. I was a previous recipient of the 2008 CCCC Scholars from the Dream Award, WMU College of Arts and Sciences Excellence in Diversity and Inclusion, WMU College of Arts and Sciences Faculty Achievement Award in Research and Scholarship, and Council of Writing Program Administrators Best Book Award.

MIKE ROSE

I've been tutoring or teaching since I was 24: elementary school; community college; university, from "basic writing" to graduate seminar;

and a range of special programs for Vietnam veterans and active-duty military, people in job-training, employees in the criminal justice system, and the general public (through UCLA Extension) interested in contemporary fiction. And almost as long as I've been teaching, I've been studying it and writing about it. I have been in education for the long haul, and it has given my life great meaning. As I try to show in a book I'm finishing now titled *When the Light Goes On*, education is a grand human enterprise, on a par with medicine or theology in the insight it gives us into the human condition, our struggles and our achievements. I feel so, so lucky to have found this work.

TODD RUECKER

My interest in working with multilingual writers was sparked by a summer working at a hotel just outside Denali National Park in Alaska. I was part of a very international housekeeping staff and my friends from the Czech Republic and Korea encouraged me to come to their countries to teach English because, as a native English speaker, I could get a job easily (a reality I've critiqued in later scholarship). After graduating and finishing a master's, which focused in part on ESL and second-language writing, I spent two years teaching English in the Czech Republic in a variety of settings. After a short time in Chile teaching English, I started a PhD program at the University of Texas at El Paso, where I was lured because of the opportunity to work with Kate Mangelsdorf while also studying and teaching in a rich, multicultural and multilingual environment. These experiences have shaped me into a teacher, scholar, and administrator who is conscious of the diverse lives of the students we work with, advocating for policies and curricula that are responsive to students' lives and languages. I am currently serving as the Director of Core Writing at the University of Nevada, Reno. In my free time, I engage in all sorts of outdoor adventures, hiking, backpacking, mountain biking, skiing, and kayaking.

IRIS D. RUIZ

I grew up in the Central Valley. I was raised by a single mom, who was a teacher turned administrator in some of the roughest areas of Fresno, California. I often accompanied her in the summers to be her teacher's aide, and I saw how dedicated she was and how much the kids loved her. I became a justice-oriented educator early on. When I decided to pursue a pre-med college path, I discovered that I loved and wanted to live to write. Writing became my passion, and my career path changed. I found what I loved to do. As a BIPOC activist scholar, I learned how to use my skills to further social justice. I've dedicated much of my life to helping others advance in their academic careers, since my own work has never been a one woman show. Never. Four books, seven articles/chapters under my belt, and most have been collaborative. I am a continuing lecturer for the UC Merced Merritt Writing Program and the founder of the professional journal *Latinx Writing and Rhetoric Studies*.

ALISA RUSSELL

I recently officially moved to the faculty side of academia—assistant professor in the writing program at Wake Forest University—but thankfully that side still includes everything I loved about being a student my whole life: digging into class discussion, annotating new scholarship, exploring the fertility of writing-in-progress, outlining through ideas, poring over syllabi, and realizing daily there's still so much to learn. Lately, my learning on sustainable program design and on "classroom genres" has been shaped by my role as WAC facilitator at Wake. Here I must give a special shoutout to my weekly AWAC Writing Group—that's where I'm writing up a recent ethnographic study that teases out the relationship between writing and access so we might better increase access through writing and writing innovations. And the student writers I'm lucky enough to encounter each semester are, as ever, the energy and inspiration driving all of this.

CECILIA SHELTON

I was a Black girl who loved words and grew up to be an assistant professor of English at the University of Maryland. Not enough of the Black girls who love words are allowed to grow up to be professors, so I'm clear that whatever I do within the academy should have resonance outside of it. I have carved a long and winding path through English studies; I started in writing centers, dipped my toes in sociolinguistics, found my footing in rhetoric and composition, and finally planted my feet in technical and professional communication.

The throughline in all of my work across these subdisciplines has been to think about communication-based solutions to systemic violences that harm vulnerable people. I'm currently an assistant professor of English at the University of Maryland where I teach language, writing, and rhetoric classes and continue to position my research to advocate for vulnerable communities. #BlackLivesMatter

JODY SHIPKA

I was born and raised in Illinois, spending the bulk of my adult life there, moving to Maryland in 2005 when I was hired as an assistant professor at University of Maryland, Baltimore County. Growing up, I don't recall having many hobbies, that is to say, having an interest in, and making time for exploring things like (analog) photography, painting, antiquing, and baking didn't come until later in life. I'm particularly interested in finding ways of connecting my hobby worlds with my scholarship—something I attempt to do with my latest book project, *Edible Rhetoric*, a text that examines people's histories with, and memories of, baking and cooking.

NANCY SOMMERS

The desire to write, to arrange the alphabet into sentences—where does it begin? Looking back, I see all the incremental moments, the overlapping encouragements and discouragements, the teachers and fellow writers who took leaps of faith, coaxing, "You come along, too." I like to think that these companions are rooting for me whenever I compose a sentence. But, really, it could have turned out differently. I grew up, in Terre Haute, Indiana, with immigrant parents who stumbled when they spoke English. They had escaped the Holocaust and English wasn't their mother tongue. Family lore has it that I became my mother's voice, speaking for her when English words weren't in her vocabulary, greeting guests with the question—"Do you want to know something?" Proceeding to tell tragic stories about the death of a pet rabbit, or about my beloved Shirley Temple doll losing her arm, I learned early on that a well-told well story finds its sympathetic listeners. As I look back on my childhood, I see that there were literacy lessons for the taking, although none of them announced, or annotated as such: lessons about words, their need to be chosen, carefully. And lessons about storytelling: start with a hook:

set the scene, develop the plot. Perhaps writing is too small a word to describe these moments—lessons at the intersection of living and writing—that seem so important in retrospect, but rarely declare themselves as such. I have been a teacher of writing, a writing program director and researcher, and a writer for forty years—a lifetime of words and stories, between and across drafts. My students' stories and mine are inevitably woven together. During our time together, we've helped each other find something to say, and a reason to say it.

CHRIS THAISS

My grandparents emigrated from Germany and what is now Slovakia around 1900 and settled in Ohio. My dad grew up on his parents' small farm, while my mom, a city girl, grew up helping her parents in their start-up dry cleaning business. Both my parents had a strong commitment to their children's education, and encouraged me to do well in school. After graduating from the University of Virginia, I was offered a job teaching at my old high school, but I chose instead to accept a fellowship in English at Northwestern, and that determined my future as the first academic in the long history of my family. After getting my degree, I taught as an adjunct at George Mason University and Northern Virginia Community College, before becoming tenure-track at GMU, where I fell in love with teaching writing, which soon turned into directing the composition program and the small writing center, then developing a WAC program, co-developing grad concentrations, and eventually chairing the department. After 30 years at Mason, my move to UC Davis helped me get closer to my family's farming roots: as director of the newly-independent University Writing Program, I began teaching writing in science, which I've been developing ever since. Retirement in 2016 gave me time to write the textbook *Writing Science in the Twenty-First Century*, build my own garden, and contribute to sensory descriptive analysis research at the Mondavi Institute for Wine and Food Science. I still occasionally teach writing in science, now virtually. You can learn more about me at http://thaiss.ucdavis.edu.

HOWARD TINBERG

I am a son of immigrants. My parents, displaced persons after WWII, came to this country seeking refuge, freedom, and a portion of the American Dream, for themselves and for their children. My parents sent us all to the public schools, including university. I have spent more than three decades teaching at a public, open-access community college, thoroughly committed to the mission of the community college to provide access and paths to success to whoever enters its doors. Having mostly taught first-year composition for roughly four decades, I believe passionately in the ennobling power of literacies—as did my parents, who, while not formally educated themselves, realized that education empowers us all. My current interest—in promoting my students' ability to transfer what they learn in first-year composition to new settings and new challenges in which composing is required—flows naturally from a career centered on student access and success.

STEPHANIE VIE

In some ways it's not surprising that I ended up focusing my research agenda on social media and digital technologies, as some of my earliest and fondest memories have to do with technology: My dad teaching me how to write the computer language BASIC when I was young and creating my own video games on a classic Apple IIe computer; playing Frogger and Adventure on an Atari 2600 and, later, getting that gray Nintendo console and Legend of Zelda games for Christmas; staying up late to chat on IRC and emailing people across the world with my first email address, back when getting emails was neat and not a drag. Today I remain fascinated by the possibilities that digital technologies hold for us, but I'm also concerned about the many ways they've been used to further inequalities and injustices. Still, I couldn't have asked for a more interesting subject to study, and much of my recent work has looked at social media pedagogy and professional uses. I've been privileged to work with colleagues at institutions in Colorado, Florida, and today Hawai'i, where I work at the University of Hawai'i at Mānoa as an associate dean of Outreach College.

ELIZABETH WARDLE

I was raised by missionaries and spent the early years of my life in a jungle in Mexico. Later, I watched my parents work as fundraisers for non-profits and as social workers for babies with attachment disorders. I began writing grant proposals for non-profits when I was still in college, and my first full-time job was as a fundraiser for a food bank. Those early experiences, and the sense that whatever I do needs to be done with conviction and a sense of mission, continues to inform how I do my work. I fell in love with teaching writing as a TA at the University of Louisville, teaching students who had worked all night at UPS and were trying to stay awake for an 8 a.m. composition course. When I struggled to explain ideas to students, my husband reminded me, "If you can only teach the students who already understand, you aren't teaching." Ever since, I have focused on how to improve teaching and curricula for more inclusive learning, whether as a writing program director (at U of Dayton or UCF), as a department chair (at UCF), or working with faculty across the curriculum (at Miami).

TARA WOOD

After spending some time bouncing from one university to the next during my early undergraduate years, I found a home at Colorado State University's English department. I'd been an English major for a while, but the focus on rhetoric and writing at CSU was the first time I felt the "these are my people" moment. I finished my BA and MA at CSU in their rhetoric and writing program and then went on to pursue my PhD at the University of Oklahoma. I've been teaching, reading, and writing in the field for about 15 years now. Currently, I'm an associate professor of English and writing program administrator at the University of Northern Colorado. I am interested in disability, writing pedagogy, and writing program administration. I have an article in *WPA: Writing Program Administration* that draws on disability theory to interrogate the roles WPAs have to play in Title IX policy and decision-making. I also serve in a couple of elected positions within the Conference on College Composition and Communication, including co-chair of the Committee on Disability Issues and as a member of the Executive Committee.

BOOKS IN THE CCCC STUDIES IN WRITING & RHETORIC SERIES

Teachers Talking Writing: Perspectives on Places, Pedagogies, and Programs
Shane A. Wood

Materiality and Writing Studies: Aligning Labor, Scholarship, and Teaching
Holly Hassel and Cassandra Phillips

Rhetorics of Overcoming: Rewriting Narratives of Disability and Accessibility in Writing Studies
Allison Harper Hitt

Writing Accomplices with Student Immigrant Rights Organizers
Glenn Hutchinson

Counterstory: The Rhetoric and Writing of Critical Race Theory
Aja Y. Martinez

Writing Programs, Veterans Studies, and the Post-9/11 University: A Field Guide
Alexis Hart and Roger Thompson

Beyond Progress in the Prison Classroom: Options and Opportunities
Anna Plemons

Rhetorics Elsewhere and Otherwise: Contested Modernities, Decolonial Visions
Edited by Romeo García and Damián Baca

Black Perspectives in Writing Program Administration: From the Margins to the Center
Edited by Staci M. Perryman-Clark and Collin Lamont Craig

Translanguaging outside the Academy: Negotiating Rhetoric and Healthcare in the Spanish Caribbean
Rachel Bloom-Pojar

Collaborative Learning as Democratic Practice: A History
Mara Holt

Reframing the Relational: A Pedagogical Ethic for Cross-Curricular Literacy Work
Sandra L. Tarabochia

Inside the Subject: A Theory of Identity for the Study of Writing
Raúl Sánchez

Genre of Power: Police Report Writers and Readers in the Justice System
Leslie Se0p3.5awright

Assembling Composition
Edited by Kathleen Blake Yancey and Stephen J. McElroy

Public Pedagogy in Composition Studies
Ashley J. Holmes

From Boys to Men: Rhetorics of Emergent American Masculinity
Leigh Ann Jones

Freedom Writing: African American Civil Rights Literacy Activism, 1955–1967
Rhea Estelle Lathan

The Desire for Literacy: Writing in the Lives of Adult Learners
Lauren Rosenberg

On Multimodality: New Media in Composition Studies
Jonathan Alexander and Jacqueline Rhodes

Toward a New Rhetoric of Difference
Stephanie L. Kerschbaum

Rhetoric of Respect: Recognizing Change at a Community Writing Center
Tiffany Rousculp

After Pedagogy: The Experience of Teaching
Paul Lynch

Redesigning Composition for Multilingual Realities
Jay Jordan

Agency in the Age of Peer Production
Quentin D. Vieregge, Kyle D. Stedman, Taylor Joy Mitchell, and Joseph M. Moxley

Remixing Composition: A History of Multimodal Writing Pedagogy
Jason Palmeri

First Semester: Graduate Students, Teaching Writing, and the Challenge of Middle Ground
Jessica Restaino

Agents of Integration: Understanding Transfer as a Rhetorical Act
Rebecca S. Nowacek

Digital Griots: African American Rhetoric in a Multimedia Age
Adam J. Banks

The Managerial Unconscious in the History of Composition Studies
Donna Strickland

Everyday Genres: Writing Assignments across the Disciplines
Mary Soliday

The Community College Writer: Exceeding Expectations
Howard Tinberg and Jean-Paul Nadeau

A Taste for Language: Literacy, Class, and English Studies
James Ray Watkins

Before Shaughnessy: Basic Writing at Yale and Harvard, 1920–1960
Kelly Ritter

Writer's Block: The Cognitive Dimension
Mike Rose

Teaching/Writing in Thirdspaces: The Studio Approach
Rhonda C. Grego and Nancy S. Thompson

Rural Literacies
Kim Donehower, Charlotte Hogg, and Eileen E. Schell

Writing with Authority: Students' Roles as Writers in Cross-National Perspective
David Foster

Whistlin' and Crowin' Women of Appalachia: Literacy Practices since College
Katherine Kelleher Sohn

Sexuality and the Politics of Ethos in the Writing Classroom
Zan Meyer Gonçalves

African American Literacies Unleashed: Vernacular English and the Composition Classroom
Arnetha F. Ball and Ted Lardner

Revisionary Rhetoric, Feminist Pedagogy, and Multigenre Texts
Julie Jung

Archives of Instruction: Nineteenth-Century Rhetorics, Readers, and Composition Books in the United States
Jean Ferguson Carr, Stephen L. Carr, and Lucille M. Schultz

Response to Reform: Composition and the Professionalization of Teaching
Margaret J. Marshall

Multiliteracies for a Digital Age
Stuart A. Selber

Personally Speaking: Experience as Evidence in Academic Discourse
Candace Spigelman

Self-Development and College Writing
Nick Tingle

Minor Re/Visions: Asian American Literacy Narratives as a Rhetoric of Citizenship
Morris Young

A Communion of Friendship: Literacy, Spiritual Practice, and Women in Recovery
Beth Daniell

Embodied Literacies: Imageword and a Poetics of Teaching
Kristie S. Fleckenstein

Language Diversity in the Classroom: From Intention to Practice
Edited by Geneva Smitherman and Victor Villanueva

Rehearsing New Roles: How College Students Develop as Writers
Lee Ann Carroll

Across Property Lines: Textual Ownership in Writing Groups
Candace Spigelman

Mutuality in the Rhetoric and Composition Classroom
David L. Wallace and Helen Rothschild Ewald

The Young Composers: Composition's Beginnings in Nineteenth-Century Schools
Lucille M. Schultz

Technology and Literacy in the Twenty-First Century: The Importance of Paying Attention
Cynthia L. Selfe

*Women Writing the Academy: Audience,
Authority, and Transformation*
Gesa E. Kirsch

Gender Influences: Reading Student Texts
Donnalee Rubin

*Something Old, Something New: College
Writing Teachers and Classroom Change*
Wendy Bishop

*Dialogue, Dialectic, and Conversation: A
Social Perspective on the Function of Writing*
Gregory Clark

Audience Expectations and Teacher Demands
Robert Brooke and John Hendricks

Toward a Grammar of Passages
Richard M. Coe

*Rhetoric and Reality: Writing Instruction in
American Colleges, 1900–1985*
James A. Berlin

*Writing Groups: History, Theory, and
Implications*
Anne Ruggles Gere

Teaching Writing as a Second Language
Alice S. Horning

Invention as a Social Act
Karen Burke LeFevre

*The Variables of Composition: Process and
Product in a Business Setting*
Glenn J. Broadhead and Richard C. Freed

*Writing Instruction in Nineteenth-Century
American Colleges*
James A. Berlin

*Computers & Composing: How the New
Technologies Are Changing Writing*
Jeanne W. Halpern and Sarah Liggett

*A New Perspective on Cohesion in Expository
Paragraphs*
Robin Bell Markels

Evaluating College Writing Programs
Stephen P. Witte and Lester Faigley

This book was typeset in Garamond and Frutiger by Mike Palmquist.
Typefaces used on the cover include Garamond and News Gothic.

CPSIA information can be obtained
at www.ICGtesting.com
Printed in the USA
JSHW051938230123
36707JS00001B/1